FEEDING THE HUNGRY

FEEDING THE HUNGRY

Advocacy and Blame in the Global
Fight against Hunger

Michelle Jurkovich

CORNELL UNIVERSITY PRESS ITHACA AND LONDON

First published 2020 by Cornell University Press

Library of Congress Cataloging-in-Publication Data

Names: Jurkovich, Michelle, 1983– author.
Title: Feeding the hungry : advocacy and blame in the global fight against hunger / Michelle Jurkovich.
Description: Ithaca [New York] : Cornell University Press, 2020. | Includes bibliographical references and index.
Identifiers: LCCN 2019048969 (print) | LCCN 2019048970 (ebook) | ISBN 9781501751165 (hardcover) | ISBN 9781501751783 (paperback) | ISBN 9781501751172 (epub) | ISBN 9781501751189 (pdf)
Subjects: LCSH: Food relief—Political aspects. | Right to food. | Hunger—Political aspects. | Food security—Political aspects. | Food relief—International cooperation. | Hunger—Prevention—International cooperation.
Classification: LCC HV696.F6 J78 2020 (print) | LCC HV696.F6 (ebook) | DDC 363.8—dc23
LC record available at https://lccn.loc.gov/2019048969
LC ebook record available at https://lccn.loc.gov/2019048970

To my grandmother, Helen Keith

Contents

Preface

I have written this book with a number of different audiences in mind. For human rights scholars, my goal is to make the case for expanding the scope of our inquiry to focus greater attention on economic and social rights and their campaigns. Our literature is severely lopsided. We now know a great deal about civil and political rights advocacy but have left an entire subset of rights—that is, economic and social rights—underexplored. This book looks at one case of an economic and social right, the right to food, and finds that many of the assumptions we make in our literature on human rights advocacy do not apply here—especially assumptions about the nature of blame and the logic of advocacy that flows from these views. I develop an alternative model of advocacy, called the buckshot model, which I argue better explains the trajectories of campaigns in this issue area. The right to food shares many important characteristics with the larger category of economic and social rights, and there may be great theoretical and empirical payoffs to focusing greater attention on this subset of rights.

For constructivists, this book explores the implications for an issue area (hunger) when there is no norm present. Constructivist work often highlights how norms make some action possible, but does not look at the logical corollary: how a lack of a norm can make action impossible or less possible. In the hunger case, the lack of a norm makes centralized pressure around a single target less likely. Additionally, for constructivist scholars of human rights in particular, this book questions the assumption that all human rights actually have norms and explores the implications of the lack of a norm on advocacy efforts on the ground.

For legal scholars and constructivists, this book seeks to encourage new thinking on the varied role of international law in legitimating advocacy campaigns. We know little about why international law is used to legitimate advocacy campaigns in some issue areas but not in others. Moreover, the hunger case highlights how norms do not translate automatically from law. This study enables us to ask new questions about the relationship between law and norms and questions the primacy of focusing on law for the fulfillment of all human rights.

Finally, for activists, this book seeks to make sense of what international anti-hunger activists already know: advocacy in this issue area is extremely difficult. The book explores the conditions that contribute to making activism challenging here with the hope that greater understanding of these conditions can be useful going forward. During interviews, the staff members of these international anti-hunger organizations frequently expressed interest in knowing how their fellow activists understood questions of blame and solutions for the hunger problem. My hope is that they find the results as interesting and telling as I did.

This project would not have been possible without the generosity of the anti-hunger activists, archivists, colleagues, friends, and family who gave of their time, wisdom, good humor, and patience to see the book to completion. I am especially grateful to the many activists fighting tirelessly for a world without hunger who shared their stories and insight despite the many other demands on their time.

I am grateful to the American Consortium of European Union Studies; the Columbian College of Arts and Sciences and the Institute for European and Eurasian Studies, both at the George Washington University; the Loughran Foundation; and the University of Massachusetts Boston for their generous financial support in funding essential research trips to London, New York City, Oxford, Rome, and Washington, DC to conduct interviews, surveys, and archival work. Special thanks are due to Patricia Merrikin for helping me navigate the United Nations Food and Agriculture Organization (FAO) library collections and to Fabio Ciccarello for his assistance in accessing the FAO archives.

Research for this project began when I was at George Washington University, and I am especially grateful to Jennifer Clapp, Kimberly Morgan, Susan Sell, and Rachel Stein for their support and guidance throughout the research and writing process. My writing/support group—Kelly Bauer, Kerry Crawford, and Jake Haselswerdt—infused the otherwise lonely task of writing early chapter drafts with baked goods and good spirit.

This book was largely rewritten during my time at the Watson Institute for International and Public Affairs at Brown University, where I benefited from a superb interdisciplinary community which pushed me to think outside the boundaries of political science. I am deeply grateful, in particular, to Jenny Greenburg for her support and insightful feedback, Gregory "Duff" Morton for our near daily conversations on core theories and concepts, Lucas Stanczyk for introducing me to new insights in philosophy, and Elizabeth Williams for her wisdom and advice on how to think about historical records. My writing group at Brown University—Maria Abascal, Casey Miller, and Perry Sherouse—helped keep me on track with chapter revisions and, as sociologists and anthropologists, provided fresh perspectives from other fields.

Over the years I have benefited from the generous feedback of so many kind souls that I have now lost count. Special thanks to Holger Albrecht, Jessica Anderson, Peter Andreas, Narges Bajoghli, Davy Banks, Rob Blair, Mark Blyth, Keith

Brown, Nitsan Chorev, Dara Cohen, Jeff Colgan, Anjali Kaushlesh Dayal, Janice Gallagher, Amy Hsieh, Katie Kuhn, Elise Leclerc-Gagné, Dov Levin, Rick Locke, Catherine Lutz, Raul Mediratta, Gabriel Michael, Jonas Nahm, Yusuf Neggers, Joseph O'Mahoney, Mara Pillinger, Mathias Poerter, Amanda Rizkallah, Andrew Schrank, Jonah Schulhofer-Wohl, Dillon Stone Tatum, Oliver Westerwinter, and Rawan Zoubi who provided valuable feedback as the book developed. Honora Chapman, Stephen Rodemeyer, and Liza Wieland provided much appreciated mentorship along the way. I am grateful to Amartya Sen for his kindness in taking me to lunch and discussing this research when I was a new junior faculty member in town. Melissa Lee and I walked through the writing and revising process for our book manuscripts at the same time, and I am very grateful for her support, feedback, and the sharing of drinks and phone calls along the way. I am grateful, too, for the excellent research assistance of Olabode George Igandan and Jane Olmstead-Rumsey.

I am deeply appreciative to the International Studies Association–Northeast for selecting this manuscript as the 2016 Northeast Circle Honoree and hosting a roundtable discussion on it. Sammy Barkin, Jamie Frueh, Andrew Ross, and Deborah Wheeler all read the entire manuscript and provided valuable feedback. A second book workshop was hosted by the Watson Institute for International and Public Affairs in April 2017 and I am especially grateful to Charli Carpenter, Michael Kennedy, Robert Paarlberg, and Wayne Sandholtz for reading the entire manuscript and providing insightful comments and suggestions as it underwent its next round of revisions. These scholars represent what is best in this profession—the incomparable generosity of spirit (and time!) in helping build new scholarship.

This book was completed at the University of Massachusetts Boston, where I am grateful to my colleagues and students for their support and insight. I am especially grateful to Sammy Barkin, Joseph Brown, Leila Farsakh, Luis Jiménez, Paul Kowert, Jeffrey Pugh, and the graduate students in my Human Security seminar for providing feedback on several chapters. The book was made stronger by the helpful feedback given by participants of workshops and seminars where I presented chapters and core ideas of the manuscript, including at Brown University, the George Washington University, Harvard University, Northwestern University, Occidental College, the Ohio State University, Reed College, the University of Alabama, the University of California Riverside, and the University of Southern California.

I owe an immeasurable debt to Martha Finnemore for her unwavering support and sage advice. I am tremendously grateful for her mentorship and friendship. Lee Ann Fujii was a mentor and friend from my early years as a graduate student and taught me how to think about research ethics, power, and positionality in the discipline. She is greatly missed.

At Cornell University Press, I had the great fortune of working with Roger Haydon. It was Roger who taught me how to start an introduction chapter, and his insightful comments and suggestions during the revision process are much appreciated. I am also grateful to the anonymous reviewers of the manuscript for their thoughtful and constructive feedback. Chapters 3 and 5 contain text first published in my article "What Isn't a Norm? Redefining the Conceptual Boundaries of 'Norms' in the Human Rights Literature," *International Studies Review* (2019), used by permission of Oxford University Press and the International Studies Association.

Friends and family made the process of researching, writing, and rewriting this book bearable. Jess Epstein, Nicolin Neal, James Orr, Trish Orr, Abby Parker, Christy Qualle, Cordie Micah Qualle, Ozge Tekin, and Lindsay Wallace lent their support, wit, and good humor and on more than one occasion also provided home-cooked food. I am tremendously grateful to Dina Bishara and Giovanni Mantilla for their steadfast friendship and for never failing to pick up the phone when I needed their advice. My family, Michael, Jeanette, Joey, Krissy, and Landon Jurkovich, tolerated long absences from Fresno as I completed the book and provided loving support when I was there. My mother made it her personal mission to ask nearly every time we spoke on the phone if I had finished my book yet. I am realizing now that it will never truly seem finished, but hopefully its appearing in print will be close enough.

This book is dedicated to the memory of my grandmother, Helen Keith, the most selfless person I have ever known.

FEEDING THE HUNGRY

THE POLITICS OF CHRONIC HUNGER

"Let me just tell you something a bit more provocative," said a senior official at Oxfam America as we began our interview. "If [anti-hunger organizations] aren't willing to use the word 'blame' or an appropriate euphemism for it . . . they don't actually believe there is a right to food."

So, then, who was to blame for hunger? Grabbing a sheet of paper, she began to draw.

"There's the person we're trying to benefit," she said, drawing a stick figure in the middle of a big circle. "She sits at the center of the universe." Dividing up the circle around her into three sections (the private sector, the state, and civil society) at three different levels (local, national, and global) she proceeded to rank each segment to identify its relative level of blame for the problem of chronic hunger. In total, nine different actors were to blame. Being able to say there is a "right to food" meant "you are capable of identifying who's responsible, talking about the nature of their responsibilities and doing something about it," she explained.

Confused, I looked at her drawing of the nine different actors she ranked as to blame for hunger: "So, who *is* responsible?"

"I've just told you," she replied.

"Lots of people, then?" I asked.

"Yeah, and you hold them *all* responsible."

Our conversation continued for several minutes before I raised the Universal Declaration of Human Rights, thinking that clearly international law had already determined that national governments were the actors who were obliged to fulfill the right to food. Interjecting quickly, she exclaimed, "We're not that legal. I mean, the reason—honestly—the reason we do rights-based work is, I walk into every room . . . I go in to any place anywhere and just say, 'Listen. I'm not going to tell you anything about the law. Who in here has the right to enough basic food to eat everyday so that they can live with dignity?' Everybody. 'What convention is it in?' 'I haven't a clue, but I have the right!' That's what you need to know, okay? I don't care if you know the name of the convention, I need you to know that the people we serve have that right and *somebody is responsible*."[1]

In the course of one hour, this senior official had taken much of what the human rights literature in international relations had come to expect from human rights advocacy and turned it on its head. We have come to expect advocacy organizations to focus blame and shame on one common target actor (almost always a national government) in human rights campaigns.[2] We expect that these activists rely on human rights law to inform their understanding of whom to target in the event that a human right is not protected or fulfilled. After all, law is what gives legitimacy to human rights claims, according to our scholarship.[3] International human rights law, in particular, ascribes responsibility to national governments for the protection and fulfillment of the human rights of those living within their borders. Once governments commit to these laws, we expect activists to use them to compel states to comply.

Over the following months, I would meet with senior and executive staff at top international anti-hunger organizations and time and again would be confronted with a very different lived reality of advocacy work around hunger. This was an issue area where everyone seemed to agree on a common goal (nobody should be hungry), but where there was no consensus among gatekeepers on a unitary actor who was to blame for the problem of chronic hunger, nor any consensus on what precisely should be done to solve the problem. Food is a human right, codified in international and sometimes even domestic laws. However, these laws did not generally motivate activists to focus pressure on national governments to fulfill this human right. For many international anti-hunger organizations I examined, the very concept of a "right" to food was justified not in legal but in moral terms. The result of the lack of consensus on such foundational questions as *who is to blame for hunger* and *how the problem should be solved* resulted in a complex aggregate of international advocacy campaigns often simul-

---

1. Interview, Oxfam America 1, May 2013, emphasis added. All interviewees are anonymous, though respondents have consented to attributing their quote to a general ranking (e.g., "senior official") under their specific organization's name. Executive and senior level staff are grouped under the common ranking of "senior official." Since identifying the gender of some respondents would make their identities obvious, all respondents are identified with feminine pronouns.

2. Keck and Sikkink 1998; Risse, Ropp, and Sikkink 1999, 2013.

3. Alston 1991; Schmid 2015; Sikkink 2011; Simmons 2009.

taneously targeting different actors to blame for hunger and making different demands of those actors in an attempt to mitigate the staggering global hunger rate. Certainly, global hunger was not a new issue that advocacy groups were only now starting to address and thus only now grappling with questions of blame, causality, and proposed solutions. International anti-hunger organizations active today have a long history, dating back to the final years of World War II, though less-organized and more limited advocacy around hunger reaches back much further.

Understanding international anti-hunger advocacy requires challenging assumptions in our literatures on human rights and transnational advocacy. For the most part, these are literatures that have focused almost exclusively on cases of civil and political rights campaigns (such as torture, enforced disappearances, suffrage, and slavery).[4] We now know a great deal, empirically, about civil and political rights campaigns and have used this knowledge to derive theoretical arguments about how and why advocacy campaigns function the way they do. But there is a gap—an entire subset of rights (i.e., economic and social rights)—that we have left underexplored.

This book addresses that gap. In focusing on international anti-hunger activism, I draw to the fore advocacy surrounding one of the most essential—or, as Henry Shue (1980) would argue, the most *basic*—of all human rights: the human right to food. Without the realization of the right to food, the fulfillment of other human rights is either impossible or substantively meaningless. The right to education, for instance, can hardly be realized when individuals are so hungry that they cannot think. It would be challenging for freedom (of assembly, of speech, of thought) to retain its full promise when experienced on an empty stomach. The liberating promise of human rights rings hollow when parents find themselves in constant worry that their children will have enough to eat, such that they can avoid the pangs of hunger and the weakness and sickness that comes with it.

And yet, hunger is a daily, lived reality for an estimated 821 million people in the world.[5] According to John Holmes, United Nations under-secretary-general for Humanitarian Affairs from 2007 to 2010, "Each day, 25,000 people, including more than 10,000 children, die from hunger and related causes."[6] To put this issue in perspective, more people die from hunger and related causes globally than in all wars, civil and international, combined. More people die from hunger

---

4. Carpenter 2011, 2014; Hawkins 2004; Hyde 2011; Keck and Sikkink 1998; Kelley 2008; Klotz 1999; Lutz and Sikkink 2000; Price 1997, 1998.
5. Food and Agriculture Organization et al. 2018, v. The estimate is for the year 2017.
6. Holmes 2008. Estimates of hunger related deaths vary. According to Black et al. (2013), in 2011 an estimated 3.1 children died from undernutrition globally.

and related causes each year than in all violent deaths (including gang violence, intentional and unintentional homicide) combined.[7] Hunger remains a problem in all countries, not only in those with the most struggling economies or those emerging from decades of civil war. The U.S. Department of Agriculture (USDA) estimated a 14 percent rate of "food insecurity" among Americans in 2014, among the highest rates in all industrialized countries.[8] Hunger is one of the most pressing global problems today, and yet the discipline of political science has spent surprisingly little time examining the role of international advocacy in this issue area.

This is unacceptable. If we think politics is about "the uneven distribution of power in society, how the struggle over power is conducted, and its impact on the creation and distribution of resources, life chances, and well-being," there are few problems as inherently political as who gets enough to eat in this world and who does not.[9] Yet, few political scientists, particularly in the United States, focus much attention on the problem of global hunger. There was a brief surge of interest in hunger and the politics of food in the late 1970s, culminating in a special edition of the journal *International Organization* titled "The Global Political Economy of Food," but the discipline's interest in the topic quickly subsided.[10] Over the coming decades, a few political scientists would conduct studies on international food aid and social movements around food,[11] apply regime theory to hunger,[12] examine the global food crisis of 2008,[13] debate the role of genetically modified organisms in modern agriculture,[14] and probe the link between food insecurity and domestic instability,[15] but such studies were comparatively rare. The subfield of international relations, in particular, has remained focused on questions of conflict and trade, with virtually no scholarship on global hunger in any of the field's flagship journals.

Instead, scholarship on hunger in the social sciences is scattered across a number of disciplines, with no clear disciplinary "home." Economists have been and continue to be interested in questions of economic demand for food, food sub-

---

7. According to Geneva Declaration Secretariat (2011, 1), "More than 526,000 people are killed each year as a result of lethal violence."

8. In 2006, the USDA removed the word *hunger* from its hunger metric, settling instead on the term *food insecurity*. The rationale for the change was that officials argued that hunger, as a sensation, was not something that could be effectively measured and thus the term should not be used. *Food insecurity* served as a more technical (and perhaps politically sterile) word that the USDA defines as "a household-level economic and social condition of limited or uncertain access to adequate food." See U.S. Department of Agriculture, Economic Research Service 2019.

9. Marsh and Stoker 2010, 7.

10. "The Global Political Economy of Food" 1978.

11. Claeys 2015; Clapp 2012; Uvin 1992; Wallerstein 1980.

12. Margulis 2013; Uvin 1994.

13. Clapp and Cohen 2009.

14. Paarlberg 2009; Zerbe 2004. See also sociologist Lang 2016.

15. Hendrix and Brinkman 2013. On the relationship between food insecurity and conflict, see Messer and Cohen 2007.

sidies, food price volatility, the effects of economic policies on nutrition, and the economics of food aid.[16] Anthropologists have conducted important studies on food insecurity in specific local contexts.[17] Sociology, like political science, has seen little scholarship on global hunger, despite the efforts of Stephen J. Scanlan to bring the study of food security into the field.[18] Hunger has, in many ways, become an "orphaned" issue: everyone agrees that it is important, but nobody knows who ought to be studying it.

Within the natural, agricultural, and earth sciences, prior scholarship has conceptualized hunger as primarily a technical problem with technical solutions: if only we could devise ways to grow more food with fewer inputs and in more environmentally friendly ways, these studies suggest, we could solve the hunger problem.[19] Yet the social sciences are especially equipped to challenge answers to complex social and economic problems that rely exclusively on technical solutions, as few benefits in society are ever distributed equally or fairly, even when scientific advancement allows resources to exist in abundance. The world currently produces more food than it needs to feed even its ever-growing population of over seven billion, and should new crop varieties and farming methods enable it to produce an even greater surplus, there would still be no guarantee that this abundance would reach the most marginalized in societies. As of 2014, the United States had roughly a 14 percent food insecurity rate, despite having the most efficient agricultural industry in the world and producing far more food than its population needs. Having been raised in the farming community of Fresno County, California, I was struck by the stark contrast of staggering rates of poverty and hunger amid the abundant groves of oranges, orchards of almonds, and the seemingly limitless supply of grape vineyards; this was a daily reminder that the existence of a resource by no means guarantees an individual any access to that resource. One might assume that simply increasing the supply of a specific commodity would automatically decrease the price to consumers (thus enabling greater access), but history reminds us that there has always been, and likely always will be, a gap between the lowest price that producers are willing to sell a commodity at to turn an acceptable profit and the highest price the poorest in society can afford to pay for the given commodity. The market alone has never been able to solve the hunger problem.

---

16. Barrett 2001; Barrett and Maxwell 2005; Drèze, Sen, and Hussain 1995; Pinstrup-Andersen 1987, 1988, 2010; Sen 1981.

17. De Waal 2004; Scheper-Hughes 1993; Taussig 1978. For a broader survey, see Pottier 1999.

18. Scanlan 2003, 2009. There has been, however, growing interest in food safety regimes (see, Epstein 2014) and in questions of global food systems (see Winders 2009; and Wright and Middendorf 2007).

19. Baldos and Hertel 2014; Bommarco, Kleijn, and Potts 2013; Burke and Lobell 2017; Godfray et al. 2010; Popp, Pető, and Nagy 2013. On growing more food in an era of climate change, see Lipper et al. 2014.

Looking specifically at famines, Nobel Prize–winning economist Amartya Sen argues that scholars must look beyond questions of food supply in order to understand the conditions under which famines might be expected to arise and persist. As Sen notes, "Starvation is the characteristic of some people not *having* enough to eat. It is not the characteristic of there *being* not enough food to eat"; instead, it is an individual's *entitlement* to food that explains who gets enough food to eat and who does not (1981, 1, emphasis in the original). According to Sen, the "entitlement approach . . . concentrates on the ability of people to command food through the legal means available in the society" (1981, 45). Entitlements, however, are complicated, socially negotiated arrangements that can and have changed over time depending on the particular social and economic issue at hand. Central to understanding entitlements is not only determining *who* is entitled to *what*, but who is obliged to provide that specific good in the event the individual is unable to command it through one of the more conventional mechanisms of entitlement (namely, trade or individual ownership). Looking back to the conversation with the Oxfam America official at the beginning of this chapter, there was little doubt she believed all humans were entitled to enough food to eat, though this belief was not rooted in any legal framework. But as this book will show, agreement on a desired goal or objective (that all people ought to have enough to eat) does not mean it is clear *how* that goal should be attained, or perhaps most importantly for the purposes of understanding social pressure, *who* should be obliged to ensure the goal is met.

The present study takes the challenge of constructing this *who* should do *what* seriously, bringing insights from across different fields to bear on the case of international advocacy to combat chronic hunger. It embraces Sen's (1981) argument that one must look to entitlements and not food supply to understand the persistence of hunger but challenges the idea that these entitlements should be (or are) viewed primarily in legal terms. This book highlights the socially constructed nature of an entitlement to food and the varied interpretations of what constitutes a human right to food, identifying challenges that hinder the construction of a norm that *good governments ought to ensure that their people have enough food to eat*. Amartya Sen and Jean Drèze (1989) have documented the ability of public pressure in open political environments to eliminate famines, but it has not had the same effect in eliminating chronic hunger. In highlighting the struggle to articulate an anti-hunger norm, this book helps to explain why.

Finally, in contrast to much of the hunger literature, this study focuses not on famines or short-term hunger but rather on international advocacy around chronic hunger. While a study of campaigns seeking emergency famine relief would be a valuable contribution in and of itself, the majority of the world's hungry suffer not from short-term famine but from long-term food deprivation.

This hunger often does not have the benefit of flashy media attention, where pictures of children with bloated bellies could perhaps sustain a brief period of sympathy for a food crisis. Ventures in response to chronic hunger require far more effort on the part of activists to construct meaningful campaigns, and how and why activists construct these campaigns matters a great deal. Put differently, it would be easy to forget about chronic global hunger. A problem of this sort cannot on its own easily sustain media or public attention. Without the advocates examined in this study, it is unlikely that this problem would receive much attention or support at all.

Rethinking Core Concepts

As this book will demonstrate, an analysis of international anti-hunger advocacy requires rethinking core theories and concepts used by human rights scholars. Our way of thinking about what constitutes a human right and a norm, as well as the relationship between rights, norms, and law, are all challenged by the important work international anti-hunger activists are currently doing in the world.

Much scholarship focuses on the primacy of law in constituting and legitimating human rights, yet advocacy around hunger and the right to food problematizes such a link. As this study will highlight, while persistent hunger can indeed be conceptualized as a rights violation, some international anti-hunger organizations choose to avoid rights language entirely, framing hunger instead as a development problem. Those who do frame the hunger problem as a violation of the human right to food, such as the Oxfam America official quoted at the beginning of this chapter, may justify this right in moral and not legal terms. This is a case in which international human rights law exists but is rarely used, even by top international anti-hunger organizations. Ronald Dworkin (1978) considers "rights as trumps," but the hunger case begs caution. As subsequent chapters in this book will discuss, the near hegemonic focus on civil and political rights in the human rights literature has limited our understanding of alternatives to legal justification of rights and encouraged models of human rights activism that assume that in cases of human rights violations activists must inherently agree on one target actor on whom to focus social pressure, the national government, because this is the actor to whom international law ascribes responsibility. Instead international anti-hunger organizations exhibit a complex understanding of blame and responsibility surrounding the persistence of hunger and focus their efforts on a wide array of targets spanning from transnational corporations to price speculators, financial institutions, and outside states, or sometimes choosing in their advocacy efforts to avoid attempts at targeting any actor at all as to blame for hunger.

The hunger case thus invites us to reconsider what constitutes and legitimates the *human right to food*. How do activists determine whom to blame in the case of violations of economic and social rights such as the right to food? If law is not the primary means of legitimating this human right, how do moral justifications serve to mobilize support for international anti-hunger campaigns? Answering these questions will require unpacking how social scientists understand the role of norms (defined as collectively shared "standards of appropriate behavior for actors of a given identity"),[20] and the relationship between norms and law. Norms are what enable focused shaming and blaming on a common actor when that actor deviates from the socially appropriate behavior expected from it. But in order to have a clear "norm violator," there must be a norm to be violated in the first place. The hunger case encourages scholars to consider more carefully the difference between shared moral principles (e.g., "people ought not be hungry") and norms (e.g., "good governments ought to ensure that their people have enough to eat if they cannot afford to feed themselves"). This book offers readers an expanded conceptual tool kit with which to understand the social and moral forces at play in human rights advocacy, moving beyond the overreliance of the norm concept to understand how norms differ from moral principles, supererogatory standards, and law in the case of international anti-hunger advocacy.

The Landscape of International Anti-Hunger Advocacy

The present study relies on interviews and surveys conducted with senior officials at top international anti-hunger organizations.[21] In total, more than seventy staff members of international anti-hunger organizations were interviewed for this project, most of whom were based at the following organizations: Action against Hunger; ActionAid; Amnesty International; the Bill & Melinda Gates Foundation; Bread for the World; CARE; the Food and Agriculture Organization (FAO) of the United Nations (UN); FIAN International; Médecins sans Frontières / Doctors without Borders (MSF); Oxfam; the Rockefeller Foundation; Save the Children; the UN's World Food Programme, and World Vision. Many of these organizations contain multiple affiliate offices based in different countries. For additional information on the non-UN organizations consulted for this study, including the specific affiliate offices (where applicable) of these organizations where I conducted interviews, see

---

20. This definition of a *norm* comes from Finnemore and Sikkink 1998, 891.
21. For additional information on research methods, and especially on the interview method, see the appendix.

TABLE 0.1   Anti-Hunger INGOs and Foundations Included in This Study

NAME OF ORGANIZATION	AFFILIATE/SECTION/CONFEDERATE OFFICE INTERVIEWED OR SURVEYED	YEAR ORGANIZATION BEGAN ANTI-HUNGER WORK
Action against Hunger/ Action Contre La Faim	Action against Hunger USA	1979 (as Action Contre la Faim)
ActionAid	ActionAid UK, ActionAid USA	1972 (as Action in Distress)
Amnesty International	Amnesty International Secretariat Office	2001 (though the organization was founded in 1961, it began economic, social, and cultural rights work in 2001)
Bill & Melinda Gates Foundation	Not a confederation	2005 (though the organization was founded in 2000)
Bread for the World	Not a confederation	1974
CARE	CARE USA	1945
Doctors without Borders / Médecins sans Frontières (MSF)	Doctors without Borders USA	1971 (as Médecins sans Frontières)
FIAN International	FIAN International Secretariat Office	1986 (as FoodFirst Information and Action Network)
Oxfam	Oxfam America, Oxfam International, Oxfam Great Britain	1942 (as Oxford Committee for Famine Relief)
Rockefeller Foundation	Not a confederation	1934 (though the Foundation was established in 1913, it began agricultural funding in 1934)
Save the Children	Save the Children UK, Save the Children US	1919 (as Save the Children Fund)
World Vision	World Vision International, World Vision US	1950

table 0.1. These organizations were selected based on prior secondary research as well as through discussions with activists themselves about important organizations working in this issue area.[22] There is no perfect metric by which to determine the definitive list of "most important" organizations working in any issue area, but here I have selected organizations that are powerful by the sheer size of their budget, scope, and scale of their operations (e.g., Oxfam) as well as those which, while far more limited in their financial resources, are nonetheless extremely influential in this issue area by nature of their very visible and vocal advocacy campaigns (e.g., FIAN International). Multiple years of fieldwork in Washington, DC, where most anti-hunger international nongovernmental organizations (INGOs) have at least

---

22. This list of top international anti-hunger organizations is, of course, not exhaustive. There is certainly important work being done by influential international anti-hunger organizations that I was unable, due to time and resource constraints, to include here. Additionally, these organizations work on diverse issues, not only hunger. Only a small part of Amnesty International's work, for instance, focuses on food. They remain in the study because of their influence in the human rights community.

some presence, as well as over a month spent at the FAO allowed me to observe which organizations were not only active in this issue area but also were influential in terms of spearheading initiatives within UN organizations and garnering both financial and popular support for large international multiyear campaigns.[23] In light of their significant influence on international anti-hunger organizations (due to their substantial funding resources), I also have included two foundations (the Gates and Rockefeller Foundations) in this study. Finally, a note about timing—the study that follows focuses on the work of these organizations generally up through 2014, with most interviews completed by 2015. More recent changes to advocacy work within these organizations, therefore, may not be reflected here.

Broadly, we can think of most international anti-hunger organizations as fitting into one of three ideal types: humanitarian, development, and human rights organizations. Most organizations blend the work of two or more of these types— for instance, humanitarian organizations which also engage in development work or development organizations which have developed human rights–based approaches to their work. Some organizations run operations, others focus exclusively on advocacy. Each of these types of work is represented by the international anti-hunger organizations examined in this study.[24]

These are organizations that work globally, and several wage a common campaign or utilize a common advocacy approach in multiple countries and regions of the world at the same time. For this reason, the present project does not ask about hunger specifically in one country or region but asks senior and executive staff at these organizations about how they understand chronic hunger generally, as this understanding informs the construction of these large multiyear and multiregion campaigns. Furthermore, while it is more common among qualitative projects in the transnational advocacy literature to examine a singular campaign or partnership in a given issue area, I have opted instead to widen the lens of this project to encompass multiple international anti-hunger campaigns across dif-

---

23. The decision to classify an organization as an international nongovernmental organization (INGO) or a nongovernmental organizations (NGO) is challenging, as the dividing line is imprecise. In this book, I refer to these organizations as INGOs because they work, either through their advocacy or operations on hunger amelioration, across borders. This does not mean all of these organizations have physical offices in multiple countries. Bread for the World, for example, is physically based only in the United States, though as their name suggests they advocate policies for reducing hunger abroad, often focusing on lobbying the U.S. government to improve policies and funding for anti-hunger efforts internationally.

24. As discussed earlier, this project focuses on chronic hunger, and because of this, I did consider omitting MSF, a highly influential international anti-hunger organization, as their work focuses more on emergency responses to acute malnutrition (and its treatment, for instance, through ready-to-use therapeutic food [RUTF]) than chronic hunger. In the case of MSF, however, I opted to keep it in the study, because it was repeatedly referenced as influential by other international anti-hunger organizations and because of its significant advocacy efforts directed toward U.S. food aid. When organizations focusing both on chronic hunger and short-term hunger (such as emergency famine relief) were interviewed and surveyed, they were asked to direct their responses to how the organization considered chronic hunger.

ferent types of organizations (including development and more purely human rights–based organizations) taking place simultaneously. Advocacy around access to food, like that surrounding access to education, health, or other economic and social rights, involves diverse organizations within its network. Broadening my focus to include this complexity allows for not only a more accurate empirical snapshot of advocacy in the hunger realm but also a more comprehensive analysis of advocacy in this issue area.

Moreover, as will be discussed in the chapters that follow, the nature of advocacy in the hunger issue area often differs from the more "aggressive" (to use the word of one senior official at Oxfam America) street protesting and rallies envisioned in much of the human rights literature.[25] Indeed, some of the participants in this study might not identify with the word *activist* and some might even hesitate to classify the work of their international anti-hunger organization as *advocacy* given its association with a specific type of more confrontational protest work. I use the terms *activist* and *advocacy* in this book because the work of all of these organizations is about enacting serious change in the way hunger is engaged with and responded to globally, even when some international anti-hunger organizations eschew approaches to activism and advocacy that reflect more conventional naming and shaming strategies. International anti-hunger advocacy takes varied forms, as will be discussed in chapters 2 and 4.

An Overview of the Chapters

This book has an unconventional structure. With the exception of chapter 1, which provides historical detail necessary to understand contemporary advocacy in this issue area, each subsequent chapter opens with its own distinct research question, geared toward better understanding contemporary international anti-hunger advocacy. In this way the book takes more of a "stepping stone" approach to discovery— in answering the question at hand, each chapter opens up a new question that readers might not have considered absent the preceding discussion. The following chapter then takes up that new question, a routine that continues throughout the book.

The book begins by placing contemporary international anti-hunger advocacy in its historical context. Building on archival research I conducted at the FAO archives, the UK National Archives, and the U.S. National Archives, chapter 1 examines how hunger evolved from a *condition*, understood as an inevitable part of the natural landscape, to a *problem*, such that state and nonstate actors would begin to see it as something to be ameliorated. Chapter 1 sets the stage for the emergence of

---

25. Interview, Oxfam America 1, May 2013.

the contemporary international anti-hunger organizations examined in this book and explores the origins of a human right to food in international law.

Chapter 2 turns its focus on contemporary international anti-hunger advocacy, describing the nature of contemporary campaigns across top international anti-hunger organizations and asking if dominant human rights models—namely, Margaret E. Keck and Kathryn Sikkink's (1998) "boomerang model" and Thomas Risse, Stephen C. Ropp, and Kathryn Sikkink's (1999, 2013) "spiral model"—are able to account for the behavior present in this issue area. Arguing that they cannot, the chapter provides an alternative model of advocacy, the "buckshot model," to describe and explain advocacy around hunger and the right to food.

Building on the insight from chapter 2 that international anti-hunger advocacy does not fit the expectations of dominant models in the literature, chapter 3 asks how it is possible that the behavior of international anti-hunger advocacy varies from the expectations of the human rights and advocacy literatures. This chapter turns its attention to critically evaluating the normative environment in which international anti-hunger advocates work. I argue that there is no norm around hunger or the right to food among top international anti-hunger organizations, and I use this insight to theorize advocacy in issue areas that lack a norm. Chapter 3 provides additional conceptual tools for scholars to make sense of the social and moral environments in which activists are working, articulating the distinction between norms, moral principles, and supererogatory standards.

If there is no anti-hunger norm within this community, this insight invites another question: Why is there no anti-hunger norm? Chapter 4 takes up this question, reconsidering how scholars understand what constitutes a human right and how issues that sit at the nexus of development and human rights (like hunger) struggle to develop socially shared expectations of appropriate behavior by specific actors (i.e., norms).

Finally, chapter 5 considers the puzzling role of international law around the right to food. Why has existing law been unable to generate norms within this advocacy community? This chapter examines the reasons why international anti-hunger organizations rarely legitimate the right to food in legal terms and how this case can challenge scholars' understanding of the relationships between norms, human rights, and law.

My objective in the present study is not simply to replace one advocacy framework with another; it is to force deeper thinking about how the constituent elements of these frameworks fit together. By breaking down standard advocacy models into their components parts and underlying assumptions and showing how the politics of blame, the assumption of established norms, and the role of law do not function as expected in the case of hunger, I can better help explain how alternative types of advocacy arise.

1

PUTTING HUNGER ON THE AGENDA

Hunger has always been a condition of humankind. It has only comparatively recently become a problem and more recently still a violation of a human right. For much of human history, hunger was understood as an inevitable feature of the natural landscape.[1] It was an expected outcome of a growing population where simple science, mathematics, and logic determined it was simply impossible to feed everyone.[2] In this sense, one would no more lament the ubiquity of hunger in the world than one would lament death itself. Hunger was simply unavoidable.

Not only was hunger not a problem for which societies or governments were obliged to look for a solution, but the use of food as a weapon was accepted military strategy. Siege tactics, despite resulting in the deliberate starvation of children, were expected practice. Even in times of peace, people were not universally entitled to food, even if it surrounded them in abundance. An individual's claim to food was rooted in their ability to command that food from the market, or through their own land and labor at home.

Hunger evolved into a problem only when its existence could no longer be seen as natural and inevitable—and, as such, unsolvable. Problems require solutions, or at least attempts at solutions. Conditions need no such thing. Moreover, conditions become problems only when the issue is made problematic to some actor, such that they should choose to invest energy in working toward its remedy.

---

1. Vernon 2007.
2. Malthus 1798.

13

While historians such as James Vernon in his *Hunger: A Modern History* have already documented the evolution of understandings of hunger up until the 1940s,[3] much of the groundwork for modern international approaches to hunger were not established until the final years of World War II and its immediate aftermath.

This chapter serves to document how responding to global hunger was put on the political agenda as a problem to be solved; the chapter also serves to identify key changes (and conversely, that which has been most immune to change) in how the international community has addressed the problem. It would be impossible to do justice to all aspects of change in how hunger was addressed in one chapter. The more modest aim herein is to highlight only that which is essential to understanding the contemporary international anti-hunger advocacy discussed in the remainder of the book, bringing front and center the process of putting hunger on the political agenda in the mid-1940s and, importantly, constructing the human right to food. This chapter relies on archival research conducted at the archives of the Food and Agriculture Organization (FAO) of the United Nations (UN) in Rome, as well as at the UK and U.S. National Archives.

Putting Hunger on the Political Agenda

At the time that the United States called for the United Nations Conference on Food and Agriculture (known as the Hot Springs Conference, as it was convened in Hot Springs, Virginia), the United States had no domestic food stamps program. Briefly, during the Great Depression, it had a temporary and limited food stamps program, but it was never envisioned as a permanent program and was disbanded in March 1943, a few months before the Hot Springs Conference was held.[4]

Looking back, then, it seems odd that the United States would have been the country to call for an international conference to address global hunger and malnutrition. It is important to note that at this point in time, there were no formal international treaties or conventions governing international approaches to hunger, and domestic food assistance programs in many countries were limited. The League of Nations had established its Nutrition Committee in the mid-1930s, which had begun to discuss how malnutrition could in fact be solvable—namely, with "the application of science to agriculture" which "would provide all food required by diets adequate for health." The committee had concluded optimisti-

---

3. Vernon 2007.
4. This despite approximately 271,635 Americans being eligible for food assistance in the final year of the program. See *New York Times* 1943a.

cally that malnutrition provided "an opportunity to eradicate a social evil by methods which will increase economic prosperity."[5] The outbreak of World War II, however, cut short the League of Nations and its efforts on this front.

President Franklin Delano Roosevelt was unable to attend the Hot Springs Conference, but Judge Marvin Jones, the chair of the American delegation, read aloud from a letter Roosevelt had provided, explaining his absence and the importance of the theme of the conference. "Society must meet in full its obligation to make available to all its members at least the minimum adequate nutrition," wrote Roosevelt, which again was a bit perplexing to assert just months after the U.S. food stamps program had been disbanded. Nonetheless, he implored participants to take seriously the work of the conference, as "the problems with which this conference will concern itself are the most fundamental of all human problems— for without food and clothing life itself is impossible."[6] The New York Times noted that the conference agenda would engage with "such basic problems as the causes and consequences of malnutrition, how more and better food can be produced throughout the world and how it can be distributed to improve living standards in low-wage areas."[7] All forty-three countries who were invited accepted the invitation to attend,[8] including China, whose delegate Kuo Ping-Wen chaired the section titled "Consumption Levels and Requirements"; the USSR, whose delegate A. D. Krutiko chaired the section "Expansion of Production and Adaptation to Consumption Needs"; Brazil, whose delegate José Geribaldi Dantas chaired the section "Facilitation and Improvement of Distribution"; and Cuba, whose delegate served as vice chairman of the section "Recommendations for Continuing and Carrying Forward the Work of the Conference" under chairman Richard Law of the United Kingdom.[9]

When the United Kingdom received its invitation to the Hot Springs Conference, it was concerned. Such a conference was "unexpected,"[10] and Britain worried

---

5. "Food and Agriculture: A Possible United Nations Approach to Economic Reconstruction," n.d. RG 83—Records of the Bureau of Agricultural Economics and Records Relating to the UN Conference on Food and Agriculture, box 1, List of Documentation and Agendas folder, U.S. National Archives.

6. Associated Press 1943.

7. New York Times 1943b.

8. New York Times 1943b.

9. See "Text of the Final Act," in United Nations Conference on Food and Agriculture Hot Springs 1943, although this differed somewhat from the planned distribution of committees by the U.S. government. Originally, for example, the United States had planned to have Brazil chair a committee on nonfood "essential agricultural products." See "Nominations by the Executive Committee of Officers of the Sections and Committees," n.d. and "United Nations Conference on Food and Agriculture: Proposed Organization of Sections and Committees," n.d. RG 83—Records of the Bureau of Agricultural Economics and Records Relating to the UN Conference on Food and Agriculture, box 1, List of Documentation and Agendas folder, U.S. National Archives.

10. "The Hot Springs Conference (1)," Official Histories: The Hot Springs Conference, MAF 152/36, UK National Archives. The document appears to have been produced in August 1944.

that the United States would use this conference to propose policies favorable to agricultural exporting states (generally at odds with Britain's interests as a net food importer). Indeed, officials at the UK Ministry of Food worried that it would be "a producers Conference, in which again we shall have to play the part of unwilling partner."[11] The United Kingdom noted that it would be "the only large importing country represented at the conference, and . . . our own interests and those of the Dominions are likely to be somewhat divergent."[12] As such, the "tactical implications" of the conference were challenging, as it "might do little more than advertise a fundamental cleavage between in [sic] the interests of the exporting countries and the farmers of the importing countries."[13] Special care was to be taken by the UK delegation to ensure that such sensitive topics as wheat and cotton schemes were not addressed,[14] though W. F. Crick of the Ministry of Food expressed concern that that the United Kingdom had already acquired the reputation of "stonewalling" and "non-co-operativeness" (put even more bluntly, as the "bad boy of the party"). "For Heaven's sake," wrote Crick to J. P. R. Maud, UK delegate to the conference, "abandon the aggrieved, supercilious or alarmist attitude. . . . Above all, suppress the cynicism which would describe the project as (I quote one of the Treasury representatives at Wednesday's meeting) 'this most ridiculous of all Conferences.'"[15]

Internal U.S. documents suggest they may not have been far off in their assessment of some of what might have motivated the United States to feign concern at global hunger, though the U.S. interest was not solely based in economic calculations.[16] Interestingly, the United States had determined that food could be a

---

11. "Letter to J.M. from WFC," March 26, 1943, Hot Springs Conference Correspondence, MAF 83/577, UK National Archives.

12. "Telegram No. II to Washington," Hot Springs Conference Correspondence, MAF 83/577, UK National Archives.

13. "The Hot Springs Conference (1)."

14. "Telegram No. II to Washington."

15. "Letter to J.M. from WFC," March 26, 1943.

16. One of the stated "Tentative United States Objectives" for the conference was the "Declaration that measures for dealing with trade barriers . . . while lying outside of the immediate scope of the conference, are essential to the solution of problems in the field of food and agriculture and that they should be dealt with on an international basis as soon as possible with a view to facilitating such solution." See: "Strictly Confidential: United Nations Conference on Food and Agriculture: Agenda of the Conference." RG 83—Records of the Bureau of Agricultural Economics and Records Relating to the United Nations Conference on Food and Agriculture, 1943, box 1, List of Documentation and Agendas folder, U.S. National Archives. The United States was also very aware that "in the course of readjustments after the war, overproduction of all industrial and food products of agriculture is likely, unless adequate measures are taken to sustain demand and otherwise facilitate consumption of these products." See "Memorandum on Consumption Levels and Requirements for Other Needed Agricultural Products," May 18, 1943, RG 83—Records of the Bureau of Agricultural Economics: Records Relating to the UN Conference on Food and Agriculture, 1943, box 1, Section 1—Reports and Recommendations folder, U.S. National Archives.

significant weapon of "psychological warfare" such that a conference around this theme should make up the first of the United Nations conferences.[17]

The link between food and psychological warfare was months in the making. Frank McDougall, an Australian delegate at the Hot Springs Conference, had invested considerable energy in convincing U.S. policy makers during his 1942 visit to Washington that, in order to make "progress in the war of ideas," the issue of food and agriculture must be placed front and center of U.S. efforts at psychological warfare.[18] "This winter," wrote McDougall, "men's minds everywhere will be concerned with food. This will be the time for the United Nations to present to the world the picture of how they propose, on the food front, to secure 'Freedom from want, everywhere in the world.'" The United States needed to be engaging not only in a physical war with Axis powers, but "our military offensive must be paralleled by our assuming the psychological offensive. Thus far, we have mainly been on the defensive—hating Hitler, despising Mussolini, loathing the Japanese war-lords. The President's Four Freedoms and the Atlantic Charter have given us sound bases from which to organize our psychological offensive but we have not yet turned these general statements into weapons in the war of ideas."[19]

If the United States could show how it would address the very pressing reality of hunger, it could more viably present itself as a potential leader of the new world order. McDougall shared his ideas (and earlier drafts of his "Progress in the War of Ideas") throughout the American political elite, meeting with President Roosevelt, Vice President Henry A. Wallace, and First Lady Eleanor Roosevelt, as well as being asked by the U.S. Department of Agriculture (USDA) to help organize a "draft program for action on food and agriculture."[20] By the time the Hot Springs Conference was organized, the United States had determined that food and agriculture "would provide the best basis for United Nations psychological warfare."[21]

---

17. See "Food and Agriculture: Agenda for Informal Discussions," n.d. RG 83—Records of the Bureau of Agricultural Economics and Records Relating to the United Nations Conference on Food and Agriculture, 1943, box 1, List of Documentation and Agendas folder, U.S. National Archives.

18. For a thorough history of McDougall and his "Progress in the War of Ideas," see Way 2013.

19. Frank McDougall, "Progress in the War of Ideas," n.d. RG 83—Records of the Bureau of Agricultural Economics and Records Relating to the United Nations Conference on Food and Agriculture, 1943, box 1, Section 1- Reports and Recommendations folder, U.S. National Archives, pp. 1, 6. Draft document with two modified versions included in the folder. Handwritten date on top of one draft reads "August 18, 1942."

20. Way 2013, 243. A draft of McDougall's "Progress in the War of Ideas" was included among the papers of the Hot Springs Conference retained in the U.S. National Archives, suggesting that it was circulated at the conference, even though according to Way (2013, 243) the earliest drafts were circulated by McDougall to senior U.S. political officials in 1942, the year prior to the conference.

21. "Food and Agriculture: Note," n.d. RG 83—Records of the Bureau of Agricultural Economics and Records Relating to the United Nations Conference on Food and Agriculture, 1943, box 1, List of Documentation and Agendas folder, U.S. National Archives.

And thus the first international conference of the United Nations came to be called around the issue of food and hunger. The relationship between freedom from hunger and President Roosevelt's "freedom from want" served as an over-arching theme to the Hot Springs Conference. In summarizing the conference, the secretary-general's report noted, "The Conference declared that the goal of freedom from want can be reached. It did not, however, seek to conceal the fact that it will first be necessary to win freedom from hunger. In the immediate future, the first duty of the United Nations will be to win complete victory in arms: as their armies liberate territories from tyranny their goal will be to bring food for the starving. The need to reach freedom from hunger before seeking freedom from want was understood, and resolutions were adopted on the subject."[22] The final act of the conference articulated several goals and commitments by attending states, though none of them were legally binding. Most notably, however, was the declaration that "the primary responsibility lies with each nation for seeing that its own people have the food needed for life and health; steps to this end are for national determination. But each nation can fully achieve this goal only if all work together."[23] This was a significant declaration, particularly in a world in which domestic food assistance programs were limited and no codified rights or entitlements to food had been established either in domestic or international law.

Perhaps the most notable outcome of the Hot Springs Conference was the creation of the intergovernmental organization of the FAO, the creation of which was called for by participants to the conference. Interestingly, the FAO, formally established on October 16, 1945, came into existence a few days prior to the official creation of the UN on October 24, 1945. Food had served as the theme for the first conference of the "United Nations," a term originally coined by Roosevelt in 1942 with the signing of the Declaration of the United Nations, years prior to the creation of the formal body of the same name.[24]

The establishment of a permanent intergovernmental organization tasked with responding to chronic hunger ensured that this particular issue would stay on the political agenda. Periodic summits or conventions can be easily forgotten, but one of the effects of setting up bureaucracies is that they can be rather challenging to disband and frequently become enduring fixtures in international affairs. In the case of the FAO, what began as a small international organization, largely staffed by technical experts and provided with a very small budget ($5 million), grew into two international organizations, the FAO and the World Food Programme,

22. "United Nations Conference on Food and Agriculture: Summation of the Work of the Conference by the Secretary General," in United Nations Conference on Food and Agriculture 1943.

23. "Text of the Final Act," 11. For a history of the FAO, see Hambridge 1955.

24. For additional information on the creation and early years of the FAO, see Phillips 1981.

the latter being at one point a division within the FAO before becoming its own independent international organization.

In a relatively short period of time—from the beginning of the League of Nation's work with nutrition in 1935 until the creation of the FAO in 1945—the condition of hunger and malnutrition was made an international problem. Far from simply a rhetorical shift in how hunger was discussed, as an issue area it went from relative obscurity in international affairs (despite high hunger rates and several notable famines) to the raison d'être of the first international conference of the United Nations and one of its first organizations. This shift was made possible, in part, because of the growing belief that science could mitigate hunger through agricultural innovation, but putting hunger on the political agenda also required political actors—namely, the United States—to see the issue as warranting attention. To the United States, selecting food and hunger as the theme for the first conference of the United Nations served what the Roosevelt administration believed were its strategic interests in setting up the country as a viable leader for the postwar system. And, interestingly, the administration believed it would be food that would win over the hearts and minds of the international community.

What Has Changed?

Of course, much has changed in how the hunger problem has been understood and engaged with since the middle of the twentieth century. For the purposes of understanding the contemporary international anti-hunger organizations discussed in this book, three changes in particular are worth noting: (1) the changing role of aspiration in international anti-hunger campaigns; (2) the rise of influence of nongovernmental organizations (NGOs) and international nongovernmental organizations (INGOs) in combatting hunger, and (3) the construction of a human right to food in international law.

The Role of Aspiration in International Anti-Hunger Campaigns

Two notable changes in how hunger has been addressed internationally since the mid-1940s have intertwined histories: the rise of influence of NGOs and INGOs in the hunger issue area and the changing role of aspiration in international anti-hunger campaigns. In light of the UN's current Sustainable Development Goals (SDGs), adopted in September 2016, and calling for, among other goals, achieving "Zero Hunger" (SDG2), it would be easy to believe that highly aspirational goals were normal for the hunger issue area. This was not always so. In fact, while there was always some degree of aspiration in how governments and international organizations addressed hunger (notably President John F. Kennedy in his address to the World Food Congress in 1963),[25] early work within the UN relating to hunger was markedly less aspirational and favoring more "realistic" standards and objectives.

This contrast is perhaps best exemplified by one of the most significant international anti-hunger campaigns launched by the FAO, which began in the late 1950s. The first head of any UN organization from a developing country, India's Binay Ranjan Sen was elected director-general of the FAO in 1956. Sen appeared to have entered his position with the idea of a global "Free the World from Hunger" campaign already in mind.[26] The purpose of this campaign would be to raise public consciousness internationally about the problem of hunger, encourage a series of academic studies to better understand how it could be solved, and ultimately to propel action by states to reduce hunger rates.[27]

Early on, Sen approached the United States to support this campaign. When he met with President Dwight D. Eisenhower in 1958, however, it became clear that the United States was uninterested in providing any additional funds to the FAO for such a campaign. Some of its objections were rather predictable, such as the U.S. desire for the FAO to invest its energies instead in encouraging agricultural trade and helping to coordinate the disposal of surplus food aid.[28] But the very idea that a UN organization would launch a campaign with such a lofty and aspirational goal was concerning to the United States. Both in public discussions at the FAO as well as in internal U.S. government position papers, the United States noted that UN organizations should not engage in "false hopes." In one internal position paper on the campaign, the United States noted, "The title should be one which is positive, does not create false hopes, appeals to reason rather than emotions, and is readily translatable into the three official languages as well as other languages."[29] The Argentine delegation similarly reported that the FAO should not launch a campaign that would "raise false hopes" and that it was important

---

25. In his address to the opening session of the World Food Congress Kennedy famously proclaimed, "We have the capacity to eliminate hunger from the face of the earth in our lifetime. We need only the will." See Kennedy 1963.

26. Bunch 2007, 12; Sen 1982, 138.

27. Interestingly, the question of what caused the problem did not appear to be on the agenda. This was likely due to the fact that the hunger problem was already framed as resulting from inefficient agricultural production and a growing population, as will be discussed at the end of this chapter. See "Report of FAO Council Ad Hoc Committee on Free the World from Hunger Campaign," April 15–17, 1959, RG 7—Ad Hoc Committee on FFHC, 1959, box 7FCL7. Food and Agriculture Organization Archives, Rome.

28. Staples 2006, 107, 109.

29. "Freedom-from-Hunger Campaign: Position Paper for Agenda Item 8," September 24, 1959, RG 59—General Records of the Department of State: U.S. Delegation Position Papers and Misc Subject Files 1946–1959, box 1, U.S. Delegation Position Papers folder, U.S. National Archives.

to be "careful as to the scope and manner" in which the campaign would be structured.[30] The Dutch delegation agreed in objecting to a highly aspirational campaign, noting,

> We, in the Netherlands, hold the view that the millions of people who are actually going hungry, will hardly find any consolation in propaganda campaigns aiming at once more drawing the attention to their privation, the more so if such actions are to culminate in nothing but just another mass congress with lengthy discussions and tons of paper.
>
> We fear that after the proposed congress a vacuum may easily arise, and that this aroused interest and expectations will be disappointed. This may well jeopardize our organization, the United Nations in general, and the Governments concerned.
>
> We therefore fully endorse the warnings which have been aired during the Council session by the delegates from the U.S.A., Indonesia, France, Canada, and at the regional conference for Latin America by the delegate from Argentine [sic], to organize and present any contemplated campaign, also by its name, in such a way that no false hopes can be entertained, and the action itself, but also *our organization will not be brought into disrepute.*[31]

The United States preferred the name International Food Campaign instead.[32] Ultimately, states agreed that the name Freedom from Hunger Campaign (FFHC) sent a less ambitious signal than Free the World from Hunger Campaign. What is most interesting in light of current, highly aspirational campaigns within the UN is how at one point states worried that the legitimacy of the FAO, as well as that of member states, would be at risk if states were unrealistic in their hunger goals.

The tension between more cautious or restrained approaches to goal setting and more aspirational approaches can again be seen between the World Food Summit (WFS) and the UN's Millennium Development Goals (MDGs). At the WFS, held at the FAO in 1996, states committed to reducing the number of hun-

---

30. "Extract from Draft Report of the Fifth FAO Regional Conference for Latin America," n.d. RG 7—Ad Hoc Committee on FFHC, 1959, box 7FCL7, Food and Agriculture Organization Archives. This document appears to be included as part of Appendix 2 for the "FAO Council Ad Hoc Committee on Free the World from Hunger Campaign: Working Paper for Meeting, Rome, April 15–17, 1959. RG 7—Ad Hoc Committee on FFHC, 1959, box 7FCL7, Food and Agriculture Organization Archives.

31. "Opening Statement by Delegate of the Netherlands: FAO Council Ad Hoc Committee on Freedom from Hunger Campaign: 15–17 April 1959," RG 7—Ad Hoc Committee on FFHC, 1959, box 7FCL7, Food and Agriculture Organization Archives, emphasis added.

32. "Freedom-from-Hunger Campaign: Position Paper."

gry people in the world by half by 2015.[33] Believing this to be unrealistic, the MDGs softened the target by calling for the reduction by half of the *proportion* of people who were hungry (not the absolute number of hungry people, which as populations increased would be too challenging to meet) from 1990 levels by the year 2015. Ultimately MDG1c (to halve the proportion of hungry people in the world) was not met, and indeed, it is likely that far less progress was made on meeting this goal than the FAO claimed.[34] Despite failing at this more limited goal, the UN adopted the extremely aspirational goal of a complete elimination of hunger by 2030 in SDG2, "Zero Hunger."

The Increasing Role of Nongovernmental Organizations

It is difficult to pinpoint a single reason for the changing role of aspiration in international anti-hunger campaigns, or why concerns about organizational legitimacy if goals were not met seemed to decline. One change which happened alongside this transformation, however, was the rise of influence of NGOs in this issue area. At the time of the Hot Springs Conference in 1943, only states were invited to attend. The Oxford Committee for Famine Relief (which would later become Oxfam) was technically established in 1942, though minutes from its early meetings highlight how the fledgling organization was mostly interested in providing emergency relief in war-torn Europe and had limited membership.[35] CARE was established in 1945, but many of the most well-known anti-hunger organizations active today (e.g., Action against Hunger, Bread for the World, FIAN International, and Médecins sans Frontières / Doctors without Borders) were not established until the 1970s or later.

It is difficult now to imagine, even within the FAO, an international anti-hunger campaign that was not influenced by civil society in significant ways. In part, the rise of influence of NGOs can be seen in how FAO director-general Sen structured the FFHC. Many states, such as the United States, had opposed any additional funding for the campaign, and so Sen looked to civil society to assist in funding its

---

33. Although this goal itself was less aspirational than the stated goal of a total elimination of hunger at the 1974 World Food Congress. It is important to highlight that while the level of aspiration is high in international anti-hunger campaigns today, the evolution of the role of aspiration in advocacy has been nonlinear, as highlighted by the debates pushing for a more restrained campaign in the FFHC to the highly aspirational goal at the 1974 World Food Congress, to the less aspirational goal of the MDGs and finally to the highly aspirational goal of Zero Hunger in the SDGs.

34. Jurkovich 2016; Pingali 2016.

35. Oxford Famine Relief Committee minutes (handwritten), October 5, 1942. Bodleian Library, Oxford University. The first entry in the minutes book lists the name as Oxford Famine Relief Committee, though the name appeared to change rather quickly to the Oxford Committee for Famine Relief.

work. The first donation ($100,000) came from the Catholic Bishops of West Germany, and Sen invited twenty-three NGOs to join an FFHC advisory committee.[36] By 1961 the FFHC had raised $1,223,740, pulling from donations across civil society organizations (many of which were religious organizations), states, private companies, and assorted other institutions and agencies.[37] NGO standing grew within the FAO, largely due to the inroads made during Sen's leadership with the FFHC. By the time of the UN's World Food Conference in 1974, 116 NGOs were granted observer status.[38]

By the 1990s, civil society organizations succeeded in forming the NGO Forum to run parallel to the 1996 WFS and ultimately the International Support Committee. Immediately prior to the WFS, a joint FAO/NGO consultation was held with representatives from 240 different NGOs to enable input on the draft Rome Declaration (which resulted in the goal of reducing the number of hungry by half by 2015). Discontent with merely commenting on the proposed declaration, NGO participants drafted their own declaration and provided copies at the WFS to member states. "This was a turning point in the process," noted former FAO employee Nora McKeon, who directed relations between the FAO and civil society, "the moment in which the civil society actors took full possession of their preparations for the World Food Summit, deviating from the route that the WFS secretariat had traced."[39] The twenty-first century has seen continued growth of NGOs and INGOs in the hunger issue area, not only within the FAO but throughout the UN more broadly. As will be discussed in greater detail in chapters 2–4, such organizations now run global advocacy campaigns, run development projects in nearly every developing country in the world, and have become vocal and active participants in constructing anti-hunger approaches within the FAO, as well as for individual member states. Anti-hunger policies can no longer be determined solely by states or even states in cooperation with UN technical organizations like the FAO, and it would be impossible to discuss anti-hunger measures without highlighting the importance of this growing civil society.

The Construction of a Human Right to Food

Finally, the analytic framing around the hunger problem ("What sort of a problem *is* hunger?") has evolved since the hunger issue was put on the international political agenda in the 1940s. When the Hot Springs Conference was

---

36. Staples 2006, 108–9, 113.
37. Bunch 2007, 61n163.
38. McKeon 2009, 19. On the importance of NGOs to the FFHC, see "Report of FAO Council Ad Hoc Committee on Free the World from Hunger Campaign," April 15–17, 1959, 5.
39. McKeon 2009, 21–33.

convened, hunger was framed as a serious problem, and as one which science might increasingly help to address, but not a violation of a human right. When Oxfam and CARE were founded, both framed hunger as an issue for charity, and accordingly targeted individual citizens (in the United Kingdom and United States) to "do their bit" to help mitigate human suffering. Campaigning in many ways circumvented the state or any state responsibility to hunger amelioration entirely, focusing instead on individuals and churches to provide assistance.

Food was deemed a human right, at least on paper, with the approval of the Universal Declaration of Human Rights (UDHR) in 1948. The right to food did not, however, appear on the initial draft of the UDHR. Its inclusion is owed to a proposal by the Panamanian delegation (who received the wording from the American Law Institute). Interestingly, while other economic and social rights, such as housing and health care, were already enshrined in domestic constitutions (often in Latin American states) before they were transported to the UDHR, *food was an entirely new right.* At the point in which it was proposed by the Panamanian delegation, no national constitution included food as a right.[40] By the second session (December 1947) of the UN Commission on Human Rights, the wording of article 25 of the UDHR listed the right to food as essential to a right to health. "Every one without distinction as to economic and social conditions has the right to the preservation of his health through the highest standard of food, clothing, housing and medical care which the resources of the State or community can provide. The responsibility of the State and community for the health and safety of its people can be fulfilled only by the provision of adequate health and social measures."[41]

According to this proposed wording of article 25, responsibility was shared between the state and "community" for the provision of this right. The U.S. delegation had several objections to this wording of article 25. In part, objections centered on the phrase "highest standard," claiming that these rights should be qualified to "affirm the right of each one to have a standard of food . . . necessary for his general well-being, so far as that can be attained, rather than the right of each to have a standard as high as the highest in the State or community." In addition to qualifying the level of social benefits to which an individual would have a right, the United States was adamant that the wording be modified to be "consistently in terms of *declaring rights* rather than prescribing as if by legislation what the State shall do to secure such rights or attempting to define the State's

---

40. Morsink 1999, 192–93.
41. "Restricted: Committee on International Social Policy: Recommendations with Respect to Specific Articles Formulated by the United Nations Commission on Human Rights at Its Second Session in Geneva in December 1947," April 23, 1948, RG 59—Dept of State Decimal File 1945–1949 from 501BD Human Rights/10-147 to 501.BD Human Rights/5-3148, box 2188, U.S. National Archives.

role in their achievement."[42] For this reason, the United States wanted the second sentence of article 25 to be removed completely.

The U.S. objection to linking rights specifically to state responsibilities is not unique to article 25 or the right to food. According to one 1947 telegram sent between two high-level Department of State representatives involved in the drafting of the UDHR, Walter Kotschnig and James Hendrik, the "Declaration should not be phrased [to] give [the] impression [to] individual citizens or governments [that] there is contractual obligation of governments or UN [to] guarantee human rights in declaration."[43] The United States outlined the explanation for its position in greater depth in an April 1948 position paper, noting,

> Since it is the proper purpose of the Declaration to set forth basic human rights and fundamental freedoms, as standards for the United Nations, it is inappropriate to state the rights in the Declaration in terms of governmental responsibility. . . . It is true that the guaranty of certain rights, such as the right to fair trial, rests exclusively in the hands of the Government. In the case of other rights, such as the right to work, the right to health and the right to social security, there are widely different theories and practices in different parts of the world as to the manner in which the Government can best facilitate the desired end.
>
> The United States believes that the Declaration should proclaim rights, but should not attempt to define the role of government in their ultimate attainment.[44]

In part the United States was interested in removing specific government responsibilities from the UDHR because it anticipated the construction of a legally binding covenant on human rights that would provide greater details on state responsibilities for human rights. And yet as the text above highlights, there was already a taken-for-grantedness in how the United States viewed the responsibility

---

42. "Restricted: Committee on International Social Policy: Recommendations," emphasis in the original. The United States was also concerned with the implication that the only way health was achieved was through food, housing, and the like, as it saw sanitation and disease control as equally important to achieving health.

43. "Restricted: Incoming Telegram: For Kotschnig from Hendrick," December 3, 1947, RG 59—Dept of State Decimal File 1945–1949 from 501BD Human Rights/10-147 to 501.BD Human Rights/5-3148, box 2188, U.S. National Archives.

44. This was in part because the covenant would have more specifics on responsibilities than the declaration. Quoted material is from a paper sent by the acting U.S. secretary of state to the U.S. representative to the UN for him, "if he sees no objection, to transmit to the Secretary General of the United Nations." See "Restricted: Committee on International Social Policy: Observations, Suggestions, and Proposals of the United States Relating to the Draft International Declaration on Human Rights and the Draft International Covenant on Human Rights Contained in Annexes A and B of the Report of the Commission on Human Rights Dated December 17, 1947," April 14, 1948, RG 59—Dept of State Decimal File 1945–1949 from 501BD Human Rights/10-147 to 501.BD Human Rights/5-3148, box 2188, U.S. National Archives.

of the state in ensuring some rights (such as the right to a fair trial) as opposed to others (such as health, work, and social security). The UK delegate Lord Charles Dukeston took this objection a step further, as he "emphasized that it was a mistake to proclaim rights without mentioning the duties of the beneficiaries" and that not making some reference to differing levels of resources in each state might "lead to [a] misunderstanding of the part played by the State."[45] The precise wording of what would ultimately constitute article 25 changed a number of times in the following drafting sessions, and at times the specific mentions of food, clothing, and housing were eliminated in favor of the more general wording proposed by India and the United Kingdom, that "everyone has the right to a standard of living adequate for health and well-being, including security in the event of unemployment, disability, old age, or other lack of livelihood in circumstances beyond his control."[46] The specific reference to the right to food and clothing was reintroduced into the article by the Chinese delegate, P. C. Chang, who argued that he "did not see what possible objection there could be to that phrase when millions of people throughout the world were deprived of food and clothing."[47] Ultimately, the Chinese amendment was adopted and the final wording of the first clause of article 25 read, "Everyone has the right to a standard of living adequate for the health and well-being of himself and his family, including food, clothing, housing, and medical care and necessary social services, and the right to security in the event of unemployment, sickness, disability, widowhood, old age or other lack of livelihood in circumstances beyond his control."[48]

When the UDHR was adopted in 1948, it was the first mention of the existence of a right to food, but it would not be the last. Ultimately, the human rights

---

45. See United Nations Economic and Social Council December 16, 1947, 15, quoted and discussed in Morsink 1999, 195. As the original quoted records are summary records, these should not be interpreted as verbatim quotes by Lord Dukeston. Additionally, the United Kingdom was publically shamed by the Soviet delegate, Alexei Pavlov for the extremely high levels of infant mortality (557 out of 1000 births) in Bombay in 1926 and for its failure to mitigate famine in India in 1935, where "three quarters of all deaths were due to diseases of exhaustion, famine, and undernourishment." Pavlov was apparently criticized by UK delegate Christopher Mayhew for providing these unhelpful remarks that "could not help to advance the business of the Committee." See "Confidential: From United Nations General Assembly Paris (UK Del) to Foreign Office," October 15, 1948. DO 35/3776, UK National Archives.

46. See United Nations Economic and Social Council May 24, 1948, quoted in Morsink 1999, 196.

47. United Nations Economic and Social Council June 28, 1948, 13, quoted in Morsink 1999, 197. As the original quoted records are summary records, this should not be interpreted as a verbatim quote by P.C. Chang. According to the summary report (United Nations Economic and Social Council June 28, 1948: 14), the delegate from China (P.C. Chang) argued that he "did not agree that the term 'standard of living' was sufficiently precise. The question involved concerned not only the quantity but also the quality of food. The Chinese representative did not understand the wish to avoid reference to the two principal factors of an adequate standard of living." Here he is referencing both food and clothing as the "two principal factors."

48. Office of the United Nations High Commissioner for Human Rights 1948, article 25.

articulated in the UDHR were split into two covenants: the International Covenant on Civil and Political Rights and the International Covenant on Economic, Social and Cultural Rights (ICESCR). Both were adopted in 1966.[49]

Under article 2.1 of the ICESCR (which includes the right to food under article 11), a state party is required "to take steps . . . to the maximum of its available resources, with a view to achieving progressively the full realization of the rights recognized in the present Covenant." The precise parameters surrounding what the right to food constituted, however, remained vague, even after the ICESCR entered into force. At the 1996 WFS, participants requested that Mary Robinson, the UN high commissioner for human rights, provide greater clarity to this right. Under Robinson's direction and with the help of legal scholar Asbjorn Eide, who first developed what became known as the "tripartite typology of state obligations" (i.e., to respect, protect, and fulfill), the UN Committee on Economic, Social and Cultural Rights (CESCR) adopted General Comment No. 12 (GC 12) in 1999, according to which, "The right to adequate food, like any other human right, imposes three types of levels of obligations on States parties: the obligations to *respect*, to *protect* and to *fulfil*."[50] The Office of the United Nations High Commissioner for Human Rights explains the meaning of these obligations in a helpful diagram (see figure 1.1).

GC 12 was significant in setting the parameters of the human right to food and served to elaborate on the specific duties governments had vis-à-vis that right in international law—namely, that they not only have to respect and protect the right but fulfill it if necessary.[51] GC 12, however, served as a *recommendation* adopted by the CESCR, which was nonbinding under international law.

In later years, the right to food would be recognized in the Convention on the Elimination of All Forms of Discrimination against Women (CEDAW), which took effect in 1981, and the Convention on the Rights of the Child (CRC), which took effect in 1990.[52] Perhaps the most comprehensive statement on the right to food was developed under the auspices of the FAO. Adopted by member states of the FAO by consensus in 2004, the Voluntary Guidelines to Support the Progressive Realization of the Right to Adequate Food in the Context of National Food Security served to "provide practical guidance to States in their implementation of the

---

49. For a helpful overview of international law around varied facets of food security, see Orford 2015. For a thorough analysis of the development of the right to food in law, see the excellent edited volume of Eide and Kracht (2005).

50. CESCR General Comment No. 12: The Right to Adequate Food, paragraph 15, emphasis original; On Robinson's reflections of her (and the UN's) work to develop the right to food, see Robinson, 2005a, xix–xxi.

51. See Way 2005, 215–16.

52. While CEDAW and the CRC do not explicitly state a right to food for all, they recognize state obligation to ensuring adequate food and nutrition to target populations (in CEDAW, pregnant and lactating women; in the CRC, children).

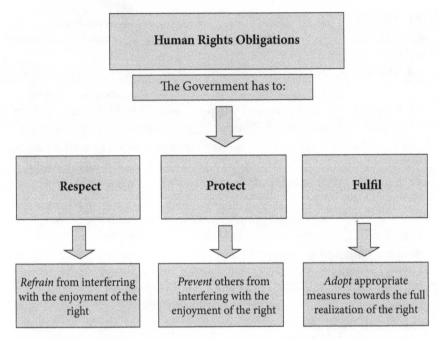

FIGURE 1.1. Human Rights Obligations under General Comment 12. Figure adapted from Office of the United Nations High Commissioner for Human Rights 2008, 11.

progressive realization of the right to adequate food in the context of national food security."[53] Interestingly, as Hartwig de Haen, former assistant director-general of the Economic and Social Department of the FAO notes, the guidelines serve as the "first attempt by governments to interpret an economic right and to recommend actions to be undertaken for its realization."[54] The guidelines are not, however, legally binding.

As articulated in table 1.1, the human right to food is now firmly established in international law. The introduction of a human right to food is an important change in how hunger has been understood, at least in terms of international law, from the 1940s until now. As we will see in subsequent chapters, however, many international anti-hunger organizations still do not conceptualize food as a human right, opting for other analytic frames. Others will use rights rhetoric but root their understanding of a right to food in moral and not legal terms, noting that the moral obligation to fulfill this right is not the exclusive domain of national governments. This will be discussed in greater detail in chapters 4 and 5.

---

53. Food and Agriculture Organization of the United Nations 2004, 9.
54. De Haen 2005, xxiii.

TABLE 1.1 International Human Rights Instruments that Recognize a Right to Food

ABBREVIATION	FULL NAME	YEAR ADOPTED	YEAR ENTERED INTO FORCE	NUMBER OF STATES THAT HAVE RATIFIED AS OF JANUARY 2017	LEGALLY BINDING?
UDHR	Universal Declaration of Human Rights	1948 (UN General Assembly)	N/A	N/A	No
ICESCR	International Covenant on Economic, Social and Cultural Rights	1966 (UN General Assembly)	1976	165	Yes
CEDAW	Convention on the Elimination of all Forms of Discrimination against Women	1979 (UN General Assembly)	1981	189	Yes
CRC	Convention on the Rights of the Child	1989 (UN General Assembly)	1990	196	Yes
—	Voluntary Guidelines to Support the Progressive Realization of the Right to Adequate Food in the Context of National Food Security	2004 (FAO)	N/A	N/A	No

Source: This table is modified from the helpful chart in Eide and Kracht 2007, xxxix.

Note: While CEDAW and the CRC do not explicitly state a right to food for all, they recognize state obligation to ensuring adequate food and nutrition to target populations (in CEDAW, pregnant and lactating women; in the CRC, children).

What Has Stayed the Same?

In many ways, far more has remained the same in how hunger is addressed and discussed internationally than has changed since the Hot Springs Conference of 1943. Perhaps most notably, the hunger problem has never escaped the twin causal claims that hunger is ultimately caused by population growth and insufficient food supply, even when academic research has seriously challenged such claims.[55] Malthusian arguments—that hunger results when the population size outgrows the food supply—were apparent at the Hot Springs Conference, clearly articulated in the early years of the FAO, and picked up speed in the 1950s and 1960s during the Green Revolution, in which the idea that hunger was primarily a supply problem was used to direct global efforts at rapid increases in agricultural

---

55. Most notably through the work of Sen 1981. On the remarkable stability over time of the "grand narrative" surrounding solutions to hunger, see Chappell 2018, 42.

production.[56] When reflecting in 1950 on lessons learned in the first five years of the FAO's existence, then director-general Norris E. Dodd stated unequivocally, "It cannot be stressed enough that this expansion of production has always been FAO's foremost objective."[57] By the early 1970s the FAO believed its mandate was "broad enough to provide for a considerable increase of FAO's population activities" given that it understood such a mandate as deriving "from its basic responsibility for raising rural living levels as laid down in its Constitution."[58] Whether through working to increase agricultural production or decrease the population size (particularly in the developing world), the FAO has frequently approached hunger as a supply problem.

In 1981, Amartya Sen published his groundbreaking *Poverty and Famines: An Essay on Entitlement and Deprivation*, arguing that famines were not caused by insufficient food supply but rather by entitlement failures, examining evidence from several cases including the 1972–74 famine in Ethiopia and the 1974 famine in Bangladesh. While the book provided no overt critique of the FAO, the study was particularly damning to an organization whose primary approach to hunger had been to treat it as, above all, a supply problem.

As Sen's argument gained publicity (and credibility), and as international criticism of the Green Revolution increased, the FAO acknowledged that hunger was not caused by insufficient food supply. And yet, even today the dominant approach to hunger in the FAO is still agricultural development, though the size of agricultural ventures has changed somewhat. The FAO now advocates for increased focus on small-scale agricultural production (though precisely what size constitutes small in scale is a subject of debate), noting that a focus on agricultural industries will result in augmenting rural incomes. And the concern regarding population continues to creep into the food advocacy area, generally in the form of looking long into the future. "Hunger might not be a supply issue *now*, but it *might* be in future generations" is generally how these conversations are framed. Whether one looks to the FAO, the World Bank, think tanks like the International Food Policy Research Institute, general interest publications like *Na-*

---

56. Much has been written about the history of the Green Revolution and its relationship to how global hunger was understood (especially by the United States). For a particularly interesting take, see Cullather 2010. On the concern over insufficient supply and a growing world population, see the FAO's "Policy Committee on Production and Distribution: Provisional Statement on Policy Issues," September 30, 1948. RG 12—Economic Analysis Branch/Div., Policy Comm. Projects (Conf. 1948)/12 ES/ECO 302 folder, Food and Agriculture Organization Archives.

57. "Working Party on Program of Work and Associated Long-Term Problems: Memorandum by the Director General" 1950, box 7FCL7, binder 1 of 2, Food and Agriculture Organization Archives, 8.

58. "FAO's Role in Population Activities," December 1, 1971, ESS:MISC/71/12, RG 8: 10DG Reg. Files FAO Activities of Interest to USA, June 1972, 80DG158 Food and Agriculture Organization Archives.

tional Geographic, or government initiatives like the U.S. Agency for International Development's Feed the Future Initiative, focusing on agricultural development and increased food production remains a commonly proposed solution to hunger.[59] As we will see in subsequent chapters, however, there is still considerable variation within INGO communities as to how they understand appropriate solutions to hunger.

The enduring focus on agricultural development as a solution to hunger may result from the hegemonic influence of agricultural ministers and agricultural epistemic communities in this issue area.[60] The FAO was established, as part of its name implies, with the idea that *agriculture* would be the solution to the hunger problem. Domestic anti-hunger programs are often housed under agricultural ministers and departments of agriculture, giving considerable influence to agricultural experts to determine solutions to hunger. In the United States, the domestic food stamps program is run through the USDA, and it is that agency that is in charge of determining how food insecurity rates will be calculated and studied in America. The emphasis on agricultural productivity is perhaps nowhere more apparent than in sub-Saharan Africa, where efforts such as the Maputo Declaration (in which states commit to combatting hunger by investing at least 10 percent of their national expenditures into agriculture and not, by contrast, into social safety nets or nutritional interventions) prioritize focus on building agricultural industries to combat high hunger rates.[61] While hunger is undeniably a health issue, in part because of the early linking of hunger with agriculture in the Hot Springs Conference and its subsequent creation of the FAO, it is an issue that generally falls under the purview of agriculture and not health. Even as the world urbanizes at unprecedented rates and food supplies have outpaced population growth such that there is a surplus of food supply globally, the hunger problem is still frequently framed as an agricultural problem with agricultural solutions.

Finally, as will be discussed in greater detail in the following chapters, responsibility for hunger remains unclear. Internal U.S. planning documents for the Hot Springs Conference highlight how the United States understood responsibility for hunger amelioration at the time as shared between national governments and the international community.[62] While one Hot Springs Conference report acknowledged that "direct acceptance of responsibility by public authorities for bringing the needed foods to the vulnerable groups is the most practical way of improving

59. Carnemark 2012; Foley 2014; Food and Agriculture Organization of the United Nations 2009; International Food Policy Research Institute 2010.
60. On the power of epistemic communities, see Haas 1992.
61. For calls to increase agricultural productivity in Africa, see Juma 2015; and Paarlberg 2009.
62. "Food and Agriculture: A Possible United Nations Approach."

their nutrition,"[63] the United States noted that "technical aid from the advanced to the more backward countries" as well as the provision of "capital assistance for the improvement of agriculture" from comparatively wealthy states would be essential.[64] The Preamble to the 1945 Constitution of the FAO highlighted the shared nature of responsibility by noting that "separate and collective action[s]" of governments were necessary to "promote the common welfare."[65] By the late 1950s, in discussing the FAO's first major campaign, the FFHC, the U.S. delegation noted that success of this campaign would require efforts beyond national government actions:

> Nations should be prepared to participate actively in the surveys and studies and to use the results in their national planning and in projects aimed at bridging the gap between needed food and available supplies. If nations are not prepared to take an active part, and to follow up with action programs of their own where these are required, the proposed campaign cannot be a success, and the idea should be abandoned. The term "nations" should not be interpreted to mean "governments"; what is intended here is that the major portion of an effort such as this should be undertaken, not by international secretariats, but by national groups, both private and official.[66]

This shared responsibility was not only linked to campaign activities. Indeed, as NGOs increased both in size and number throughout the 1970s and 1980s, they began to pick up development programs and projects as falling under their individual organizational mandates.[67] Civil society began the process of irrigating fields, opening feeding centers, sponsoring school lunches, and providing funding for agricultural development, at times relying on state funding and at times private donations. Potential legal responsibilities of corporations and the private sector to human rights fulfillment were debated in the early twenty-first century

---

63. "Report of Section I, Committee 2: Measures for Improving Standards (Levels) of Food Consumption," n.d. RG 83—Records of the Bureau of Agricultural Economics and Records Relating to the UN Conference on Food and Agriculture, 1943, box 1, Section 1—Reports & Recommendations folder, U.S. National Archives.

64. "Food and Agriculture: A Possible United Nations Approach."

65. Although to be precise, the Preamble opens with a call to "The Nations accepting this Constitution," though as it is governments who approved the document I find it appropriate to assume by "nations" the Preamble were referencing "governments." See: "Constitution of the Food and Agriculture Organization of the United Nations." Printed by the U.S. Government Printing Office Washington 1947. RG 59-General Records of the Department of State. US Delegation Position Papers and Misc. Subject Files 1946-1959. Box 4, FAO: Constitution, Legislation, etc. folder.

66. "FAO Council Ad Hoc Committee on Freedom From Hunger Campaign: Opening Statement by Delegate of United States," April 15–17, 1959 RG 7—Ad Hoc Committee on FFHC, 1959, box 7FCL7, Food and Agriculture Organization Archives.

67. For a very helpful review on the increased relevance of development NGOs, see Fisher 1997.

by the UN Sub-Commission on the Promotion and Protection of Human Rights, which approved its Norms on the Responsibilities of Transnational Corporations and Other Business Enterprises with Regard to Human Rights in 2003. Ultimately the UN Commission on Human Rights did not approve the Norms initiative, though the Guiding Principles on Business and Human Rights were endorsed by the UN Human Rights Council, opening up the door for future efforts to codify in law the responsibility of the private sector (not only the state) in ensuring human rights. These efforts are described in greater detail in chapter 3.

While international human rights law ascribes responsibility to national governments for the protection and fulfillment of the right to food, in practice responsibility remains unclear in the hunger issue area. For all of the attention given to technical innovations, the application of science to agriculture, over seventy years of international conferences, summits, and conventions attended by the most powerful states, the creation of two UN organizations tasked with responding to the hunger problem and the proliferation of large anti-hunger INGOs, the core question of who is ultimately responsible for ensuring people are fed and who is to blame when people are hungry remains contested.

HOW TO THINK ABOUT ADVOCACY

What is the shape of contemporary international anti-hunger advocacy? Can our dominant human rights models make sense of advocacy in this important issue area? While chapter 1 served to provide necessary historical context concerning how responsibility for hunger has been understood in the past, this chapter turns its focus to contemporary international anti-hunger advocacy. Its first objective is to describe in broad strokes the shape of some contemporary international anti-hunger campaigns (for which greater empirical detail is provided in chapter 4). Holding up these examples to the theoretical expectations of dominant models in the human rights literature, I argue that existing models are unable to make sense of international anti-hunger advocacy. In response, I put forward an alternative model of advocacy, the buckshot model, which is better equipped both to describe and explain international advocacy surrounding hunger. Using the hunger case to set up a contrast with more often studied civil and political rights campaigns that have disproportionately informed our theoretical models in the human rights literature, I identify the hidden assumptions behind our dominant human rights models and explore their limitations.

The Contemporary Landscape
of International Anti-Hunger Advocacy

A snapshot of contemporary international anti-hunger advocacy reveals a highly varied, and at times seemingly chaotic, array of campaign targets, strategies, and demands. What unites the diverse array of campaigns is agreement that all people ought to have access to adequate food, though who should do what to ensure that access varies considerably across the campaigns (and at times is unclear even within a single campaign). Let us look at just a few contemporary examples of the types of advocacy work by top international anti-hunger organizations. As explained in the introductory chapter of the book, most interviews with international anti-hunger activists were completed by 2015 and the advocacy work reflected in this chapter (and book) focuses generally on contemporary campaigns and efforts up through 2014.

The 1 Billion Hungry Project

In 2010 the Food and Agriculture Organization (FAO) of the United Nations (UN) launched its 1 Billion Hungry Project, a celebrity spokesperson for which was actor Jeremy Irons. A campaign promotional video features a visibly angry Irons, talking to (and at times yelling at) the camera. "Everyone knows things are bad," Irons begins. "It seems like we're stuck in a world where we can't change a thing but the climate. Every time we check the news we've been hit by a quake or a storm or a financial disaster. We know things are bad, worse than bad, they're crazy!" At this point, Irons screams into the camera, "It looks like everything, everywhere, is going crazy so we don't go out anymore, but we still think we're connected with all the people of the world, but that's not true. People around the world suffer hunger. Chronic hunger. One billion people. One billion of us—now, that's bad! Worse than bad, that's crazy! And we've got to get mad! I want you to get mad! I want you to get up right now, stick your head out of the window and yell 'I am mad as hell. I am mad as hell. I am mad as hell and I'm not going to let one billion people go hungry!' You tell 'em!" The screen then goes to black, with the URL for the website of the campaign centered in bold white lettering.

The 1 Billion Hungry Project, like many international anti-hunger campaigns across the varied landscape of organizations working in this issue area, was a highly emotive campaign, though it was never very clear *at whom* individuals should be "mad as hell." As evident in the campaign's banner hanging on the side of the FAO headquarters in Rome (see figure 2.1), the symbol of the campaign—a yellow whistle to be blown at rallies—symbolized well the message that supporters should vocalize their anger and their resolve that such hunger should be stopped. According to Jacques Diouf, FAO director-general at the time, "We should be extremely angry for the outrageous fact that that our fellow human beings continue to suffer from hunger. If you feel the same way, I want you to voice that anger. All of you, rich and poor, young and old, in developing and developed countries,

FIGURE 2.1. Campaign Banner Hanging on FAO Headquarters, Rome. Photograph by Michelle Jurkovich, May 2012.

express your anger about world hunger by adding your names to the global 1billion hungry petition."[1]

The global petition, however, was directed simply to "governments" (no specific government was mentioned) to "make the elimination of hunger their top priority." No specific policy "asks" were stated on the petition. Whether it was national governments who were obliged to ensure that their own people were fed, or developed states who were obliged to ensure adequate aid was given to developing states, was not articulated.[2] As is common across many contemporary antihunger campaigns, the mobilization tactic was to leverage emotion (in this case,

---

1. Food and Agriculture Organization of the United Nations 2010.
2. Although in an October 2010 "FAO Uganda Information Bulletin," developing and developed states are both highlighted as explicitly targeted under this campaign, with developed states urged to provide more aid and developing countries urged to spend more on agricultural development nationally: "In the developed countries, we want to see governments spending on fighting hunger rise higher on the political agenda and for them to fully commit to the promise of $20 billion for agriculture and food security made at the G8 meeting last year.

anger) without clarifying precisely who the villain was or what should be done to solve the problem. Indeed, in the same year that the 1 Billion Hungry campaign was launched, the then FAO director-general Jacques Diouf delivered a speech at the World Food Day Ceremony at the FAO headquarters in Rome, the theme of which was "United Against Hunger." In his address he both praised the 1 Billion Hungry campaign and noted that "Responding properly to the hunger problem requires urgent, resolute and concerted action by all relevant actors at all levels. It calls for the need for all of us to be united. . . . It underlines that achieving food security is not the responsibility of one single party; it is the responsibility of all of us."[3] The clear message here is that responding to hunger should be an urgent imperative but that responsibility to do so is diffuse.

Behind the Brands and GROW

Oxfam, in its global Behind the Brands campaign, took a different approach. Highlighting the wealth of the "Big 10" transnational food and beverage corporations (Coca-Cola, General Mills, Mondelēz International, and Nestlé, among others), Oxfam lamented that "making sure everyone always has enough nutritious food to eat has not been the focus of these powerful members of the global food system." Such corporations "have the power to exert substantial influence over the traders and governments which control and regulate global food supply chains."[4] According to Oxfam, if big corporations engaged in better land and labor practices, hunger rates would be lower. As such, these were actors that should be targeted in international anti-hunger campaigns.

Behind the Brands falls under Oxfam's overarching, multiyear GROW campaign, which it was running in approximately forty countries by 2013.[5] Many actors were to blame for hunger, according to this campaign, and responsibility for resolving the problem was similarly diffuse. According to Oxfam's June 2011 report *Growing a Better Future: Food Justice in a Resource-Constrained World*,

> Hunger . . . is a by-product of our broken food system. A system constructed by and on behalf of a tiny minority—its primary purpose to delivery profit for them. Bloated *rich-country farm lobbies*, hooked on handouts that tip the terms of trade against farmers in the developing world and force rich-country consumers to pay more in tax and more for food. *Self-serving elites* who amass resources at the expense of

In the developing countries, we want investment in agriculture to be priority in national planning and spending." See Food and Agriculture Organization of the United Nations July-September 2010, 3.

3. Food and Agriculture Organization of the United Nations October 15, 2010.

4. Hoffman 2013, 5, 6.

5. Interview, Oxfam America 1, May 2013.

impoverished rural populations. *Powerful investors* who play commodities markets like casinos, for whom food is just another financial asset. . . . *Enormous agribusiness companies* hidden from public view that function as global oligopolies, governing value chains, ruling markets, accountable to no one. The list goes on.[6]

Indeed, the list does go on in who Oxfam identifies as to blame throughout its multifaceted GROW campaign. At times pushing for reform in biofuel policies from the Global North, increased aid from developing countries, government commitments to reducing greenhouse gasses, and ultimately a "new global governance" of food,[7] GROW targets a wide variety of actors with an at times dizzying array of demands. For the most part, however, the activities Oxfam organizes under GROW are not especially confrontational (for instance, the shaming of national governments through street protests), though Behind the Brands does feature petitions and protests against the Big 10 food corporations, largely in Europe and the United States.

Tax Justice and Food Not Fuel

ActionAid, another large international anti-hunger nongovernmental organization (INGO), launched its multiyear Tax Justice campaign, which targets companies which evade taxes when working in developing countries for robbing these countries of resources that could be used to increase funding for agricultural development to reduce hunger rates, increase funding for education, and improve health care.[8] In addition to the Tax Justice campaign, ActionAid also launched its Food Not Fuel campaign, arguing that increased use of biofuels has served to "undermine food security and fuel hunger around the world."[9] According to ActionAid USA, hunger rates would be lower if agricultural lands now used to grow corn, soy, or sugarcane for the purposes of creating ethanol or biodiesel had instead been used to grow food crops. Additionally, demand for biofuels—from the United States, in particular—has incentivized land grabbing in developing countries, ActionAid argues, as well as food price volatility.[10]

Globally, ActionAid maintains an active "network of passionate campaigners" in more than twenty-five countries,[11] with ActionAid UK highlighting one cam-

---

6. Bailey 2011, 6, emphasis added.
7. Bailey 2011, 50.
8. The Tax Justice campaign used to be called Tax Power. This campaign is not focused solely on reducing hunger, as fighting tax havens served a broader agenda of increasing resources to developing country governments in efforts to reduce poverty. See ActionAid International 2013.
9. Stone 2015, 4.
10. Stone 2015.
11. ActionAid UK 2019.

paign photo with a group of villagers in northern Guatemala holding up a "Food Not Fuel" sign and raising their fists in protest against biofuel production.[12] Guatemala has one of the highest rates of chronic undernutrition in the world, and 46.5 percent of its children under the age of five are stunted in growth, according to the World Food Programme.[13] Notably absent from the Food Not Fuel campaign is a push for the Guatemalan state to improve its social safety nets or the targeting of the Guatemalan state as to blame for its country ranking as among the most chronically hungry in the world.

Enough Food for Everyone IF

ActionAid UK linked its Food Not Fuel campaign into the collaborative Enough Food for Everyone IF campaign, launched in 2013 in the United Kingdom, targeting land grabs and biofuel policies as to blame for hunger in the developing world. The IF campaign briefly united such influential anti-hunger organizations as ActionAid UK, Oxfam Great Britain and Save the Children UK to influence the June 2013 G8 Summit in Northern Ireland. According to the IF campaign,

> We believe there can be enough food for everyone . . .
> - **IF** we give enough aid to **stop children dying from hunger** and help the poorest families feed themselves
> - **IF** governments **stop big companies dodging tax** in poor countries, so that millions of people can free themselves from hunger
> - **IF** we **stop poor farmers being forced off their land** and we grow crops to **feed people not fuel cars**
> - **IF** governments and **big companies are honest and open about their actions** that stop people getting enough food.[14]

The IF campaign leveraged the G8 meeting to focus attention on the responsibility of advanced industrialized states and transnational corporations for reducing hunger internationally.

These brief examples of contemporary international anti-hunger advocacy work are not intended as an exhaustive list of campaigns active in this issue area. There are many more, some of which will be discussed in detail in chapter 4. The purpose of providing a few examples here is to highlight the varied list of actors targeted in contemporary anti-hunger advocacy (national governments, outside states, transnational corporations, U.S. demand for biofuels, etc.) and the diverse

---

12. ActionAid UK. n.d.
13. World Food Programme 2019.
14. Oxfam GB 2013, emphasis in the original.

policy "asks" from international campaigns. In this issue area there is no unitary target actor across advocacy campaigns, nor is there consensus on how the problem of chronic hunger should be solved.

Modeling Human Rights Advocacy

The human rights and transnational advocacy literatures in international relations focus almost exclusively on cases of civil and political rights campaigns. Studies of campaigns against torture, enforced disappearances, apartheid, land mines, and chemical weapons have transformed the way we think about the possibilities for promoting and protecting human rights and the kinds of actors that can successfully do this work.[15] We now know a great deal about civil and political rights campaigning and have used these cases to derive theoretical insights about human rights advocacy generally. And yet many of today's largest and most pressing advocacy campaigns center not on civil and political rights but on economic and social rights. What happens when we apply the lessons of this literature to the case of one essential economic and social right—the right to food? Can they explain the shape and logic of international anti-hunger advocacy?

The remainder of this chapter critically evaluates the assumptions behind our two most dominant models of advocacy in the scholarly literature—Margaret E. Keck and Kathryn Sikkink's "boomerang model" and Thomas Risse, Stephen C. Ropp, and Kathryn Sikkink's "spiral model."[16] These models are both descriptive and explanatory, as they seek both to describe the linkages, shape, and structure of activism around human rights but also explain why activism takes this particular shape. And yet, as I argue here, these models' expectations do not hold in the case of international anti-hunger advocacy. They neither describe nor explain the type of advocacy present in this case. In response, I put forward an alternative model of advocacy, the buckshot model, which I argue is better equipped to explain international anti-hunger advocacy.

Why should it matter if advocacy around one human right cannot be explained by our dominant models? Theoretically, this matters because it highlights weaknesses in some of the core assumptions behind these models—namely, (1) that activists necessarily agree on a unitary target for human rights campaigns, (2) that

---

15. See, for example, Carpenter 2011, 2014; Hawkins 2004; Hyde 2011; Keck and Sikkink 1998; Kelley 2008; Klotz 1999; Lutz and Sikkink 2000; and Price 1997, 1998.

16. Citation counts are imperfect metrics for determining impact, but at the time of this writing, Keck and Sikkink 1998, which provided the boomerang model has been cited over 19,000 times in the literature. The spiral model provided in Risse, Ropp, and Sikkink (1999, 2013) builds off the boomerang model; at the time of this writing, the 1999 version alone has been cited over 3,600 times.

transnational advocacy networks rely on a specific directionality where local NGOs reach out first to international nongovernmental organization (INGOs) for assistance, instead of the other way around, and (3) that UN organizations or other intergovernmental organizations (IGOs) will assist advocacy campaigns in focusing pressure on a common target actor. As we will see in the hunger case, these assumptions do not hold, calling into question some of our core theoretical claims regarding the nature of human rights advocacy.

Existing Models in the Literature

More often than not, when the human rights literature in international relations discusses human rights, activists, and their campaign trajectories, it refers almost exclusively to civil and political rights (or physical integrity rights even more narrowly).[17] In part, this bias toward civil and political rights is an understandable legacy of the Cold War, during which the U.S. government in particular favored an emphasis on civil and political rights, and media coverage generally focused far more on campaigns against violations of these sorts of rights (e.g., torture, enforced disappearances, lack of free speech, etc.) than violations of economic or social rights (e.g., inadequate food, shelter, health care, or education).

The academy followed suit. Noticing patterns in how transnational actors could compel national governments to improve their human rights records, particularly in the case of civil and political rights, Keck and Sikkink (1998) and Risse, Ropp, and Sikkink (1999, and most recently in their updated 2013 edition) developed what are still the two dominant advocacy models referenced in the human rights literature. Their boomerang model and spiral model, respectively, sought to describe and explain how advocacy networks could change the behavior of target actors, often through social pressure.[18] These models functioned on the basis of a common (essential) assumption—that blame could be centered on a common target actor, almost always a "violating" national government, such that pressure could be focused by transnational actors onto the target actor to compel change.[19]

---

17. There are some notable exceptions here. See for example Hertel 2006. For an excellent analysis of right-to-education campaigns, see Mundy 2010. On the right to health in South Africa, see Heywood 2009.

18. Keck and Sikkink 1998; Risse, Ropp, and Sikkink 1999, 2013.

19. In their updated 2013 edition, Risse, Ropp and Sikkink include cases targeting private actors and rebel groups. While the boomerang model is drawn to focus on violating states (e.g., "State A" and "State B" in the model), Keck and Sikkink (1998) also acknowledge advocacy targeting Nestlé, a private corporation. The focus on civil political rights specifically is also common outside the constructivist literature on human rights. Lebovic and Voeten 2006 and Simmons 2009 also focus, with few exceptions, on questions of state commitment to civil and political human rights. See also Goodliffe and Hawkins 2006; and Moravcsik 2000.

And the models worked. From cases of forced disappearances in Guatemala to torture in Kenya, racial discrimination in South Africa and arbitrary arrest in the Philippines, scholars were able to explain national governments' acquiescence to international pressure in the form of changed behavior vis-à-vis political and civil human rights.[20]

But while these models have been an extremely useful point of departure for the literature on transnational advocacy, they are less clear in articulating their scope conditions. Risse and Ropp note that the spiral model works best when not dealing with cases of "limited statehood."[21] Keck and Sikkink note that the boomerang model should work best when vulnerable groups serve as victims (notably, children) and when causal chains are short.[22] And yet, hunger exists in a great many countries with high levels of state capacity (the United States comes immediately to mind) without the expected type of advocacy expected in the spiral model. Turning to the scope conditions articulated in Keck and Sikkink, there are certainly a great many hungry children in the world without the sort of advocacy expected by the boomerang model. And while causality is complex in the hunger case, I would argue that causality is almost *always* complex around human rights violations. Consider the case of torture. When Amnesty International shamed then president George W. Bush for acts of torture committed during his time in office the argument was not that he, himself, was the individual physically torturing detainees. The argument was instead that the president was ultimately responsible for ensuring that this sort of violation does not happen and that by authorizing "enhanced interrogation techniques" he should be investigated for violating international law. According to Amnesty International, the president "did not take all necessary and reasonable measures in his power as Commander in Chief and President to prevent" the acts of torture that took place.[23] The causal chain between former president George W. Bush and specific acts of torture may have been complex, but this did not mean that there was confusion in *who was ultimately to blame* if torture took place. The purpose of raising this case is only to note that causality around human rights violations is almost always complex, and when we believe it to be simple or obvious it is more likely due to much effort by activists to convince us that causality and responsibility are simple or obvious, and not an inherent feature of the case itself. Chapters 3 and 4 will further engage with this argument.

---

20. Black (1999); Gränzer (1999); Jetschke (1999); Keck and Sikkink (1998); Klotz (1999); Risse, Ropp and Sikkink (1999, 2013); Schmitz (1999); Thomas (1999).
21. Risse and Ropp 2013, 4.
22. Keck and Sikkink 1998, 27. They also reference that advocacy may be more successful when "involving legal equality of opportunity."
23. Amnesty International 2011, 1.

The Spiral Model

In 1999 Risse, Ropp, and Sikkink wrote one of the foundational texts for the human rights literature, arguing that they created a model of "human rights change" which mapped the socialization process of "human rights norms" in a way that was "generalizable across cases irrespective of cultural, political, or economic differences of the countries."[24] Their 2013 edition of this argument, however, acknowledged that state capacity—in particular, in the case of weak or failed states—would affect compliance with human rights and that nonstate actors could also be targeted as human rights violators.[25]

The spiral model is designed to explain key phases of human rights change as the result of a dynamic process of interaction between the state, domestic society, and international/transnational actors. More specifically, it theorizes types of socialization processes and identifies five phases where the state's response to a given human right can change because of the power of international norms and the state's interaction with domestic society or the international community. It is worth noting that not all human rights campaigns are expected to follow all five of the phases or do so in the same order. Rather, the spiral model is "a causal model which attempts to explain the variation in the extent to which national governments move along the path toward improvement of human rights conditions. . . . Thus, the 'spiral model' serves to operationalize the theoretical framework of norm socialization . . . to identify the dominant mode of social interaction in each phase . . . and, ultimately, to specify the causal mechanisms by which international norms affect domestic structural change."[26]

The Boomerang Model

Risse and Sikkink note that their spiral model builds upon on the earlier boomerang model (figure 2.2) developed by Keck and Sikkink, with the spiral model containing "several 'boomerang throws.'"[27] Briefly, the boomerang model hypothesizes linkages between domestic NGO groups, INGOs, and outside states which can work together to apply pressure to a norm-violating state to compel behavior change. According to the model, when unable to successfully apply pressure alone to a norm-violating state, domestic NGOs can link with INGOs to gain leverage (through increased resources) in partnership with other states and intergovernmental organizations (IGOs) to pressure the norm-violating state to

---

24. Risse and Sikkink 1999, 3, 6.
25. Risse and Ropp 2013, 3–4.
26. Risse and Ropp 2013, 18–19.
27. Risse and Sikkink 1999, 18.

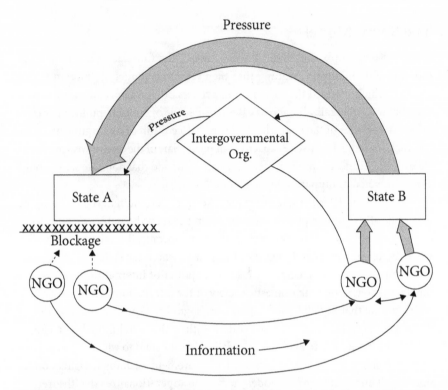

FIGURE 2.2. The Boomerang Model. Reprinted from *Activists Beyond Borders: Advocacy Networks in International Politics*, by Margaret E. Keck and Kathryn Sikkink. Copyright © 1998 by Cornell University. Used by permission of the publisher, Cornell University Press.

change its behavior.[28] For their part, domestic NGOs provide legitimacy and necessary information about the rights violations to INGOs.

Taken together, the boomerang and spiral models have effectively generated a vibrant research program examining how activists can effectively leverage social pressure to compel behavioral change among violators of some human rights. These models rely on a number of assumptions, however, which are made especially problematic in light of the hunger case. I take each of these in turn.

Agreement on a Unitary Target Actor

Both models operate from the assumption that all actors involved in the advocacy network (IGOs, INGOS, NGOs, and states) *agree on a common, unitary*

---

28. Keck and Sikkink 1998, 12–13.

target for a rights violation. Generally the target actor for a rights violation is the national government. As shown in figure 2.2, the boomerang model labels the sole target of an advocacy campaign explicitly as "State A" and the spiral model labels the target as "State," though both acknowledge nonstate actors could also be targets.[29] According to Keck and Sikkink, "Governments are the primary 'guarantors' of rights, but also their primary violators. When a government violates or refuses to recognize rights, individuals and domestic groups often have no recourse. . . . When channels between the state and its domestic actors are blocked, the boomerang pattern of influence characteristic of transnational networks may occur: domestic NGOs bypass their state and directly search out international allies to try to bring pressure on their states from outside. This is most obviously the case in human rights campaigns."[30]

But are national governments the obvious target for all human rights campaigns? Whom do activists target in their many international advocacy anti-hunger campaigns? Far from focused pressure on a single actor that advocates agree is to blame for hunger, international anti-hunger organizations are waging campaigns against a diverse array of targets: transnational corporations, national governments, outside states (usually developed states), or other actors, though sometimes they choose to blame no one at all for the hunger problem. Examples provided earlier in this chapter from INGOs such as ActionAid and Oxfam highlight the diversity of targets in contemporary international anti-hunger advocacy campaigns. In this issue area there is no centralized pressure by advocates (even within the same organization) on a single target; rather, international anti-hunger campaigns target a wide array of actors, often at the same time.

As one senior official at Oxfam International told me, "There's no way that we could only target national governments. That would be tremendously naive. It's not the way the world works."[31] Food is a human right, but the understanding of this "right" across advocacy communities is not always what we would expect it to be from an international legal standpoint where national governments are "primary guarantors." According to one Oxfam Great Britain senior staffer in discussing her work with the Behind the Brands campaign, "Both influencing governments *and* influencing the private sector, I think they're both relevant to a rights-based approach."[32] While there certainly is agreement among these influential anti-hunger organizations on a common

---

29. For example, Risse, Ropp, and Sikkink (2013) acknowledge the need to focus on nonstate actors such as private actors and rebel groups. Keck and Sikkink 1998 document advocacy against some private actors, such as Nestlé, though the "boomerang model" itself identifies the advocacy target as the state.

30. Keck and Sikkink 1998, 12.

31. Interview, Oxfam International 1, July 2015.

32. Interview, Oxfam Great Britain 2, July 2015, emphasis added.

goal (ameliorating hunger), there is not the expected consensus across actors on a common unitary target that would be expected in either the boomerang or spiral models.

Directionality in Transnational Advocacy Campaigns

In both the boomerang and spiral models, campaigns involving INGOs are expected to originate at the level of domestic civil society groups. Domestic actors make the first move in these models, appealing to their larger international counterparts for assistance in campaigns begun at the local level. In the case of the boomerang model, it is in part the need for *information* which solidifies partnerships between local activist groups and larger, wealthier (and often more powerful) NGOs and INGOs. While Keck and Sikkink acknowledge that information goes both ways (from grassroots organizations to larger NGOs and INGOs and the reverse), they note that "most nongovernmental organizations cannot afford to maintain staff people in a variety of countries. In exceptional cases they send staff members on investigation missions, but this is not practical for keeping informed on routine developments. Forging links with local organizations allows groups to receive and monitor information from many countries at low cost. Local groups, in turn, depend on international contacts to get their information out and to help protect them in their work."[33]

In issue areas like hunger, however, the existence and even the scale of the problem is already documented at the international level, as IGOs such as the FAO control and disseminate the authoritative "hunger count" for each country. Certainly this is not to say that the production of hunger statistics is without controversy. Indeed, the production of hunger statistics remains fraught with methodological and political problems.[34] However, unlike in the cases of some civil and political rights where widespread prevalence data may not be collected nor disseminated through IGOs and where local NGOs are needed to provide information on the existence of the violation to INGOs, multiple sets of hunger statistics are collected and disseminated regularly, including the Food Insecurity Experience Survey (FAO/Gallup), the Prevalence of Undernourishment indicator (FAO), and stunting, wasting, and underweight anthropometric indicators (World Health Organization), to attempt to capture

33. Keck and Sikkink 1998, 22.
34. On the methodological problems of hunger statistics, see Jurkovich 2016; Lappé et al. 2013; and Svedberg 1999.

the scale of the problem of hunger across countries and, in the case of some statistics, subnationally.[35]

In practice, this means local community organizations serve a slightly different purpose for larger INGOs. Instead of providing information on the existence or scale of hunger, these groups provide human stories and faces to the campaigns waged by INGOs. They may also provide details on specific farmer groups that have been displaced from their land or local land grabbing which has taken place in a given community. INGOs do not, however, need local groups for information on the existence (or extent) of the hunger problem in a given country.

Instead, in this issue area directionality runs both ways in transnational advocacy campaigns. One Oxfam America official reflected on an instance when Oxfam wanted to launch a campaign against land grabbing but needed to find appropriate cases. Oxfam asked "Where is a good case example of a land grab that we can use?" and decided on a case in Uganda.[36] Here, Oxfam first had decided this was an important issue around which to campaign and then selected a country case that it thought would be most effective for such a campaign. GROW, the largest campaign Oxfam has ever run (and its signature international anti-hunger campaign), was primarily designed in a top-down fashion where, according to one Oxfam senior official, "we see globally that we can work together to pressure, you know, global targets and then . . . shoot down into the country level, so that we can . . . bring out national cases to be global examples and that we can also stimulate national work that will be coherent with the types of things that we're doing globally."[37] It is "a little of both," another Oxfam America official noted, when asked if campaigns originate with local communities or at the level of the INGO.[38] Another official at Oxfam Great Britain lamented that more campaign work was not "bottom-up" when thinking about her time working on Behind the Brands:

> And we'd like it to be much more bottom-up, I think. That would be the best way forward. But with Behind the Brands, it's largely come more . . . we started basically with our ten companies. And we know who they are. We've chosen them because they're the ten biggest food and beverage companies. And we think that they have the most leverage, and therefore, the best targets. And because of that we have then looked to kind of pick up on specific issues with companies where we think they're

---

35. That does not mean, however, that these statistics are without controversy or even that the data UN organizations provide is always reliable. See Jurkovich 2016; Lappé et al. 2013; and Svedberg 1999. On the fraught nature of development statistics, especially in Africa, see Jerven 2013.

36. Interview, Oxfam America 2, May 2013.

37. Interview, Oxfam America 2, May 2013.

38. Interview, Oxfam America 3, April 2013.

not doing enough. And then, we have kind of looked into these companies' supply chains and looked for examples in countries. So it has kind of gotten fairly top-down. But I think ideally, if we're to kind of develop a campaign in something, we'd like to think about is how to have a more kind of bottom-up approach, perhaps more led by more by country programs.[39]

A senior official at ActionAid USA responded that determining linkages (between INGOs and NGOs) was "complicated." Reflecting on a case of land grabbing in Tanzania, she recalled that "people in the [local] communities were coming to ActionAid Tanzania about this problem," which she described as "a U.S. company that was actually partnering with [a U.S. university] that was engaged in a land grab in Western Tanzania." And yet, "communities were divided about the land. So . . . there wasn't necessarily a straightforward strategy emerging from the ground. But we looked at it in the big picture of the new alliance and said, you know, what are the policy initiatives that are pushing for this type of development, and raised our critique from that angle."[40] While campaigns may originate at the level of local NGOs, in the hunger issue area it appears equally likely that INGOs will use data available to them to determine an effective campaign framing and reach out after they have done so to find local partners in campaigns largely designed within the INGO itself.

Intergovernmental Organizations as Partners in Applying Social Pressure

Finally, IGOs, which serve in the boomerang and spiral models to empower advocacy INGOs and join with them to apply pressure to target national governments, do not play the same role in international anti-hunger advocacy. The FAO, established in 1945 with a mandate to ameliorate global hunger, has become the main authoritative voice in the UN for all matters related to chronic undernourishment. The World Food Programme, once a division within the FAO but now its own independent IGO, serves as the UN's largest humanitarian organization focusing on the provision of food assistance globally. Neither organization publicly pressures specific governments about their state obligations to respect, protect, and fulfill the right to food in their countries or shames them for noncompliance with these obligations, though the core purpose of both organ-

---

39. Interview, Oxfam Great Britain 2, July 2015.
40. Interview, ActionAid USA 2, June 2015.

izations is to assist in the realization of this human right. While the 1 Billion Hungry Project did direct its petition to "governments," it was never specific in *which* governments were obliged to act in a particular way to ameliorate hunger; no individual governments were singled out or shamed. When asked about whether the FAO could blame or pressure a national government, one senior FAO employee responded, "But this we can't do . . . no . . . [the FAO] cannot. It can support countries. It can raise awareness. It can support countries that are interested to implement the right to food"[41] The FAO can provide support and guidance if governments want help in developing agriculture or even implementing legislation on right-to-food provisions, but the organization does not use the mechanisms of focused shaming or blaming, as might be expected in the boomerang or spiral models. Another senior FAO official, who had worked for decades in the organization, quipped that while the FAO Council and FAO Conference (organizational governing bodies) were supposed to "give advice to government," she "never quite understood what that means."[42]

Instead the FAO highlights many varied possible causes of hunger and many possible solutions in its seemingly limitless reports, conventions, and summits. In recent years, climate change, gender inequalities, poverty, land tenure systems, and price speculation are all highlighted as "to blame" for global hunger. That is not to say that the FAO does not, on paper, embrace food as a right for which national governments are responsible. Indeed, it helped to organize and develop the FAO Voluntary Guidelines to Support the Progressive Realization of the Right to Adequate Food in the Context of National Food Security (adopted by the FAO Council in 2004), though as one senior FAO official involved in the drafting process noted, "To be very frank, no, that was not desired from management in the FAO to engage in that . . . debate [over] our right to food." Instead, some at the FAO pushed back on efforts to organize the Voluntary Guidelines, arguing that this was a "matter for the United Nations . . . not the FAO."[43] Indeed, the FAO often has to be dragged into more contentious right-to-food work, somewhat reluctantly—quite the far cry from how the role of an IGO is understood in the boomerang model. Moreover, as the FAO Council is driven by "the desire to do everything by consensus, which is the worst," it tends to result in "wishy-washy" positions in the FAO.[44]

---

41. Interview, FAO 8, May 2012. This was reiterated by another senior FAO employee who noted that the FAO was not in the business of holding states accountable. Interview, FAO 1, May 2012.

42. Interview, FAO 9, July 2011.

43. Interview, FAO 2, May 2012.

44. Interview, FAO 9, July 2011.

The Buckshot Model

In the case of international anti-hunger advocacy, therefore, instead of boomerangs or spirals we see buckshot (see figure 2.3).

There are a few significant differences between the boomerang and buckshot models. Most notably, the buckshot model does not have a second arm of the boomerang pattern focused squarely back on the "norm-violating" national government ("State A" in the boomerang model). Instead, INGOs and IGOs involved in the hunger issue area "buckshot" blame to multiple different actors, linking to different causal frames. Individual INGOs may target two or three actors as "to blame" in any individual campaign and then start a new campaign soon after that targets different actors (such as Oxfam with Behind the Brands and GROW). Or, alternatively, INGOs may run multiple campaigns at the same time around the hunger issue, focusing blame on varied actors and varied causes of hunger (such as ActionAid with its Tax Justice and Food Not Fuel campaigns). It does, however, occasionally happen that an INGO will wage a campaign applying pressure and blame back at the national government, but overt, aggressive naming and shaming is comparatively rare in this issue area, for which reason they are marked

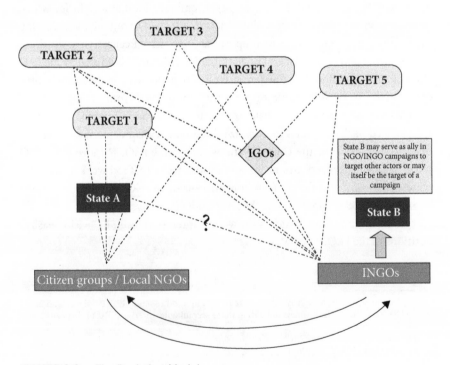

FIGURE 2.3. The Buckshot Model.

with a question mark in figure 2.3.[45] Furthermore, INGOs may attempt to partner with IGOs, like the FAO, but IGOs in this issue area do not serve to focus pressure on a singular "violating" state. Rather, they may join in campaigns highlighting
varied causes of hunger which are not aggressively targeting a specific state, or
they may refrain entirely.

An outside state ("State B") also functions differently from how we would
expect in the boomerang model. While INGOs may reach out to outside states
to serve as allies in their campaigns against diverse target actors, it is more
common that "State B" may find itself a target of the advocacy campaign (for
things like increasing foreign aid or reducing greenhouse gas emissions to
curb climate change). As will be discussed in greater detail in chapter 4, because
hunger as an issue area sits at the nexus of development and human rights
frameworks, campaigns sometimes target outside states (generally advanced
industrialized states) as actors that ought to be blamed for chronic hunger
elsewhere in the world.

Additionally, while retaining part of the first arm of the boomerang, the buckshot model expects that partnerships can be initiated by either local NGOs or
INGOs. This is in part because local NGOs are not needed to provide information in the same way expected in the boomerang model. Some anti-hunger IN-
GOs are just as likely to decide the direction of a campaign back in an affiliate or
confederate office in the United Kingdom or United States and then reach out
for local partners, as they are receptive to local partners taking the initiative.

Finally, the buckshot model does not assume that advocacy necessarily takes
a confrontational approach to the target actor. While both Keck and Sikkink
(1998) and Risse, Ropp, and Sikkink (2013) acknowledge the importance of less
confrontational approaches to advocacy (notably, through persuasion), many of
the applications of these models highlight a more antagonistic relationship between advocacy organizations and target actors (especially states) than may be
present in advocacy around hunger.

Certainly shaming and blaming plays an important role in some international
anti-hunger advocacy, especially against private-sector targets. And yet, the type
of advocacy here is far more nuanced. One senior official at ActionAid USA
described the organization as "the best friend and worst enemy of every

---

45. FIAN International is one INGO that does consistently wage campaigns which take similar
forms to the boomerang model (i.e., blame is centralized back on the national government), but not
exclusively, and this practice is not common among anti-hunger INGOs. The case of FIAN International and its campaigns will be discussed in both chapters 4 and 5. It is more likely—particularly
with hybrid development-rights INGOs like Oxfam—that when national governments are "targeted" it will be with far less aggressive pressuring than the boomerang model would suggest, as IN-
GOs in this issue area worry about protecting relationships with national governments in order to
preserve their active in-country development missions.

government."[46] One Oxfam Great Britain official described the organization's relationship with the private sector targeted in its Behind the Brands campaign as a "critical friend relationship."[47] Put more bluntly, a senior official at Oxfam America said, "You know what my line that I use a lot in this office is? 'I want to hear your best passive-aggressive approach to getting this solved.' Aggressive will get you kicked out. Passive is 'Go do World Vision.' I want passive-aggressive. I want you to get shit done and change the power without being in people's faces."[48] A senior official at World Vision International noted that, having been kicked out of Somalia once already, the organization was more apt to use "not a confrontational approach but . . . a collaborative approach."[49]

This does not mean that international anti-hunger organizations never use shaming or blaming or social or reputational pressure in their work. They certainly do. Behind the Brands is a campaign which attempts to shame the private sector into better labor and land policies vis-à-vis food. ActionAid's Tax Justice campaign did not shy away from blaming the financial services company Barclay's for helping corporations to evade tax responsibilities in the developing world. FIAN International attempted to shame the Philippine government for not making good on land tenure reform which FIAN argued was contributing to hunger in the region. And yet, when these organizations do run campaigns which rely on social pressure, they are generally less aggressive, especially in campaigning against developing country governments, than the civil and political rights campaigns envisioned by those using the boomerang and spiral models. Advocacy, moreover, takes many varied forms in this issue space, with traditional campaigns being only one kind of advocacy. Alternative forms of advocacy, for example, may take the form of lobbying the U.S. Congress for reforms to foreign aid to benefit food assistance programs abroad or advocating for change within donor government development agencies for reforms to their international food security programming or policies.

When asked why advocacy tended to be less aggressive, especially toward governments, staff at ActionAid, Oxfam, and World Vision noted that they struggled with questions of legitimacy in telling other governments, in particular, how to spend their money. One senior official at World Vision International explained a lack of aggressive campaigning against national governments by saying, "You're from the outside. You're not part of the country, you don't feel necessarily that you should be having a political view because, of course, people then say, well,

46. Interview, ActionAid USA 1, June 2013.
47. Interview, Oxfam Great Britain 1, July 2015.
48. Interview, Oxfam America 1, May 2013.
49. Interview, World Vision International 1, May 2013.

that's an outside entity pushing their views on us."[50] One senior official at Oxfam America expressed a similar concern:

> Oxfam is a northern NGO for the most part. And there is, we have to be careful about Oxfam lecturing developing country governments about what they should be doing. Our voice is most credible, most authoritative, and has the most legitimacy in speaking to our own governments and our own home-based activist-like corporations and our own publics. . . .
>
> We recognize developing country governments as important and maybe more important targets. . . . But it doesn't change our—it doesn't inherently change whether our voice is legitimate. . . . We're comfortable reaching out to global audiences to bring pressure on global targets. And we're comfortable with activists in Bolivia criticizing the United States or activists in Bolivia criticizing Coca-Cola. We're not comfortable with activists in America criticizing the government of Bolivia and we're not—well, it's not Oxfam's role.[51]

A common refrain was that northern-based INGOs lacked legitimacy when telling developing country governments how they should spend their national budgets. Interestingly, however, the concern over legitimacy did not necessarily extend into how members of these organizations viewed advocacy over other issue areas within their organizations. In another meeting with a senior Oxfam America official we discussed comparing Oxfam's work across a number of different rights, in particular focusing on how Oxfam's understanding of state obligation across different rights would vary:

> MICHELLE JURKOVICH: So with other economic and social rights issues, you mentioned education and health care, if you were to . . . look at how Oxfam deals with the right to education, right to health care, right to food—and perhaps using the term *right* isn't even applicable—do you think that the campaigns . . . target in the same way? Or is it that with food you target the private sector more than you would education, for example . . .
>
> OXFAM AMERICA SENIOR OFFICIAL: Well, it depends on the role. I mean, you know, Oxfam's work on health and education is that this is a responsibly of the public sector, so . . .
>
> JURKOVICH: Governments?
>
> OXFAM AMERICA SENIOR OFFICIAL: Yes. So it's . . .
>
> JURKOVICH: But food is not?

50. Interview, World Vision International 1, May 2013.
51. Interview, Oxfam America 3, April 2013.

OXFAM AMERICA SENIOR OFFICIAL: Providing food. Providing an education and health service is our position that governments have the obligation to provide health care and education services.

JURKOVICH: That's interesting. But not food?

OXFAM AMERICA SENIOR OFFICIAL: No, governments don't provide food.

JURKOVICH: This fascinates me . . .

OXFAM AMERICA SENIOR OFFICIAL: But, I mean, to provide food, sure . . . a safety net is an issue. A safety net is, you know, I mean, we're much further in getting recognition of free health care and education than we are safety nets. I mean, there's many more countries where you have . . . basic health care and education, and you don't have safety nets. So safety nets still, you know, the basic social safety net is still a struggle to get, a lot because of cost, I think. . . . And so I would say . . . the right to food is similar to—well, I don't know, I guess I've never really thought about that. I was going to say it was similar to the right to housing, you know? It's not the government that provides the house, but it's the right to . . . like the right to water, the right to food, the government doesn't provide the water, you know, the government provides the framework to enable, that is, I think, is the issue. But in health care and education, we believe that governments should provide services.[52]

Underpinning questions of legitimacy appears to be a lack of a consensus that national governments really ought to be responsible for ensuring access to adequate food for its citizens such that an advocacy group would be entitled to point fingers and shame a government into fulfilling its responsibility regardless of where that organization is headquartered.

As subsequent chapters will demonstrate, the type of advocacy generated around hunger is nuanced. The "critical friend" or "passive-aggressive approach" referenced by activists means that while international anti-hunger organizations will at times blame and shame targets, they also attempt other strategies such as partnering with governments to build more effective policies through providing additional research or information to the target actor.

The Significance of Buckshot Advocacy

The buckshot model appears complex, but conveying this complexity is essential to understanding the logic of advocacy in the hunger issue area. It is in the seem-

---

52. Interview, Oxfam America 2, May 2013.

ingly chaotic nature of advocacy that we not only can challenge hidden assumptions in previous models but better understand the potential effects of this type of advocacy. This is especially true in creating openings for political manipulation and the deflection of responsibility. Buckshot advocacy—by which I mean advocacy in issue areas where, despite a shared common campaign goal (e.g., reducing hunger), IGOs, INGOs, and NGOs focus their campaigns on diffuse targets, often simultaneously—poses challenges both to activists who engage in this style of advocacy and to scholars attempting to study issue areas where there remains no single "villain" around which campaigns may be targeted.

To activists, the long-term effect of this strategy may be a failure to effectively hold any single actor (namely, a national government) to account for persistent problems of chronic hunger. As the old adage goes, "If everyone is responsible, nobody is accountable." While scholarly debates surrounding the strategy of advocacy framing often focus on meaning-making through framing, how frames are constructed, and why some frames "resonate" more than others,[53] the buckshot model encourages attention to target cohesiveness. Jeremy Shiffman and colleagues examine a series of public health problems to determine why some succeed in attracting attention and funding while others (of similar characteristics and importance) do not. They argue that issue networks are more likely to succeed in attracting funding and attention in cases where "members construct a compelling framing of the issue, one that includes a shared understanding of the problem, [and] a *consensus* on solutions and convincing reasons to act" (Shiffman et al., 2016, 110, emphasis added).

When advocacy organizations lack a cohesive frame attributing responsibility to a shared actor for a shared policy "ask," they may unintentionally create space for targeted actors to deflect responsibility onto other actors or institutions. Take, for example, former president of Guatemala Álvaro Colom declaring a "state of public calamity" because of staggering hunger rates but blaming the problem on climate change.[54] Government officials in Mali in 2015 similarly blamed global warming for widespread chronic hunger in their country.[55] In the case of Nigeria, the minister of agriculture, Chief Audu Ogbeh, acknowledged in August 2016 that "there is a cry in the air that Nigerians are hungry and we hear them loud and clear" but declared that such hunger was not the fault of the Nigerian government. Instead, blame for hunger resided with the Global North, especially because of forced currency devaluations dating back to 1986 and the Nigerian state being "forced to open our doors to importation."[56] Of course,

---

53. Benford and Snow 2000; Goffman 1974; Sell and Prakash 2004; Snow and Benford 1988.
54. Buchanan 2009.
55. Arsenault 2015.
56. Ripples Nigeria 2016.

government leaders can also attempt to deflect responsibility for hunger without relying on previously legitimated targets. Venezuelan president Nicolás Maduro, for example, blamed the Central Intelligence Agency for food shortages in his country.[57]

How (Is Buckshot) Possible?

Understanding that international anti-hunger advocacy cannot be explained by dominant human rights models helps us to identify problematic assumptions in our literature on human rights advocacy, but it also raises a new question: How is it possible that international anti-hunger advocacy behaves so differently than our expectations in the human rights and transnational advocacy literatures? This is, by nature, a constitutive question, and answering it requires careful thinking about the normative environment in which international anti-hunger advocates are working.[58] We turn to answering this "How is it possible?" question in chapter 3.

---

57. Lopez 2013.
58. On the difference between constitutive and causal questions, see Finnemore 2003, 14–15; and Wendt 1999, 77–78, 83–85.

NOT ALL HUMAN RIGHTS HAVE NORMS

Taking as a starting point what we discovered in chapter 2—that international anti-hunger advocacy does not fit the expectations of dominant models in the field—we are left with another question: How is it possible that international anti-hunger campaigns behave so differently from our expectations in the human rights and transnational advocacy literatures? In order to answer this question, we need to understand the social and normative environment in which activists are working. This chapter argues that the lack of a norm around hunger and the right to food among executive and senior staff of top international anti-hunger organizations is essential to explaining the trajectory of advocacy campaigns in this important issue area.

Implicit in the human rights literature is the assumption that all human rights have norms, and thus we expect they make up a fixed part of the social landscape in which activists engage in advocacy work. This chapter challenges this assumption and broadens the conceptual tool kit available to human rights scholars by highlighting the distinctions between norms, moral principles, and supererogatory standards. Clarifying what a norm is (and, importantly, what it is not) improves our analytic equipment and theories, but the inquiry is not purely a theoretical exercise. In the case of hunger, clarifying the norm concept enables us to understand how the nature and shape of advocacy may vary based on the normative environment in which activists are working. If activists are engaging in an issue area around which there are established moral principles but no norms, or if activists are working in an issue area for which behaviors by specific actors to ameliorate a condition are understood as optional but not obligatory, we should expect that this will affect the logic and shape of their advocacy campaigns. Constructivist work often highlights how norms make some action *possible* but often does not look at the logical corollary: how a lack of a norm can make action *impossible* or *less possible*. When a norm is present, it can constitute one type of environment in which human rights activists may work. A lack of a norm constitutes a different kind of environment. The constructivist literature generally focuses on cases where there *are* norms and these norms can be leveraged by activists. It rarely stops to ask what happens when *there is no norm* to be leveraged in the first place. This chapter begins to fill in this gap.

The chapter opens with a general discussion on what constitutes a norm and how norms differ from moral principles and supererogatory standards. It then provides evidence of a lack of norm around hunger, drawn from surveys and interviews with senior and executive staff at top international anti-hunger organizations. The surveys show that there is no consensus across these senior staff on an actor who is to blame for chronic hunger or on how the problem should be solved. The chapter concludes with a discussion of the implications for a lack of a norm both for activist efforts and for the shape of international anti-hunger advocacy.

What Constitutes a Norm?

Scholarly discussion of norms has now permeated all theoretical approaches in international relations (IR). Rationalists and realists speak of norms even if they argue that norms matter less in influencing behavior than constructivists might expect.[1] Perhaps because of the regularity with which norms are discussed in IR, scholars now rarely define what they mean by the concept, which may contribute to the blurred boundaries of the concept in contemporary scholarship.

Earlier scholarship was much more careful in setting the parameters of the norm concept. Ronald L. Jepperson, Alexander Wendt, and Peter J. Katzenstein (1996, 54) define norms as "collective expectations about proper behavior for a given identity."[2] Martha Finnemore and Kathryn Sikkink (1998, 891) define a norm in similar terms as "a standard of appropriate behavior for actors with a given identity."[3] While some scholars have focused on disaggregating norms into

---

1. See, for example, Abbott and Snidal 1998; Morrow 2007; Schweller and Pu 2011; Simmons 2009; and Walt 2009.
2. This serves as the definition of the term *norm* throughout Katzenstein 1996.
3. Within the field of sociology we see a similar categorization of the norm as including a sense of oughtness combined with an actor and an expected action or behavior. See, for instance, Parsons 1937: "A norm is a verbal description of the concrete course of action thus regarded as desirable, combined with an injunction to make certain future actions conform to this course. An instance of a norm is the statement: 'Soldiers should obey the orders of their commanding officers'" (75).

various types (e.g., legal, social, prescriptive, regulatory, and descriptive norms, among others),[4] for the most part constructivist scholarship in the field of IR speaks of a norm as a single concept, without qualifiers. When scholars do provide a definition for norms in their work, they tend to rely on either the Jepperson, Wendt, and Katzenstein (1996) or Finnemore and Sikkink (1998) definitions, as do I in setting the contours of the norm concept.[5] Of course, scholars are free to define a norm differently than I do here, but doing so would require them to similarly articulate the analytic costs and benefits to an alternative definition. As I will argue in this chapter, these early definitions of a norm are not only conceptually appropriate but are analytically useful to the field. Moreover, the increased flexibility in how the term *norm* is used in contemporary scholarship may result in diminished analytic payoff.

As these early definitions highlight, norms have three essential component parts: (1) a moral sense of oughtness (as signaled by the words "proper" and "appropriate" above) (2) a defined actor "of a given identity," and (3) a specific behavior or action expected of that given actor. A norm must also meet the condition that these three component parts are *collectively shared* within a particular society (distinguishing a norm from an individual's private belief) and that these component parts are sufficiently specific such that it is possible for a violator to be identified. Importantly, if any of these component parts (actor, action, or oughtness) is missing, I argue scholars are not observing a norm but a different aspect of the social fabric entirely. The Venn diagram is a useful format for visualizing the edges of the norm concept, once the core component parts of norms are identified. In the interest of clarity, I have constructed one (see figure 3.1).

Often it is the sense of oughtness embedded in a norm that gets the most attention in constructivist theory. This may be a product of scholarly history. When the field of IR resurrected its interest in sociological approaches, which brought with it renewed interest in the power of norms, scholars were deeply invested in debating distinctions between the logic of consequence and the logic of appropriateness (i.e., oughtness).[6] That individuals (or states) could act in accordance with social rules determining appropriate behavior and not solely on the basis of strategic calculations was itself fodder for extensive conversation.[7] The idea that such a thing as social appropriateness mattered in enabling or constraining action was a key takeaway from these debates.

---

4. Brauer and Chaurand 2010; Elster 1989; Gibbs 1965; Kratochwil 1989.
5. See, for example, Blyth 2003; Checkel 1997; Keck and Sikkink 1998; Murdie and Davis 2012; Payne 2001; and Risse 2000. Citation counts are, of course, imperfect metrics for assessing the influence of articles, but for reference, at the time of this writing, the Finnemore and Sikkink (1998) article has been cited over eighty-five hundred times.
6. March and Olsen 1998.
7. Goertz and Diehl 1992; Katzenstein 1996; Price 1998.

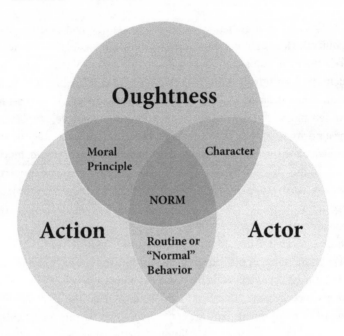

FIGURE 3.1. The Norm Concept.

Indeed, norms must have a moral dimension (the sense of oughtness). This oughtness, moreover, is of a particular type. When we refer to the moral sense of oughtness in a norm, we understand this to mean that engaging in a particular expected behavior is socially acceptable and, should an individual *not* comply with the norm, doing so would be understood as unacceptable. In other words, these claims of oughtness are not understood as *optional*, such that a social community would react in the same way whether individuals complied or did not comply with a given norm. Should one opt not to comply with a norm, we should expect a reaction from the social group to signal disapproval with that person's deviant behavior.[8]

Not all socially expected behaviors have a moral component. If you had an expected behavior from a particular actor without any sense of oughtness, you would be describing routine or "normal" behavior, but not a norm. Take for instance the following example: "American adults drink coffee in the morning." Here we have a clear group of actors (American adults) and an expected behavior (drinking coffee), but no sense of oughtness or appropriateness. Drinking coffee might be customary or routine behavior, but if an American adult did *not* drink coffee in the morning they would not be socially shamed for that behavior,

---

8. Of course, the word *moral* should not be understood to mean "religious," but rather understood in its philosophical sense as distinguishing "the appropriate."

as there was no moral component to this statement of custom or routine.[9] Drinking coffee in the morning might be normal behavior, but not *a norm*.[10]

Norms, however, require more than just a sense of oughtness. They must also link a specific actor to a specific expected action. It is in linking an actor to an action that the relevant social rule is constructed and the norm becomes powerful and effective in enabling social pressure. The attribution of a specific expected behavior to a specific actor in the construction of a norm relies on socially shared beliefs about the character of the actor in question (labeled "Character" in figure 3.1), such that the specific behavior would fit within what is expected from the character of the actor.

I use the term *character*, instead of *identity*, for the sake of precision. Constructivist scholarship has long been interested in unpacking how identities are constructed,[11] but while the concept of identity encompasses moral attributes or virtues assigned to a particular actor (what I define as character), it also includes a number of attributes that are not necessarily justified in moral terms. Character is certainly an important part of the identity of the United States, for instance, but its identity is also constituted by the structure of its political bureaucracy in ways that rely on technical and legal attributes as much as moral ones. Identity can encompass a wide array of moral, technical, legal, bureaucratic, and strategic variables. For the purpose of norm construction, it is the specific moral virtues which constitute a particular actor that matter for justifying why a particular behavior would be expected of that specific actor in the first place.

IR scholarship does not often conceptualize actors independent of any action or behavior, making examples of what would fill the "Character" block in figure 3.1 less obvious. Conceptually, this category would be filled by examples such as "Good democracies are tolerant" or "Good Christians are compassionate."[12] Such statements identify not only an actor (a democracy or a Christian) but a moral virtue that constitutes that actor. It is the character of these actors (that they are tolerant or compassionate) that is used to justify why a particular action would be expected of them in the construction of a norm.

---

9. On the importance of oughtness in distinguishing norms from "behavioral regularities," see Florini 1996. Gibbs (1965, 589) uses the example of Americans drinking coffee to highlight customary behavior absent a sense of oughtness though he does not believe that what he calls "collective evaluations" are a necessary component to all norms.

10. Some work utilizing practice theory in IR, for example, would seek to understand the power of habit or routine in IR, as opposed to norms, focusing on better theorizing this conceptual area. There remains, however, variation in where practice theorists draw the boundaries of their "habit" or "practice" concepts. See Adler and Pouliot 2011; Hopf 2010; and McCourt 2016.

11. Katzenstein 1996; Wendt 1994.

12. I thank Daniel Levine and the participants of the University of Alabama Department of Political Science forum for the example "Good Christians are compassionate."

Take, for instance, the following norm: "Good governments ought to regulate elections to ensure they are free and fair." Here we see all three requisite component parts of norms: a sense of oughtness, the government as the defined actor, and the regulation of elections as the expected action by that actor. The action or behavior (regulating elections) is expected of this particular actor (government) because it is seen as consistent with the character of this actor (i.e., we understand the government as constituted by certain virtues such that this behavior is consistent with those virtues).

A society may agree that elections ought to be regulated, or that it is appropriate that elections be regulated, but not link this particular desired outcome to a particular actor. This by itself would constitute a *moral principle* ("Elections ought to be regulated"). Moral principles function as passive voice goals. In contrast, the construction of a norm requires more than articulating an expected action and a sense of oughtness about it. Norms must specify an actor from whom a behavior is expected. In this way, while all norms are moral principles, not all moral principles are norms. Under the broader category of moral principles, the subcategory of norms requires the specification of a particular actor from whom an appropriate behavior is expected.

Moral Principles as Passive Voice Goals

Clearly distinguishing between moral principles and norms allows scholars to better understand a significant challenge to norm construction—the social process of determining *from whom* an appropriate behavior is expected. Determining who is obliged to behave in a particular way is a serious challenge for any effort at norm construction, and has been especially problematic for the hunger issue area, as well as the broader category of economic and social rights. It is one thing to convince publics that it is wrong that people should go hungry in the modern age, but it is quite another to create a shared social understanding that any particular actor, such as a national government, is obliged to ensure that people have access to adequate food. Indeed, one of the greatest challenges to norm construction around economic and social rights in particular has been the struggle of determining from whom society expects a particular behavior such that that actor could be held accountable through social sanctions if they deviated from the behavior society expected from them.

One important characteristic (and benefit) of a norm as opposed to a moral principle is that norms can have identifiable "violators," and the existence of a norm violator may enable more effective shaming by social groups. We see this benefit at play in both the boomerang and spiral models discussed in chapter 2.

When a norm exists around a human right, this necessitates a shared understanding that a specific actor is obliged to behave in a specific way to fulfill that right. When this actor deviates from this expected behavior, we should expect a social response to that deviation, often in the form of shaming or social pressure. The existence of a norm constitutes a type of environment where such a response is possible.

When a norm is absent for a particular issue area, even when moral principles are present, the social environment in which advocates are working is constituted differently than when norms are present. Moral principles, unlike norms, do not supply social communities with the answer of *who* ought to be targeted when a shared social goal is not met. The moral principle "Nobody should have to live on the streets" may be shared across all members of a society, but the result of this principle may be no more than a shared sense of sadness or tragedy at the high rates of homelessness in a given community. Individuals may choose to respond to this moral principle by donating to charities (or not) or opening up their homes (or not), but absent a norm linking an expected behavior to a specific actor such that the persistence of homelessness could be linked to a norm violator, constructivist theory gives little reason to believe the social tactics and strategies available to influence changes in behavior (like shaming) would be effective.

Many human rights may lack norms but have no shortage of moral principles, especially when dealing with economic and social rights. In the case of hunger and the right to food, there is certainly a shared moral principle among international anti-hunger advocates that nobody should go hungry. But *who* is obliged to do *what* to ensure all people have enough to eat? As we shall see later in the chapter, despite a shared moral principle that nobody should go hungry, there is no anti-hunger norm within this community.

Supererogatory Standards, but Not Norms

Not all claims of good or moral behavior are alike, and in the case of many economic and social rights and the case of hunger in particular, understanding the difference between norms and supererogatory standards is essential. As we shall see here, not all behaviors that are socially praiseworthy or good are understood as obligatory. And when behavior by specific actors might be laudable but entirely optional, we should expect this to constitute a very different social environment than when such behavior is both socially expected and obligatory.

Understanding the difference between these two concepts requires a deeper analysis of what constitutes the sense of oughtness in a norm. Of critical importance to the norm concept is that the embedded oughtness claim is understood as *not optional* but, rather, obligatory. When we say there is a norm among states that "Good states ought not plunder other countries,"[13] compliance to the norm, among the society of states, is understood as obligatory. Should a state *not* comply with the norm, we should expect a social response to the norm's *violation*, as such behavior would be seen as an act of deviance. We understand compliance with the norm as marking "good" or "appropriate" behavior and noncompliance as "bad" or "inappropriate." We would expect, in other words, a different reaction from the social group to noncompliance with the norm than we would from compliance with the norm.

But what about nonobligatory actions that are understood by a social community as morally good if they are done, but not morally bad or inappropriate if they are not done? Referred to as "supererogatory" by philosophers such as J. O. Urmson (1958), John Rawls (1971, 117), and Susan Wolf (1982), supererogatory acts are understood as morally praiseworthy if done but *are not required*. If an individual performed a supererogatory act, it would be seen as morally good, but if they did not, they would not be shamed for noncompliance. Supererogatory standards of behavior, in contrast to norms, are nonobligatory.

A frequently cited example of a supererogatory act is articulated by Urmson. Contrasting understandings of duty with the supererogatory, he considers the following:

> We may imagine a squad of soldiers to be practicing the throwing of live hand grenades; a grenade slips from the hand of one of them and rolls on the ground near the squad; one of them sacrifices his life by throwing himself on the grenade and protecting his comrades with his own body. . . . But if the soldier had not thrown himself on the grenade would he have failed in his duty? . . . If he had not done so, could anyone have said to him, 'You ought to have thrown yourself on that grenade?' . . . The answer to all these questions is plainly negative. We clearly have here a case of moral action, a heroic action, which cannot be subsumed under the classification [duty] whose inadequacy we are exposing. (1958, 202–3)

The supererogatory constitutes a category of behavior that extends all the way to the heroic or saintly,[14] but also includes anything which is one step above what is understood as one's "duty." As Urmson notes, "It is possible to go *just beyond* one's duty by being a little more generous, forbearing, helpful, or forgiving than fair dealing demands, or to go a very long way beyond the basic code of duties

---

13. Sandholtz 2007.
14. Urmson 1958; Wolf 1982.

with the saint or the hero" (1958, 205, emphasis added). The concept of duty, understood by philosophers as conceptually distinct from the supererogatory, functions similarly to how constructivists understand a norm. Both duty and norms are constituted by shared expectations of appropriate behavior by specific actors.

Consider discussions about a norm of charity or a norm of charitable giving.[15] Is the term *norm* really capturing what is taking place when individuals, for instance, donate to a specific charity? Consider the following example. A woman visits her friend at her home for coffee. Noticing a child sponsorship card on her fridge—a picture provided by a nongovernmental organization (NGO) of a child in Rwanda she supports through her monthly charitable giving—the friend remarks how good it is of her to donate to support this child.

Certainly, the act of donating to an NGO to support a child in Rwanda is seen by this friend as a praiseworthy thing to do. And yet, had this woman *not* donated to charity, we would not expect her to be shamed for not doing so. Donating to charity is a supererogatory act. It is morally good to do, but not required. It is not a norm.

Much behavior may be laudable, but this praise may not be evidence of any norm compelling this behavior. Bringing us back to the case of hunger, consider U.S. foreign assistance to Guatemala, a country where chronic hunger has become such a pervasive problem that an estimated 46.5 percent of its children under the age of five are stunted in growth, according to the World Food Programme.[16] In fiscal year 2018, USAID's Office of Food for Peace contributed $21.5 million to Guatemala. This was certainly a praiseworthy response to the crisis, but would such praise constitute evidence that there was a norm among the society of states that developed states were *obliged* to provide aid to other countries when people were hungry? It would not. Donating in response to high rates of chronic hunger may constitute supererogatory acts by states. In this sense, while laudable, they would not elicit the same type of social response to noncompliance than would the violation of a norm that "Good developed states ought to provide sufficient assistance to other countries in times of humanitarian crises." Should the United States reduce or freeze its funding, would we expect social costs from among the society of states? This particular case of U.S. aid to Guatemala is instructive on this point, as in March 2019 the United States announced

---

15. For an interesting discussion of "quasi-moral" and "utility-based norm of charity," see Elster (2011, 332). Some would also argue that in the context of certain communities (such as religious communities) there may be strong beliefs in the importance of charity (Ferris 2011; Lazarev and Sharma 2017). Whether this translates to a norm depends on whether donating to charity is socially required.

16. World Food Programme 2019.

it would suspend foreign aid to Guatemala, causing NGOs to cut planned food assistance programs.[17] There was little public response at all by other states to this cut in aid.

Distinguishing between supererogatory acts on the one hand and norm-driven acts on the other requires that scholars look for social response to noncompliance or violation (i.e., shaming or social sanctions). Supererogatory acts do not elicit shaming or social costs if the acts are not performed, as they are nonobligatory. Norm noncompliance *does* elicit social sanctions or social costs. Far from simply a minor characteristic of norms, the threat of social sanctions for noncompliance is what gives norms their power to enable and constrain behavior. This is a key attribute of norms, as articulated in constructivist theory, but one that requires a very particular type of an oughtness claim which is absent when dealing with supererogatory standards. Response to violation, then, provides both necessary and sufficient evidence of a norm. Praise is neither necessary nor sufficient to provide evidence of a norm (though verbal shaming in response to violation would), as such evidence may be signaling a supererogatory standard instead.

Norms as a Spectrum

At first glance, the conceptualization of norms put forward in this chapter may not appeal to those who instead understand a norm as a very broad concept under which all social life falls along a spectrum of "weak" to "strong." According to this way of thinking, there is no aspect of social life that cannot be placed at least on the very weakest end of this conceptual spectrum. Using this perspective as a lens through which to view moral principles surrounding hunger, one might say that what we observe here is a weak norm (since *no norm* is conceptually not allowed in this spectrum approach to normativity).

My response to this alternative conception is that we may gain greater analytic leverage not by understanding a norm as a very broad concept encompassing all of the social world on a single spectrum but rather by understanding the social world as constituted by *many different types of social concepts*, of which the norm is only one. Norms have specific component parts, which provide important analytical leverage. Other social concepts, like moral principles or supererogatory standards, have others.[18] Blurring the diversity of all social life into one concept (the "norm") on one spectrum gives us less analytic leverage in part

---

17. Moloney 2019. On FY 2018 Food for Peace funding in Guatemala see USAID 2020.
18. For more on the distinction between norms, moral principles, and supererogatory standards, see Jurkovich 2019.

because spectrums, by design, only allow for variation on one dimension (in this case, norm "strength"). Conceptualizing any social concept as existing primarily as on a spectrum heightens analytic focus on only one aspect of variation (e.g., level of strength) but blurs our ability to see other important points of variation (such as whether or not there is any consensus on the actor from whom specific behavior is expected, whether or not the oughtness claim is obligatory, etc.).[19]

Discussing social life as all fitting on a norm spectrum of weak to strong also runs into trouble when we try to decipher what scholars actually mean when they say a norm is strong or weak. If using a spectrum approach to understanding norms, it is essential that the single dimension on which the concept is allowed to vary is very clear and well-defined. And yet there is remarkable fuzziness on the concept of strength. To some scholars, norm strength means the degree of *internalization* the norm may have, which reflects how committed a social group is to the norm. To others, strength refers to how *widely held* the belief in the norm is within a community. Do only the residents of San Francisco share this norm? Or do all Americans? Or Americans and the British? Or all global citizens? According to this logic, the larger the community to hold the norm the stronger the norm is. So *strength* can refer simultaneously to both how internalized (i.e., deeply held) a norm is in a community *and* how widely shared this norm actually is among a larger population. At this point we can already see the challenges to spectrum approaches to a concept that we believe can actually vary on more than one dimension (i.e., internalization *and* size of the intersubjective community). My point here is not to get into a lengthy discussion of why spectrums can be a challenging conceptual tool. Rather, my aim is to highlight the analytic leverage provided by considering the social world as constituted by different *types* of social concepts instead of considering the norm as a grand concept in which the diversity of social life all fits along a spectrum.

Identifying Norms

As the previous sections have suggested, it is difficult to identify the existence of a norm. Empirically, how would we know whether or not there was a norm around a human right? Only looking for a shared goal or desired outcome can mean conflating moral principles with norms. Simply observing what behavior is common in a community runs the risk of conflating routine behavior (like drinking

---

19. And, of course, such an approach would run into problems with the vast literature on "norm entrepreneurs" who "create" new norms. If you can create a norm, this implies it did not previously always exist.

coffee in the morning) with norm-driven behavior. Looking solely for praise from a community in response to a particular behavior may result in confusing supererogatory standards with norms.

Constructivist scholars generally point to societal reaction to norm violation as evidence of the existence of a norm. If an actor's behavior elicits a reaction from society as inappropriate, this provides evidence both that there *was* an appropriate behavior expected by society from this particular actor (i.e., a norm) and that the individual failed to behave in that way.

In the case of the right to food, evidence of a norm would come from the observed response to a given actor's violation of its expected appropriate behavior. If, for instance, we wanted to know if there were a norm among the society of states that *good governments ought to feed their people if they cannot feed themselves,* we would expect that when a country has persistent hunger rates (especially when it is a comparatively wealthy country) there would be a social cost imposed by the society of states for violating this norm. By this logic, we would expect the United States to be shamed by other states for its persistent domestic hunger problem, or be met by some social cost, or for instance the United Kingdom to be shamed for the roughly four million Britons (as of 2012) struggling with food insecurity in that country.[20] And yet no such response has occurred. Neither the United States nor the United Kingdom are shamed at UN meetings for persistent hunger within their domestic populations. Using response to violation as evidence of a norm among the society of states, then, we would conclude that no norm had been violated by the persistence of domestic hunger in these countries.

Another way to measure the existence of a norm, at least among civil society active in this issue area, is to see if gatekeepers within its advocacy organizations can name a common *subject* and *verb* at play in ensuring a particular human right. *Who* should do *what* to ensure the right to food is realized? In order to keep *response to violation* central to the method, the question would need to be framed to pick up not theoretical or technical understandings of responsibility but rather whom members of this community would see as *to blame* in response to the persistence of a given condition (in this case, chronic hunger). This approach also allows scholars to avoid the risk of conflating supererogatory standards with norms.[21]

In the human rights literature in the field of IR, much attention is focused in particular on international nongovernmental organizations (INGOs) as important catalysts for improving human rights around the world. The staff at these

---

20. McGuinness, Brown, and Ward 2016.
21. See Jurkovich 2019. Since supererogatory behavior is nonobligatory, we should not expect blame if such behavior is unfulfilled.

organizations work to improve human rights conditions across multiple regions and very different political landscapes. These actors matter, according to IR human rights scholars, because they serve to set and vet important international human rights agendas, apply pressure to human rights violators, and lend legitimacy to human rights campaigns. They are often better financed and connected than their domestic NGO counterparts, and can harness their visibility, legitimacy, and financial resources to compel behavioral change.[22] They are not always effective in doing so, but they remain one of the most consequential actors for IR human rights scholars.[23]

For this reason, while one could look for evidence of a norm in many different contexts, I chose to examine if a norm were present across twelve of the top international anti-hunger organizations: Action against Hunger USA, ActionAid USA, Amnesty International, the Bill & Melinda Gates Foundation, Bread for the World, CARE USA, FIAN International, Médecins sans Frontières / Doctors without Borders USA (MSF), Oxfam America, the Rockefeller Foundation, Save the Children US, and World Vision.[24] In order to determine if there was a norm around hunger within these organizations, I surveyed executive and senior staff regarding their beliefs about who was to blame for continued existence of chronic hunger and what should be done to solve the problem. Where possible, multiple senior staff were surveyed within the same organization, with a total of twenty-one senior and executive staff surveyed. While the opinions of employees at all levels of the organization would be valuable, executive and senior staff were selected because they are the most likely to be able to "speak for the organization," and their decisions can directly shape the nature of the advocacy in these INGOs.[25]

Officials surveyed were asked to direct their responses to how they understood chronic hunger specifically.[26] The top of each survey noted, "When a question

---

22. Barry, Clay, and Flynn 2013; Carpenter 2014; Keck and Sikkink 1998; Murdie 2014a, 2014b; Murdie and Davis 2012.

23. On the efficacy of naming and shaming as a strategy, see especially Ausderan 2014; Hafner-Burton 2008; and Murdie and Davis 2012.

24. One of the respondents from World Vision worked with World Vision International and the other with World Vision USA. Otherwise, all survey respondents worked within the same confederate/affiliate office of the given INGO. In the case of Amnesty International and FIAN International, survey respondents worked in the International Secretariat. Members of other confederate/affiliate offices of these INGOs were at times interviewed (and those interviews referenced in this chapter) but were not surveyed.

25. These interviews averaged roughly one hour in length and were, with very few exceptions, conducted one-on-one with myself and a single interviewee. All surveys were conducted one-on-one.

26. There can be some ambiguity, however, in the dividing line between short-term or emergency responses to acute hunger versus responses to chronic hunger. Operations that begin with the expectation of providing emergency assistance for severe malnutrition for a short period of time can end up becoming multiyear operations responding to chronic hunger. At times, organizations can focus on both providing for cases of severe malnutrition (for instance, through the use of ready-to-use therapeutic foods [RUTFs]) as well as chronic hunger. When I asked respondents to focus their responses

refers to 'hunger,' it is referring to endemic malnutrition (i.e., chronic hunger), not short-term famines." Chronic hunger constitutes a far greater share of the hunger problem in the world, and when interviewed and surveyed, respondents were directed to answer with reference to how they understand this larger problem.[27]

Survey Results

If there were a norm around hunger within this important advocacy community, we would expect gatekeepers within these international anti-hunger organizations to be able to name a common subject and verb (*who* should do *what*) in response to chronic hunger. More than simply a shared understanding that hunger is morally wrong or a shared belief that *people ought not go hungry*, a norm in this issue area would require a shared understanding of a specific actor who was obliged to behave in a specific way, such that if it did not we should expect a social cost. The survey was designed to test this by asking not only about understandings of who was to blame for chronic hunger but also what should be done to ameliorate it.

The surveys were designed to be brief (they took roughly five to ten minutes), and I conducted them at the beginning of a one-on-one interview which lasted about an hour on average.[28] Surveys were conducted across the twelve organizations between February and November 2013.

In the survey portion of the interview, respondents were asked five questions, of which the following three are of importance to the chapter at hand:

1. In your view, who is to blame for hunger? If you believe there are multiple actors to blame for hunger, please rank all that apply.
2. In your view, which of the following are the best solutions to hunger? Please rank the top three (3).
3. Would any of the platforms or campaigns of the anti-hunger organizations you have worked for disagree with or differ from your choices in #1 or #2? If so, how?

---

on how they understood chronic hunger and not short-term hunger or famines, I cannot recall any respondent asking me to clarify my meaning, but I am cognizant of some ambiguity in terms here.

27. Additionally, these are organizations that work globally and at times wage a common campaign (or use a common approach or advocacy effort, as not all organizations would say they "campaign") in multiple countries in multiple regions of the world at any given point in time. For this reason, the project does not ask about hunger specifically in one country or region but asks senior and executive staff at these organizations about how they understand chronic hunger generally, as this understanding informs the construction of these large multiyear and multiregion efforts and campaigns.

28. There were a few exceptions to this, where surveys were not the first part of the interview. This was the case for the Bread for the World surveys, one Oxfam America survey, and in a very few instances when an interviewee wanted first to start the interview before completing the survey.

All respondents qualified their responses with certainty scores on a range from 1 to 10 (with 1 representing "very uncertain" and 10 representing "very certain" of their choices).

Interestingly, there was at times considerable variation in the answers given by the senior/executive level staff members interviewed and surveyed within the same organization, though almost all of them answered that the platforms and campaigns of their organization would neither disagree with nor differ from their survey answers.

In response to the "who is to blame?" question, respondents were asked to rank as many (or as few) actors as they thought necessary and to provide a certainty score (i.e., how confident they were in their response). The response options listed were derived from the anti-hunger campaign literature available. Responses are displayed in figure 3.2.[29]

If respondents did not believe anyone was to blame for hunger, they could select this option. If the respondent did not believe any of the options listed were applicable, they could select "Other." Among those who responded "Other," one (from the Gates Foundation) elaborated that *blame* is not the word they would use, but rather *responsibility*: national governments were the most *responsible* for hunger but so, too, were lack of foreign assistance and poor local agricultural development. The second respondent listing "Other" (from MSF USA) qualified the response, saying a combination of factors were to blame (e.g., distorted markets, price speculation, and poor focus of national government policies). The third (from World Vision USA) said that "blame is not the word we use, but rather [we talk in terms of] causes." To this individual, poor productivity, poor local knowledge of nutrition and hygiene, and gender disparities were behind hunger. An additional respondent (from World Vision International) selected "Other," stating that the "world is bent and broken" and that "we are all to blame for hunger." One respondent from Amnesty International stated that international financial institutions were also to blame for hunger, and the respondent from Save the Children US added a "lack of political will" as to blame for hunger but did not link this lack of will to a singular actor. One official at Bread for the World noted "poor governance at all levels" both national and international was to blame, though her first reaction to the question of who was to blame was to say "Everyone!" The FIAN International respondent added intergovernmental organizations

---

29. The option of "lack of capacity" as to blame was not included on the survey during the first three times the survey was administered (all at Bread for the World). It was a Bread for the World official who, in writing in this response as "other," convinced me to add it to the survey. It is possible that one of the individuals surveyed prior to this point at Bread for the World (who is discussed above as writing "poor governance at all levels" was to blame for hunger) might have categorized that response as fitting under "lack of capacity" if that option had been available. My best judgment, however, is that she would not have done so.

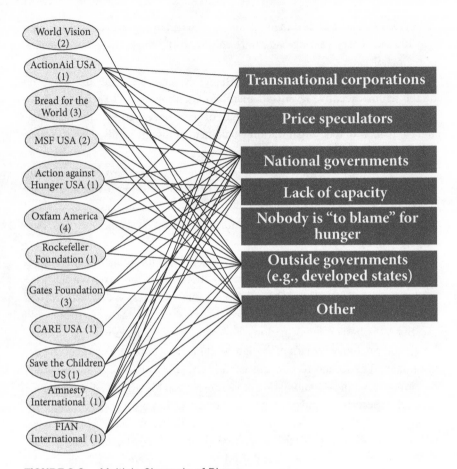

FIGURE 3.2. Multiple Channels of Blame.

Note: The numbers in parentheses represent the number of survey respondents from this organization. There were, for example, three respondents from the Gates Foundation. All were taken from the same affiliate office of the organization with the exception of World Vision, where one respondent worked at World Vision US and the other at World Vision International. Only one line was provided linking an organization to a particular response. If multiple people from the same organization listed the same response, only one line was provided for the sake of visual clarity.

to those blamed for hunger. Finally, one respondent from Oxfam America selected "Other," noting that "economic injustice" was to blame for hunger, but did not specifically blame any of the actors listed on the survey.

Responses to the survey are displayed in the above form not to analyze the data but to visually convey the diversity of responses. Had there been a common understanding about a single target actor expected to behave in a specific way, we would expect a common response to who is to blame for chronic hunger. There was no such consensus.

TABLE 3.1 Who Is to Blame for Chronic Hunger?

	NUMBER OF RESPONDENTS (WITH CERTAINTY SCORE OF 6+)	PERCENTAGE OF RESPONDENTS (WITH CERTAINTY SCORE OF 6+)	PERCENTAGE OF TOTAL RESPONDENTS (N=21)
National governments	13	65%	62%
Outside governments	12	60%	57%
Other	9	45%	43%
Lack of capacity	7	35%	33%
Transnational corporations	4	20%	19%
Price speculators	1	5%	5%
Total	20	100%	95%

If we remove responses about who is to blame with low certainty scores (scores 1–5, representing "very uncertain" to "neither certain nor uncertain"), we are left with the following responses (see table 3.1). One respondent listed low certainty scores for each actor on the blame question, for which reason that individual is omitted from the table below (which is why the N = 20 for those with at least one response with a certainty score of 6+). Additionally, only one point per respondent was attributed to "Other" (if they selected "Other") regardless of the number of additional actors or factors listed. It is important to note that no respondent listed only one actor as to blame for hunger. That national governments, outside governments, and "other" received higher response rates is indicative of the fact that they were mentioned at least once on many individuals' surveys, but they were never listed on a survey as the sole actor to blame for hunger.[30] If there were a clear norm around who should act to provide food, we would expect convergence among activists on a common actor as to blame for hunger, but no such consensus exists.

One response in particular illuminates the fragmented nature of blame in this issue area. As was mentioned in the introduction to this book, when I asked one senior official at Oxfam America who was to blame for hunger, she asked for a piece of paper and drew a diagram. She noted there were three types of blameworthy parties (the private sector, the state, and civil society organizations) which exist at three levels (the local, national, and the global level). Drawing a stick figure in the middle, representing the hungry individual, she then proceeded to

---

30. Although, in the case of the senior official at the Gates Foundation referenced earlier, who noted that blame is not the word Gates would use but rather responsibility, despite noting that many factors contributed to responsibility for hunger (such as inadequate foreign assistance and poor local agricultural development), in the end she would have ranked only the national government as "responsible" for chronic hunger.

map out the multiple levels of blame by drawing rings around the hungry individual, ranking each actor in order of how much it was to blame for hunger. In total, she ranked nine actors, all to blame for hunger. In ranked order of blame, they were: (1) national governments; (2) national businesses and corporations; (3) outside governments and intergovernmental organizations; (4) transnational corporations; (5) local governments; (6) local private sectors; (7) global civil society organizations; (8) national civil society organizations; and (9) local civil society organizations.[31] Blame for hunger did not rest solely on one actor, according to this official. It was shared by many.

But can blame be conflated with responsibility for an issue area? In other words, if no single actor is seen as *to blame* for hunger (or right to food violations), can there at least be an agreement around *responsibility* for the problem?

Yet, to activists, even responsibility is diffuse for economic and social rights like the right to food. Take, for instance, Amnesty International's discussion of responsibility for economic and social rights. Amnesty International has not been shy about blaming governments for human rights violations, particularly in the civil and political realm. But in the case of economic and social rights, as explained in its *Human Rights for Human Dignity: A Primer on Economic, Social, and Cultural Rights*, the organization notes, "*Responsibility* for denial of economic, social, and cultural rights frequently lies not only with governments but also with individuals, groups, and enterprises" (Amnesty International, 2005, 43, emphasis added). The report acknowledges that "primary accountability in international law rests with the state in whose jurisdiction the violation occurs," but that there should also be "corporate accountability for human rights abuses" as well as responsibility on the part of international financial institutions like the International Monetary Fund and World Bank. Additionally, "states that provide international development assistance and cooperation should be held responsible for the human rights impact of their policies outside their borders" (43–46).[32] Indeed, the chapter in this report entitled "Who is responsible?" begins with the following quote by Mary Robinson, former UN high commissioner for human rights, highlighting the complexity of responsibility around economic and social rights: "In the interest of ensuring that ESC rights are taken more seriously as obligations, international human rights organizations should not

---

31. Interview, Oxfam America 1, May 2013.

32. This is not to say Amnesty International does not see the state as the primary actor responsible for ensuring the right to food for its people. Its brief discussion of the right to food in this report highlights this responsibility. The broader point here is that responsibility for economic and social rights, even within organizations that have a history of rooting understandings of responsibility in international law, can still be multifaceted and include diverse actors.

be unduly limited in identifying the targets of their naming and the means of their shaming."[33]

The relatively recent push for the responsibility of corporations (particularly transnational ones) for human rights is especially interesting. In 2003, the United Nations (UN) Sub-Commission on the Promotion and Protection of Human Rights approved its *Norms on the Responsibilities of Transnational Corporations and Other Business Enterprises with Regard to Human Rights*, which stated,

> States have the primary responsibility to promote, secure the fulfillment of, respect, ensure respect of and protect human rights recognized in international as well as national law, including ensuring that transnational corporations and other business enterprises respect human rights. *Within their respective spheres of activity and influence, transnational corporations and other business enterprises have the obligation to promote, secure the fulfillment of, respect, ensure respect of and protect human rights recognized in international as well as national law, including the rights and interests of indigenous peoples and other vulnerable groups.* (2003, 4, emphasis added)

The *Norms* were, unsurprisingly, a contentious proposal, pitting corporations—who argued that human rights protection was the exclusive domain of states (not the private sector)—against some human rights activists, who believed corporations should be obligated to protect and ensure human rights as well.[34] Ultimately, the Commission on Human Rights did not approve the *Norms*, instead asking for more research on the legality and history of involving the private sector in human rights protection.[35]

On recommendation of the Commission on Human Rights, UN secretary-general Kofi Annan appointed a special representative for business and human rights, a position he gave to political scientist John Gerard Ruggie. According to Ruggie, the Commission believed an individual expert was needed to "'identify and clarify' existing standards for, and best practices by, businesses, and for the role of states in regulating businesses in relation to human rights; and to research

---

33. Amnesty International 2005, 43. See also their second edition to this report, which retains the same wording: Amnesty International 2014, 103. This Mary Robinson quote is taken from her article "Advancing Economic, Social, and Cultural Rights: The Way Forward," and continuing the original quote to the sentence that follows drives home the point of multifaceted responsibility for economic and social rights particularly well: "Governments, corporations, and international financial institutions can be named and can be shamed in new and imaginative ways that result in advancing the promotion of ESC rights" (Robinson 2004, 870).

34. Ruggie 2013, xvii.

35. For the response of the UN Commission on Human Rights, see Office of the United Nations High Commissioner For Human Rights 2004.

and clarify the meaning of the most hotly contested concepts in the debate, such as 'corporate complicity' in the commission of human rights abuses and 'corporate spheres of influence' within which companies might be expected to have special responsibilities" (Ruggie 2013, xviii).

The rejection of the *Norms* initiative, even when coupled with the creation of the new special representative for business and human rights, angered many human rights activists. According to Ruggie, "the main international human rights organizations did not accept that the 'Norms' initiative had come to an end, having invested heavily in it. Amnesty International USA, for example, hailed the 'Norms' as 'representing a major step toward a global legal framework for corporate accountability'"(2013, xix). Ultimately Ruggie presented the UN Human Rights Council (which was formerly the Commission on Human Rights) with his Guiding Principles on Business and Human Rights, which the Council unanimously endorsed (xx). The Guiding Principles (known informally as the Ruggie Rules or Ruggie Principles) essentially recommended that in the realm of human rights "states must protect; companies must respect; and those who are harmed must have redress" (xxi). For organizations such as Human Rights Watch (HRW), the Ruggie Rules were "woefully inadequate," as they provided no enforcement mechanism, either to ensuring corporations fulfill their human rights obligations or that governments ensure regulation of those corporations.[36]

What is interesting for our purposes here is that even responsibility for human rights can be a contentious issue, with activists pushing for donor states, national governments, and corporations to all share in the responsibility for ensuring human rights. While it is a fair point to distinguish blame from responsibility, both are contentious issues.

In the hunger realm, then, who is to blame and who is responsible for hunger may be unclear, but is it clear *what should be done*? The issue area may lack consensus on the *actor* or *subject* required for the norm, but is there still a commonly expected specific *appropriate behavior*?

Survey results again indicate that there is no consensus on appropriate behavior among activists in this issue area. Respondents were asked to rank the three best solutions to chronic hunger.[37] As with the question on blame, respondents

---

36. Albin-Lackey 2013, 4.
37. During the life of the survey some adjustments to the solution options were made to allow for greater nuance in two areas. First, the solution option of "gender equality in wages" (originally the only gender solution option) was expanded to include an additional option for "gender equality in access to credit, farming technology, and markets." Second, the solution option "agricultural development with a focus on increasing farm worker wages" expanded to include an additional option of agricultural development "increasing small farmer income (i.e. income of small farm landowners)." While informative, these expanded options were not available to earlier respondents, so the responses described in figure 3.3 and table 3.2 are grouped more generally to account for all responses (e.g., gender equality in either wages, access to credit, farming technology, or markets). Col-

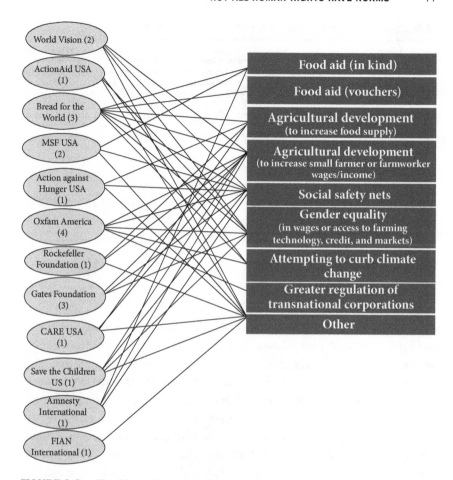

FIGURE 3.3. The Many Varied Solutions to Hunger.

Note: The numbers in parentheses represent the number of survey respondents from this organization. There were, for example, three respondents from the Gates Foundation. All were taken from the same affiliate office of the organization with the exception of World Vision, where one respondent worked at World Vision US and the other at World Vision International. Only one line was provided linking an organization to a particular response. If multiple people from the same organization listed the same response, only one line was provided for the sake of visual clarity.

had a list of options to choose from, drawn from campaign materials as well as international organization reports in this issue area. Respondents could also select "Other" and write in a response if they believed the appropriate solution(s) were not provided on the list. If there were a norm, we would expect consensus around

---

lectively, it is possible that had these expanded options been available to two Bread for the World and two Oxfam America respondents (other respondents' answers would not have been affected), their responses to the solution question might have varied. I doubt this, however, as there would have been the option to convey this by selecting "Other" and writing this in. That was not done.

TABLE 3.2   How Do You Solve the Problem of Chronic Hunger?

	NUMBER OF RESPONDENTS *(WITH CERTAINTY SCORE OF 6+)*	PERCENTAGE OF RESPONDENTS *(WITH CERTAINTY SCORE OF 6+)*	PERCENTAGE OF TOTAL RESPONDENTS (N=21)
Agricultural development (focus on small farmer and farm worker wages)	12	63%	57%
Agricultural development (focus on increasing food supply)	4	21%	19%
Social safety nets	10	53%	48%
Gender equality	9	47%	43%
Other	8	42%	38%
Curbing climate change	3	16%	14%
Regulating transnational corporations	2	11%	10%
Food aid (in kind)	2	11%	10%
Food aid (vouchers)	1	5%	5%
Total	19	100%	90%

three common answers across international anti-hunger organizations active in this issue area, though perhaps some variation in terms of how these three solutions were ranked. There was no such consensus. Responses are provided in figure 3.3.

"Other" was selected several times, with a wide range of additional solutions provided (including improving nutritional practices/behaviors, improving water and sanitation conditions, government regulations on land distribution, providing employment outside the farming sector, reduction of disparity, human rights accountability, the primacy of human rights law, universal social protection, and improving resilience of the food supply, among others).[38] In short, there was no agreement on a singular appropriate action around which activists could generate a norm.

As with the question on blame, if we were to remove responses with a low certainty score (scores 1–5, representing "very uncertain" to "neither certain nor uncertain") we see the results indicated in table 3.2. For this question, two respondents listed low certainty scores for each potential solution they ranked, for which reason those individuals are omitted from the table below (which is why N = 19 for respondents with at least one response with a certainty score of 6+).

---

38. One benefit to conducting the surveys myself as part of a lengthier interview was the ability to recognize the complexity and nuance in how officials thought about solutions to the problem of chronic hunger. For example, one respondent (from World Vision International) is coded as selecting gender equality, but her view on this was complex. She believed that gender *discrimination* should be eliminated but did believe there were (and should be) differences in gender roles. In this way, she did not see "gender *equality*" as the key concern. She wanted to see additional effort put into "empowerment for men" to encourage men to be more responsible in the family unit. Another respondent (from the Gates Foundation) selected social safety nets as a top solution for chronic hunger but noted that she understood programs like food aid vouchers as fitting under this broader umbrella.

Additionally, if individuals ranked more than three options, only the top three were included in table 3.2, though the full array of responses is included in figure 3.3. As with the blame question, only one point per respondent was attributed to "Other" (if they selected "Other") regardless of the number of additional solutions added in this category. As is evident, there is no consensus on what should be done to effectively solve the hunger problem. If there were a clear anti-hunger norm, we would expect a consensus not only on *who* to target but on *what* that actor should do. Given that actors were asked to list the top three solutions to the problem of chronic hunger, we would expect to see consensus across those three solutions, but no such consensus exists.

No Single Norm, but Many Norms?

Even if there is no single norm around hunger, might there be *a great many norms* prescribing the varied responses we see? If this were the case (and if we assumed there were a norm within this advocacy community that these organizations *ought* to target the violator of such a norm, as suggested by the Oxfam America official mentioned in the introduction to this book) we would expect a reaction from the relevant community when one of these norms was violated, yet we do not see this. There are no instances of shaming INGOs for targeting the "wrong" actor for hunger. For example, when Oxfam launches an anti-hunger campaign but does *not* blame national governments for chronic hunger, they are not shamed for failing to target the national government. Had there been a norm here that they violated by not targeting the national government, we should expect some response to norm deviance. Instead, what we see is more akin to "parallel play" on the part of these international anti-hunger organizations. These organizations hold diverse understandings of blame and solutions to the hunger problem, and they advocate (and where applicable wage different campaigns) reflecting these beliefs (such as the campaigns targeting transnational corporations, developed states, and tax evaders, among others).

Why a Lack of a Norm Matters

Understanding that not all rights have norms allows us to problematize prior understandings of how human rights campaigns function and the role of blame in advocacy campaigns; and it encourages us to be careful when making blanket statements about human rights or thinking about a common normative landscape across all human rights. Broadening our conceptual tool kit to include not only norms but moral principles and supererogatory standards enables us to understand that not all issue areas exist in the same type of social or moral environment. In asking how it is possible that human rights campaigns might "boomerang" or "spiral," scholars must first examine the normative environment in which activists are working. The presence of norms can enable specific behavior (like focused advocacy on a single common target actor) and the absence of norms can enable a different type of behavior ("buckshot" advocacy). Not all human rights have norms, and when an issue area is replete with moral principles or supererogatory standards but no norms (as is the case with the right to food), we should expect this to make a difference in how advocacy functions.

Had a norm existed around the right to food, we should have expected advocacy to function differently. When I talked through a hypothetical scenario with one Oxfam Great Britain senior official we discussed how advocacy might function differently if there were a norm that national governments were obliged to ensure the right to food of their citizens. She responded, "So, obviously, if the state has clearly got a legal responsibility to deliver something, and it's *recognized* that they have a legal responsibility to deliver it, then it's easier for us . . . and, yes, then we would go harder after the government."[39] If society believed that indeed the state was obliged to ensure the right to food, this would enable an environment conducive to blaming the state. And yet, reflecting on the rise of privately run food banks in the United Kingdom, she lamented, "Food as a human right is not a thing that exists, I would say"—at least not "if human right means the state is obliged."[40] There is certainly law attributing responsibility to national governments for ensuring the right to food of their citizens, but according to this anti-hunger activist, this law did not walk hand in hand with a norm in society recognizing this state obligation. And this lack of a norm mattered in explaining the nature and shape of advocacy.

More than simply serving as a precursor to advocacy focused on a single violator of the sort expected in the boomerang or spiral models, a lack of a norm can deter some influential activists from getting involved in an issue area to begin with and potentially make advocacy efforts less effective. The primary mechanism by which activists enable and constrain the behavior of states is through pressure, generally in the form of shaming and blaming (even if, as discussed in chapter 2, this advocacy may be more or less aggressive depending on the issue area). Targets can most effectively be shamed if activists (and their audience) understand the target to have done something *wrong*—to have violated a particular norm or standard of appropriate behavior. Clear violation allows activists to join together to shame the actor into compliance. Yet only if a specific actor is linked to a specific expected appropri-

---

39. Interview, Oxfam Great Britain 1, July 2015, emphasis added.
40. Interview, Oxfam Great Britain 1, July 2015.

ate behavior can such a norm be constructed. In the absence of a norm, where it is unclear who is to blame and what should be done, we should expect shaming to be less effective. Kenneth Roth, the executive director for HRW, notes how the struggle over ascribing blame and appropriate action has affected campaigns in his experience, and how diffuse blame may make shaming less effective:

> Although there are various forms of public outrage, only certain types are sufficiently targeted to shame officials into action. That is, the public might be outraged about a state of affairs—for example, poverty in a region—but have no idea whom to blame. *Or it might feel that blame is dispersed among a wide variety of actors. In such cases of diffuse responsibility, the stigma attached to any person, government, or institution is lessened*, and with it the power of international human rights organizations to effect change. Similarly, stigma weakens even in the case of a single violator if the remedy to a violation—what the government should do to correct it—is unclear. (Roth 2004, 67, emphasis added)

In practical terms, norms are useful to activists in prioritizing an actor as responsible for a given action and rallying support in order to shame actors who violate their normative responsibilities. But in my interview with a senior official at HRW on why the organization did not campaign around the right to food, she noted that it would be very challenging for HRW to be effective in this issue area. HRW could release a report, she noted, documenting the extent of hunger in the United States, but "I'm not sure we'd get all that much attention at all or that it would be that shameful." And in terms of successfully shaming governments, she noted, "we are successful . . . only if we can contrast their conduct with what a relevant public feels is moral or proper conduct" for them to have engaged in in the first place.[41] In cases such as this, where the HRW methodology of shaming is less likely to be effective, HRW is less likely to get involved in the first place.[42]

The lack of an anti-hunger norm is not only constitutive of the environment in which activists work in this issue area but also makes some campaign outcomes (e.g., centralized pressure on one singular actor) less possible and makes others (e.g., scattered campaigns blaming multiple actors for the hunger problem) more possible.

How is it possible that international anti-hunger campaigns behave so differently from the expectations of dominant models in the literature? What explains the

---

41. Interview, Human Rights Watch 1, October 2014.
42. Interview, Human Rights Watch 1, October 2014.

"buckshotting" of advocacy in this issue area? This chapter has argued that the normative environment around hunger is crucial in making sense of advocacy in this issue area and in so doing has challenged the assumption that all rights have norms, providing evidence for the lack of an anti-hunger norm from surveys of senior international anti-hunger advocates. If we believe that norms can be powerful in enabling and constraining action, as constructivist scholars certainly do, then understanding that not all human rights have norms is an important insight to have for those of us seeking to understand advocacy in this issue area. This chapter has also expanded our conceptual tool kit for making sense of the social world by distinguishing norms from moral principles and supererogatory standards.

Understanding that the hunger issue area lacks a norm is important, but knowing this raises two deeper questions: Why does this issue area lack a norm? What are the primary challenges to norm development around hunger and the right to food? Chapter 4 takes up these questions, and chapter 5 explores the inability of international human rights law to effectively translate into norms in this case.

HUNGER AT THE NEXUS OF RIGHTS AND DEVELOPMENT

If norms matter in explaining the shape and nature of advocacy around human rights, and not all human rights have norms (as argued in chapters 2 and 3), the pressing question that follows is why some rights may struggle to generate norms. In the hunger case, specifically, what are the challenges to norm development? This chapter argues that one of the most significant obstacles to the development of an anti-hunger norm is the issue's placement at the nexus of development and human rights frameworks.

The human rights meets development nexus can be especially challenging to navigate as development and human rights frameworks understand responsibility for hunger amelioration in different ways. Food is a human right, codified in international law,[1] but it is also seen as one of the world's greatest development problems, even the *main* development problem for the post-2015 development agenda.[2]

But why should this be a problem? Are human rights and development not natural bedfellows? After all, according to Navi Pallay, United Nations (UN) high commissioner for human rights, "The litmus test of development is the degree to which any strategies and interventions satisfy the legitimate demands of the people for freedom from fear and want, for a voice in their own societies, and for a life of dignity."[3] These development objectives sound quite similar to the objective of

1. For a discussion of international legal instruments that recognize the right to food, see chapter 5.
2. United Nations 2013.
3. Navi Pallay, quoted in Office of the United Nations High Commissioner for Human Rights, n.d.

human rights campaigns, particularly in their focus on the empowerment of individuals in their own societies. UN member states affirmed the interdependence of rights and development in the 2005 World Summit Outcome document, stating, "We recognize that development, peace and security, and human rights are *interlinked and mutually reinforcing*."[4] In 2003, the UN Development Group adopted the Common Understanding of a Human Rights-Based Approach to Development Programming (also known as the UN Common Understanding). According to the Common Understanding,

1. All programmes of development co-operation, policies and technical assistance should further the realisation of human rights as laid down in the Universal Declaration of Human Rights and other international human rights instruments.
2. Human rights standards contained in, and principles derived from, the Universal Declaration of Human Rights and other international human rights instruments guide all development cooperation and programming in all sectors and in all phases of the programming process.
3. Development cooperation contributes to the development of the capacities of 'duty-bearers' to meet their obligations and/or of 'rights-holders' to claim their rights.[5]

At least at the level of the UN, development and human rights approaches are perceived as inherently intertwined, ultimately interdependent, and internally consistent approaches.

But are these approaches truly consistent with each other? Do they encourage similar types of activism, a shared actor as responsible, or a common understanding of how the problem should be solved?

The hunger case suggests that the intersection of rights and development can be a complicated place to navigate. Issue areas at the crossroads of rights and development share advocacy space across multiple *types* of nongovernmental organizations (NGOs) and international nongovernmental organizations (INGOs) (namely humanitarian, development, human rights, and hybrid organizations).[6] In the case of hunger, these organizations have had different histories dealing with the issue area, different mobilization strategies, and different types of programming and advocacy work. Most significantly for our purposes here,

---

4. United Nations General Assembly 2005, p. 2, emphasis added. On the integration of rights into development see also: World Bank and the Organisation for Economic Co-operation and Development 2013.

5. United Nations Development Group 2003, 1.

6. We will discuss hybrid INGOs later on in the chapter. These generally refer to INGOs which began exclusively as development or humanitarian organizations but have since added on a human rights dimension.

these different histories and conceptualizations of the problem lead to very different understandings of who is to blame for hunger (if anyone), who should be targeted by advocacy efforts, and how they should be targeted.

Why should any of this matter? The intersection of rights and development is a relatively new phenomenon, and the challenges that this nexus brings to international anti-hunger advocacy are likely also experienced, or soon to be experienced, by campaigns around other economic and social rights. And these are challenges that are poorly understood, at least in the human rights literature.[7] Put differently, issues that could theoretically be understood as economic and social *rights* (food, health care, housing, education) were in the past dealt with internationally exclusively as *development* concerns,[8] but this is changing. International human rights organizations that had previously expressed little interest in claiming economic and social rights have entered the advocacy space over these issue areas, and the UN has begun intentionally linking rights with development concerns. Understanding the effects of this new amalgamation of actors and approaches is important to burgeoning discussions on transnational advocacy surrounding economic and social rights more broadly.

This chapter begins with a brief discussion of the history of the intersection of development and human rights within the UN and across anti-hunger INGOs in the twentieth century. It then examines human rights, development, and "hybrid" frames around the issue among anti-hunger INGOs, generally up to the year 2014. The chapter then concludes with a discussion of how these varied frameworks contribute to "buckshotting" in this issue area and reduce the likelihood that a norm around hunger will be established in the near future.

A History of Linking Development and Rights

In 1997 the UN formally began "mainstreaming" human rights into its development work. Then UN secretary-general Kofi Annan singled out human rights as key to UN reform, noting that "the integration of human rights into all principal United Nations activities and programmes" was to be a "priority area" for the UN going forward.[9] In the following decade, UN agencies such as the UN Children's

---

7. The practice literature, however, has examined this intersection, particularly from the perspective of development and rights organizations and international organizations. See Alston and Robinson 2005; Gauri and Gloppen 2012; Hickey and Mitlin 2009; Tomasevski 1993; and World Bank and the Organisation for Economic Co-operation and Development 2013.

8. There are some exceptions here, particularly in communist countries where economic rights in particular took center stage early on in the Cold War.

9. United Nations General Assembly 1997.

Fund (UNICEF), the UN Development Programme, and the World Health Organization included rights language in their own mandates and programming.[10]

There had certainly been some, albeit gradual, movement toward the integration of rights and development in the UN prior to 1997. In 1986, the UN General Assembly adopted the Declaration on the Right to Development, affirming

> the existence of serious obstacles to development, as well as to the complete fulfillment of human beings and of peoples, constituted, inter alia, by the denial of civil, political, economic, social and cultural rights, and considering that all human rights and fundamental freedoms are indivisible and interdependent and that, in order to promote development, equal attention and urgent consideration should be given to the implementation, promotion and protection of civil, political, economic, social and cultural rights.[11]

Soon afterward UNICEF took up an active role in encouraging the successful adoption of the Convention on the Rights of the Child (CRC), which resulted in the link between its development work and its support for the rights of children.[12]

That said, the integration of rights into development work (and vice versa) is a relatively new phenomenon. At the level of INGOs, development and human rights groups had, until recently, occupied distinct terrain, embodying very different strategies, programs, and understandings of their individual missions. As political scientist Peter Uvin aptly puts it, "Individual development practitioners may well have been card-carrying members of, say, Amnesty International; they may have discussed worrying human rights trends in the countries they worked in with colleagues during the evening, with a beer on the veranda, but they did *not* think that any of this was *their* job . . . they vaccinated, built schools, disseminated agricultural techniques, advised ministries. Human rights were . . . clearly somebody else's job" (2004, 1, emphasis in original). Certainly, as specific donor governments (notably the Netherlands, the Nordic states, Switzerland, and the United Kingdom) and the UN began to push for greater linkages between human rights and development work,[13] NGOs and activists had incentives to blend their work as well. But there was another, perhaps even more powerful, reason for this union that came as a shock within the development community: the Rwandan genocide.

---

10. Robinson 2005b, 29.

11. United Nations 1986.

12. Alston and Robinson 2005, 2. The CRC was adopted in 1989. Ultimately, however, the integration of rights language into UNICEF would be difficult. See Munro 2009.

13. Robinson 2005b, 29.

In the months prior to the genocide, Rwanda was touted by the development community as a success story. It was experiencing steady economic growth. Social indicators of development looked promising as well: access to clean water, sanitation, and vaccination rates were all on the rise.[14] And it was more densely populated with NGOs than most African countries.[15] According to development indicators, Rwanda was a model country. Then it shocked the development community by rapidly descending into mass violence. The Rwandan case highlighted the danger of a development approach divorced from all concerns about human rights. And development INGOs (with Oxfam International leading the way), began to explicitly integrate rights work into their mandates. This is not to suggest that a rights framework among INGOs could have prevented the genocide, but rather that the development community took this incident as a sign that their work should incorporate "rights" elements. On the other side of the aisle, human rights advocacy groups like Amnesty International and Human Rights Watch also publicly committed to expanding their work into economic and social rights.[16]

Finally, the UN Millennium Declaration in 2000 solidified the new mentality of the international community that rights and development should be interlinked.[17] The eight Millennium Development Goals embody this union, as they blend traditional development concerns like poverty amelioration with rights concerns such as the empowerment of women. Additionally, actors that had previously been more averse to engaging in "rights rhetoric," such as the World Bank, have begun to more explicitly link their development work to human rights objectives.[18]

Anti-hunger INGOs in the Twenty-First Century

Following the reemergence of interest in economic and social rights after the Cold War and the UN's efforts to integrate rights into development programming in the late 1990s, the hunger issue area in particular found itself at the crossroads of rights and development frameworks. Practically, this meant that an issue which had historically been dominated by humanitarian and development frameworks

---

14. Uvin 1998, 47. Although, Uvin notes that there may be reason to doubt the reliability of some of this data.

15. Uvin 1998, 48.

16. Robinson 2005b, 30.

17. "We will spare no effort to promote democracy and strengthen the rule of law, as well as respect for all internationally recognized human rights and fundamental freedoms, including the right to development." See United Nations General Assembly 2000.

18. See Wolfensohn 2005, 19–24.

was now exposed to rights rhetoric in ways that had previously been quite rare. The result of this change was twofold. First, advocacy efforts now straddled humanitarian, development, and rights foci, dependent upon the particular anti-hunger organization; second, a new breed of hybrid INGOs emerged—previously development-oriented organizations which now began to classify themselves as human rights-based organizations (e.g., ActionAid and Oxfam).

In terms of INGOs and activists, however, the union between rights and development has, at times, been a challenging one. Development professionals worry that human rights approaches are too "political," "unrealistic," "abstract," and "unable to cope with time . . . [as] it is never acceptable for policy makers to 'go backwards' at one point in order to go forwards later on."[19] Human rights activists are also perceived as placing too great an emphasis on state responsibility and law, when the poor tend to avoid the state at all costs and seek assistance from local communities instead.[20] From a rights perspective, development work is also suspect, as it may favor economic reforms that alienate or displace a few for the sake of the many. For rights activists, for example, moving a small indigenous group from their land, even if this means providing for a new highway that could modernize an economy, would be seen as a rights violation. For development workers, these decisions are less black and white, as collective benefit to a community may outweigh the cost to some individuals.

Most significant for our purposes here, however, is that development and rights approaches are based on different analytic frameworks, rely on different advocacy strategies, have historically taken different trajectories, rely on different understandings of blame and responsibility, and have very different practical considerations regarding programming. Issue areas that find themselves at the crossroads of these two approaches are likely to face varied (at times even competing) understandings of the problem. This makes the development of a single norm around the issue area very difficult and encourages and perpetuates the "buckshotting" of campaigns discussed in chapter 2.

Human Rights Organizations

To "pure" human rights organizations (by which I mean those with no development or humanitarian legacies), we would expect national government responsibility for rights to be linked to traditional understandings of human rights law.

---

19. Robinson 2005b, 32–36.
20. Robinson 2005b, 36–37. On the difficulties of using law to fulfill economic and social rights, see also Gauri and Gloppen 2012, 498–99. The use (or nonuse) of law will be discussed in greater detail chapter 5.

National governments are responsible for ensuring the human rights of their own citizens, of "progressively realizing" economic and social rights, and of "respecting, protecting, and fulfilling" all human rights, whether civil, political, cultural, economic, or social. The buck, so to speak, stops with states, particularly the national government of the particular state where the specific human right is being violated. Whether the state itself is doing the violating directly, or simply failing to stop another actor from violating a right is of little importance in terms of international law (i.e., acts of commission verses omission), at least in terms of the core human rights covenants. That said, acts of commission are far easier to organize campaigns around than acts of omission, as we will see below in how human rights organizations have campaigned in the hunger issue area.

FIAN International, founded in 1986, is one influential organization in the hunger network which has no development or humanitarian organizational legacies and takes a more conventional human rights approach to its anti-hunger work—though it is a relatively small organization in relation to organizations like CARE or Oxfam.[21] In its own words, "FIAN's mission is to expose violations of people's right to food wherever they may occur. FIAN stands up to unjust and oppressive practices that prevent people from being able to feed themselves."[22] When asked about their approach to hunger, one senior official at FIAN International stated,

> We are a human rights organization. Therefore we depart from a framework that is not defined by us—that is defined by human rights law . . . human rights is a way to regulate power, not only of the state but to regulate power of the private sector and any other big actor, you know, political parties, religious groups, that for any reason impinge on or abuse the human rights of other people. We say human rights are about the regulation of power. It is about the government not going beyond what it is supposed to do and impinging on rights. It is about asking the states and governments, as the manager of the public good, to guarantee that all people have equal rights . . . and the third level is demanding from states that they play their role to reduce inequality and to promote human dignity. This is what we believe is our mission. Let's put it this way: it is defined by the framework of human rights. It is not decided by us, but by the peoples and committed by the governments to a certain extent.[23]

Naming and shaming is central to the work FIAN does, and the organization is not shy about focusing this pressure on national governments. In 2014, for

---

21. FIAN's income for the year 2012 was roughly €1.64 million (approximately US$2.3 million), compared to Oxfam America's revenue of approximately US$69 million in fiscal year 2012.

22. Stronthenke and Carrigan 2013, 4.

23. Interview, FIAN International 1, July 2013.

example, FIAN International waged a campaign against the Philippine state for the right-to-food violations of the Hacienda Luisita farmers (which number roughly 6,200).[24] FIAN initiated a letter-writing campaign, for individuals of all countries, to send letters to the president, the secretary of agriculture, and the secretary of agrarian reform of the Philippines to remind them,

> The Philippines is a State Party to the International Covenant on Economic, Social and Cultural Rights (ICESCR) and therefore obliged to protect and fulfill the right to food of its people, including the farmworker beneficiaries of Hacienda Luisita. Secured access to land is fundamental for the rural population who depend on cultivating land to feed themselves adequately. The Philippine government breached its protect-bound obligation under the right to food by not regulating the unjust arrangements of the ariendador that enforced farmworkers' dependency. Finally, the government of the Philippines has failed to fulfill the right to adequate food of the Hacienda Luisita farmers by not duly implementing the CARP [Comprehensive Agrarian Reform Program]—a program which aims to distribute land to landless farmers and to provide essential social protection measures and support services to guarantee their right to adequate food.[25]

This is consistent with the behavior that the human rights literature has come to expect from human rights campaigns: activists assert pressure on governments to comply with their commitments under international law. FIAN does not only focus this pressure on national governments, however. In 2013 it concluded a campaign against the Swedish government for financing tree plantations in Niassa Province in Mozambique.[26] FIAN argued that these plantations displaced peasants from their land and infringed on their ability to grow their own food, thus violating the peasants' right to food. Citing the Maastricht Principles on Extraterritorial Obligations of States in the Area of Economic, Social and Cultural Rights,[27] FIAN urged individuals around the world to send letters to a variety of departments within the Swedish government to urge them to conduct a study to

---

24. FIAN International 2014.
25. FIAN International 2014
26. This campaign was active from October 2012 through April 2013. See FIAN Netherlands 2012.
27. According to the Maastricht Principles,

> A State has obligations to respect, protect and fulfill economic, social and cultural rights in any of the following:
> a) situations over which it exercises authority or effective control, whether or not such control is exercised in accordance with international law;
> b) situations over which State acts or omissions bring about foreseeable effects on the enjoyment of economic, social and cultural rights, whether within or outside its territory;

examine if there had been rights violations, to stop violations that had happened, and to open up a complaint mechanism whereby local residents could disclose right-to-food violations.[28] The Maastricht Principles, however, were largely a construct of human rights scholars and activists, and had not been signed or ratified by states. In this instance, we observe the naming and shaming strategy that is common in human rights campaigns, but it is focused on outside governments. To one senior official at FIAN, however, the practice of targeting national governments, outside states, intergovernmental organizations, and corporations should not be understood as fragmented but rather as firmly rooted in international human rights law, which this official interprets as ascribing responsibility to states not only for their behavior inside their borders but outside their borders, as well as through their influence in intergovernmental organizations and through their permission with corporations operating under their influence.[29]

What we observe with the case of FIAN is both the closest example to a "pure" human rights approach to the hunger problem but also the appeal of campaigns around clear instances of commission (instead of omission). Particularly in issue areas that lack the benefit of a norm clearly ascribing responsibility in a society to a given actor, the burden of proof for activists is higher to make a compelling case to justify their target selection. As will be discussed in chapter 5, this means that FIAN often finds it difficult to gather enough evidence to wage compelling campaigns against national governments for not fulfilling the right to food.[30] FIAN does wage campaigns which blame national governments for failing to meet their obligations under international law vis-à-vis the right to food, but it also capitalizes on acts of commission committed by other actors (either outside governments or corporations) which it can leverage to construct compelling campaigns.

Development and Humanitarian Organizations

Humanitarian and development organizations, in contrast to a "pure" human rights approach, often place responsibility *outside national governments* and onto

---

c) situations in which the State, acting separately or jointly, whether through its executive, legislative or judicial branches, is in a position to exercise decisive influence or to take measures to realize economic, social and cultural rights extraterritorially, in accordance with international law.

This is only a small piece of the larger Maastricht Principles. See ETO Consortium 2013.

28. FIAN Netherlands 2012.

29. Interview, FIAN International 1, July 2013.

30. On the difficulty of making a compelling case for governments failing to fulfill the right to food, see Windfuhr 2007, 340–41.

development organizations themselves and the donations of developed states. This is due in part to the history of these organizations' involvement in country missions. As will be discussed later in the chapter, path dependence keeps development organizations (even those that have taken on rights frameworks, such as Oxfam) approaching hunger in relatively consistent ways over time, even if this varies from how traditional rights-based approaches would suggest.

Historically, development NGOs started constructing houses, irrigating fields, digging wells, and vaccinating children *because the state was unable or unwilling to do so*.[31] Organizations such as CARE or Oxfam, for example, started on the heels of World War II in order to provide relief to war-torn Europe. In the case of Oxfam (originally the Oxford Committee for Famine Relief), meetings began in October 1942. With a membership of five, the committee discussed "the food situation in each of the plundered countries," noting that "our task needs be very difficult. The problem is to mitigate the famine without invalidating the Allies' blockade."[32] In the aftermath of the war (and under blockade), states could hardly be expected to provide food or health care effectively for their populations, and NGOs helped to fill this gap. In order to do so, they developed very particular fundraising and mobilization strategies, encouraging the (comparatively) well-off in developed states to provide cash or in-kind aid to the humanitarian organization which would then funnel necessary goods and services abroad to those in need. CARE, in particular, gained recognition for its delivery of "CARE packages": the organization would fly over war-torn areas and drop boxes of supplies from planes.[33]

Often, as was especially the case in Latin America, development and humanitarian INGOs became active in countries on the heels of structural adjustment policies demanded by international financial institutions (notably, the International Monetary Fund) which required states to refrain from direct spending on such economic and social rights as food, housing, and health care. In the era of the Washington Consensus, INGOs served as the *replacement* for the state, which was prohibited from necessary social spending as a condition to their loans.[34] Indeed, the raison d'être of development and humanitarian organizations was generally to provide for services that they perceived national governments as unable (or unwilling) to provide.

---

31. Mitlin and Hickey 2009.
32. Oxford Famine Relief Committee minutes (handwritten), October 5, 1942. Bodleian Library, Oxford University.
33. Though CARE is most commonly known by its one-word acronym, it was originally named the Cooperative for American Remittance to Europe and is now officially named the Cooperative for Assistance and Relief Everywhere. It classifies itself as a humanitarian organization, but notes, "CARE works in more than 90 countries, reaching over 50 million people through over 950 poverty-fighting development and humanitarian aid programs," CARE International, n.d.
34. See Mitlin and Hickey 2009.

Shaming or blaming national governments, as a strategy, makes little sense if you understand a problem as outside the capacity of the state to solve. When asked about whom World Vision blames (if anybody) for hunger while conducting the survey, one senior official responded:

> WORLD VISION US SENIOR OFFICIAL: That's a tough question [*laughs*]. See, I wouldn't say "nobody's to blame," but I don't think the groups you've listed here are to blame necessarily. I mean, it's a combination of factors.
>
> MICHELLE JURKOVICH: If blame doesn't make sense, then it's okay to say, "We don't think in terms of blame."
>
> WORLD VISION US SENIOR OFFICIAL: Yeah, I'll definitely mark that down.[35]

This official then wrote, "Blame is not a word we use, rather 'causes'" on the survey question pertaining to blame and, selecting "Other," wrote in "poor productivity," "poor knowledge, especially for nutrition and hygiene," and "gender disparities."[36] When given a list on the survey including national governments, outside states, transnational corporations, and price speculators, no particular actor resonated as "to blame" for hunger.

Similarly, when I surveyed a senior staff member at CARE USA about who is to blame for chronic hunger, the individual remarked, "I don't think, you know, I've come across any kind of government or anybody who really wants . . . to have a population that's hungry. I think it's a lack of capacity, actually."[37]

As of 2014, CARE worked in ninety countries around the world, including sponsoring child and maternal nutrition programs in comparatively developed states like India, as well as continued programming in Brazil and South Africa.[38] CARE also provides aid in the aftermath of natural disasters, even in developed states, and as of 2012 was continuing to provide assistance in northern Japan after the 2011 earthquake and tsunami there.[39] CARE also works in places like the Democratic Republic of the Congo, Gaza, and South Sudan, where development and humanitarian assistance would be more expected than in Brazil or India or comparatively economically advanced states like Japan and South Africa.

It might appear puzzling that a senior official for CARE USA would dismiss the idea of blaming national governments for high hunger rates (citing a lack of capacity), when CARE works in places like India, where 38 percent of children

---

35. Interview, World Vision US 2, May 2013.
36. Survey result, World Vision US 2, May 2013.
37. Interview, CARE USA 1, May 2013.
38. CARE India n.d.; CARE International 2014. For an updated list of where CARE works, see CARE International, n.d.
39. On CARE International's assistance programs in Japan, see CARE International 2012.

are stunted in 2015, but the country is part of the G20.[40] This is even more inter-esting when one contrasts this approach with local grassroots movements (not driven by INGOs) for the right to food in India, which were successful in getting the national government to agree to the 2013 National Food Security Act as well as allowing citizens to seek redress for right-to-food violations in domestic courts.[41] But it is less puzzling when one considers the history of how hunger has been understood within development and humanitarian organizations like CARE. Since the organization's founding in 1945, hunger has been conceptual-ized primarily as a humanitarian and development problem in which aid organ-izations either provide assistance directly to those in need or work with local communities to help them build capacity to provide their own food security. When anti-hunger missions began in organizations such as Action against Hunger, CARE, and World Vision, state capacity in the developing world was highly sus-pect and advocacy efforts approached hunger as a problem for charity (generally relying on funding and donations from developed countries and their citizens). In this way, while one might question the argument that countries like Brazil or India *lack the capacity* to improve the food security situation in their countries, the hunger-as-development-problem frame continues to encourage organizations with this historical legacy to approach the problem in this way. Over time these organizations have embraced greater partnerships with developing country gov-ernments, but also continue to retain active on-the-ground staff and operations providing food assistance and nutritional supplements, irrigating fields, and running agricultural training programs.

The *construction of state (in)capacity* is a particularly interesting feature of anti-hunger advocacy, and likely economic and social rights advocacy more broadly. In the case of civil and political human rights, the need for strong state capacity may be less obvious, though as David Beetham argues, all rights require state action to fulfill.[42] In the case of economic and social rights, however, and the right to food in particular, the question of *what measures a state can reasonably do* hovers over ac-tivist efforts. Who decides if Guatemala can (and should) do more to ensure the right to food of its citizens? How do we know if Malawi has the capacity to reduce malnutrition rates within its borders? Who makes these determinations?

Generally activists, either domestic or international, make the determination regarding what a state should be held accountable for doing for its citizens. It is

---

40. United Nations Children's Fund, World Health Organization, and World Bank, 2015.

41. See, in particular, People's Union for Civil Liberties (PUCL) v. the Government of India and Others, Writ Petition (Civil) No. 196 of 2001, Supreme Court of India. After early rulings calling for government action to use existing public grain stores and other public programing to address hun-ger, the case was ultimately dismissed in 2017. For more on grassroots right-to-food advocacy in India, see Hertel 2015.

42. Beetham 1995, 51.

these actors who historically pressure governments to pick up additional responsibilities and provide (new or better) programs and services. And this is inherently a subjective call. While we could imagine in theory a world where international law demarcated these responsibilities clearly (and more objectively), this is not the world we live in for economic and social rights, as will be discussed in chapter 5. International law leaves states open to "progressively realize" the right to food and other economic and social rights. How fast they ought to realize this right, and through what means, is not explicitly stated in international law. Absent a state taking the initiative itself, perhaps due to electoral incentives,[43] it is left up to activists and their organizations to do so.[44]

For this reason, the analytic framework activists and INGOs use to make sense of hunger is especially significant. If hunger is perceived of through a development framework where state incapacity is generally assumed and reiterated through the perpetuation of in-country missions, even in economically more advanced countries, it should not be particularly surprising that such organizations do not shame and blame national governments to improve hunger conditions in their countries. It may not be entirely clear who *should* improve these conditions, but shaming national governments in developing states is generally not an approach that follows from this framework.

Action against Hunger USA, a member of the Action against Hunger/ Action Internationale Contre la Faim (ACF) International Network, sums up its approach in the following way:

> For 40 years, across nearly 50 countries, we have led the global fight against hunger. *We save the lives of children and their families.* We are there for them before and after disaster strikes. *We enable people to provide for themselves*, see their children grow up strong, and for whole communities to prosper. We constantly search for more effective solutions, while *sharing our knowledge and expertise* with the world. We push for long-term change. We will never give up. Until the world is free from hunger.[45]

Framed in this way, it is an INGO (Action against Hunger) which will save hungry children and support hungry communities through the knowledge and

---

43. This was certainly the case with Luiz Inácio Lula da Silva, who championed the Bolsa Familia and Fome Zero conditional cash transfer programs in Brazil. He proposed these programs as part of a populist campaign designed to win him the presidency, and it worked. But examples such as this are comparatively rare.

44. On the question of "minimum core obligations" of states to ensure economic and social rights, however, we have seen recent efforts by scholars (at times in partnership with IGOs like the World Bank) to consider what basic efforts states must make at minimum to ensure these rights and the legal and philosophical justifications for doing so. See for example Tasioulas (2017) and Young (2008).

45. Action against Hunger USA, n.d., "Countries" (website), emphasis added.

expertise the organization itself has and the funding it receives.[46] Contrast this traditional understanding of a humanitarian and development approach (which tends to view assistance as provided by the Global North to the Global South) with a traditional rights approach (i.e., demanding national governments fulfill their obligations vis-à-vis their citizens under international law). The fundamental logics of both approaches are different. Their understandings of who *ought to do the providing* are different. Their campaign strategies (mobilizing citizens to blame governments versus rallying citizens in developed states to give money directly or through their governments to fund programs or projects the INGO will run in developing states) are fundamentally different.

When dealing with civil and political rights, these realms could remain separate, as development organizations had little interest in these issues. And for most of the twentieth century, international human rights groups were uninterested in economic and social rights in general, focusing almost exclusively on civil and political rights. Development organizations thus reigned over issue areas like hunger, education, health care, and access to water. But in the mid- to late 1990s, with the rise of "rights rhetoric" in the UN, the mandate to focus on human rights across UN development programming, and the internal shock to the development community (in the case of the Rwandan genocide), things began to change.

But what happens when INGOs traditionally perceived of as development organizations which historically dominated issue areas like hunger begin to broaden their mandate to include a rights focus? What does activism look like in these INGOs regarding issue areas like hunger?

New "Hybrid" (Development/Rights) INGOs: Oxfam and ActionAid

Instead of engaging in more traditional human rights approaches of naming and shaming national governments over right-to-food violations, Oxfam has engaged in a different strategy: a combination of continued active programming work, as well as advocacy campaigns, often targeting private corporations. In this way, it continues development work much as before through active in-country operations, yet also takes up the hallmark human rights strategy of naming and shaming, but often in a less aggressive way than one might imagine campaigns around civil and political rights and with a focus on multiple target actors, including private corporations.

---

46. See Action against Hunger USA, n.d., *2014 Annual Report and Financials*. In 2014 a mix of U.S. government, private corporation, and private citizen donations made up the largest share of financial contributions.

Oxfam now uses "rights rhetoric" and classifies itself as falling under a rights framework, but does not direct the majority of its more aggressive naming and shaming to national governments or have a significant focus on international legal obligations of states vis-à-vis the right to food. What is interesting about the "rights-based" work in this new generation of hybrid INGOs is that they largely eschew the traditional aggressive state-centered campaign foci that the literature has come to expect from human rights activist campaigns and embrace alternative strategies of shaming the private sector, and insufficient donations and aid from developed states, for hunger in developing states. In INGOs such as these, in issue areas that cross rights and development frameworks, we see a new form of activism, one which uses rights rhetoric to legitimate the goal of the campaign (ending hunger) but chooses to leave behind the legal frameworks provided for human rights in international law.[47]

It is worth briefly reviewing the specifics of Oxfam's international anti-hunger programming and campaign work. Much of what Oxfam does one might expect of a traditional development organization. In fact, as of 2013, roughly 90 percent of all spending within Oxfam (as aggregated across all Oxfam confederate offices) went toward "development and humanitarian" programming, while only 10 percent was spent on what is referred to in Oxfam's annual report as "influencing" (i.e., advocacy) programs.[48] Oxfam provides relief in the aftermath of natural disasters or war; in the case of Oxfam America, supports farmers associations;[49] and provides training and education on agricultural techniques,[50] among many other development-oriented projects.

But in conjunction with its integration of a "rights approach," Oxfam has expanded its focus on advocacy in a way that is distinct from the work of traditional development agencies. Interestingly, however, as of 2014 the primary target to the largest unified advocacy effort within Oxfam was the private sector. Behind the Brands, part of Oxfam's flagship GROW campaign, targets the "Big 10" transnational food and beverage corporations: Associated British Foods Coca-Cola, Danone, General Mills, Kellogg's, Mars, Mondelēz International (previously Kraft Foods), Nestlé, PepsiCo, and Unilever.

According to Oxfam, the Big 10 controls approximately 10 percent of the global economy, but "these companies have grown prosperous while the millions who supply the land, labor and water needed for their products face increased

---

47. The relative lack of reliance on international law in international anti-hunger campaigns will be discussed in detail in chapter 5.

48. Oxfam International, n.d., *Oxfam International Annual Report, 2012–2013*, 70.

49. For instance, Oxfam America has supported two farmers associations in Haiti. See Ferguson 2013.

50. Ferguson 2013.

hardship."[51] What links the Big 10 to global hunger? Oxfam constructs the following causal chain in its campaign literature:

> Overall, up to 80 percent of the global population considered 'chronically hungry' are farmers, and the use of valuable agricultural resources for the production of snacks and sodas means less fertile land and clean water is available to grow nutritious food for local communities. And changing weather patterns due to greenhouse gas emissions-a large percentage of which come from agricultural production-continue to make these small-scale farmers increasingly vulnerable.[52]

Oxfam argues that the Big 10 use resources that, if allocated directly to hungry people, could be used to grow food and provide clean water, therefore reducing global hunger. Furthermore, these large corporations (or their supply chains) produce greenhouse gases, which leads to climate change, which in turn leads to volatile farming conditions for poor farmers and food price increases for consumers. Additionally, dependent on the particular corporation, Oxfam levies allegations ranging from the use of child labor, engaging in land or water grabs, abusing natural resources, and engaging in environmentally degrading practices.[53]

The solution to this problem, according to Oxfam, is to wage an international shaming and accountability campaign, where Oxfam ranks the Big 10 on a "scorecard" based on the corporations' policies on seven themes, which as of 2014 were: "transparency, farmers, workers, women, climate change, land, and water."[54] Primarily, its interest is on investigating the supply chain upon which these corporations rely.[55] Oxfam exposes poor corporate policies on these seven themes and then encourages citizens around the world to pressure these corporations for change (in part by providing form letters for them to send).

What is interesting, however, is how much effort is exerted to *construct causal chains that link global hunger primarily to the actions of ten, albeit quite large, food and beverage industries.* When an international legal framework already exists to legitimate national governments as responsible for ensuring (and fulfilling if necessary) the right to food within their countries, we might expect a group with a rights focus to leverage this to blame national governments for persistent hunger within their borders. Moreover, it would seem to be much easier to construct a short causal chain between government neglect and hunger within the state's

---

51. Hoffman 2013, 1.
52. Hoffman 2013, 9. Oxfam cites a WordPress blog for the statistic that 80 percent of the world's chronically hungry are farmers; this number should be taken with caution.
53. Hoffman 2013, 2.
54. Oxfam International 2014, 1.
55. Oxfam International, n.d., "Behind the Brands: About" (webpage).

borders than argue that Kellogg's or Mars is responsible for global hunger. But then why do we see comparatively little aggressive blaming of national governments and instead a focus on the private sector?[56]

Publically, Oxfam justifies its focus on the private sector as a target of the Behind the Brands campaign in the following way:

> Of course, these companies are not the only ones responsible for hunger and poverty in the world. But, as described in this report, their success has hinged on the availability of cheap land and labor supplied by poor communities around the world. Additionally, the Big 10 today have the power to exert substantial influence over the traders and governments which control and regulate global food supply chains. They are also the most visible part of the industry, and are putting their own reputations at risk as consumers grow more concerned about what they buy and from whom.[57]

In other words, the Big 10 take advantage of both people and natural resources in developing countries, and they are extremely powerful actors, perhaps even more powerful than governments. Privately, however, when asked why Oxfam engages in much more aggressive shaming of corporations than national governments, one Oxfam America senior official responded that corporations cannot deny visas, though governments can. Oxfam retains active in-country missions in developing countries, and by contrast "don't operate in the lobby of these [corporations]." Oxfam relies on the goodwill of national governments to maintain their more traditional development programming, but they have no such dependency on the goodwill of corporations.[58]

There was a marked tension and defensiveness expressed by the senior staff I interviewed at Oxfam America regarding the extent of pressure Oxfam places on national governments. As one official put it,

> We get our legitimacy, as opposed to a think tank, or a Bread for the World, or a One, by being based in these ninety-two countries. We also argue that we are not the same as World Vision because we are willing to hold the powerful accountable, like I said to you earlier. We're willing to name names, to launch national campaigns. Yet to launch a campaign in a country against people . . . who are the corrupt, with private

---

56. There are, however, some individual campaigns (namely, in Guatemala and the Philippines) where Oxfam partners with local groups to participate in rallies against national government land policies, linking the evictions of people off their lands to their subsequent hunger; see Oxfam International n.d., *Oxfam International Annual Report, 2012–2013.*

57. Hoffman 2013, 6.

58. Interview, Oxfam America 1, May 2013.

interests, then we have to be convinced that the good we will do with that national campaign will exceed the risk we will draw our programs into, which some of which are very traditional, because we do campaigning but we also do some basic stuff. That is my battle. . . . [Amnesty International], they don't have operations. They don't have to balance that.

She went on to explain that before 2010 Oxfam had "no work in countries holding national institutions accountable for the failure of a policy or to put in place a policy they don't have." As of 2013, Oxfam was working in roughly forty focus countries for its GROW campaign, and,

Somebody in that government wishes [Oxfam] would go away. I think a third of our work goes in that world. Like, somebody in the government, if you asked them, they'd wish it wasn't there because it creates a discomfort. I'd say one-third . . . maybe it's a massive transparency initiative—all we're trying to do is find out who's buying up all the land. We're not, you know, my line that I use a lot in this office is, "I want to hear your best passive-aggressive approach to getting this solved." Aggressive will get you kicked out. Passive is "Go do World Vision." I want passive-aggressive. I want you to get shit done and change the power without being in people's faces.[59]

Oxfam carries over a strong development legacy even in its current rights focus. It maintains significant in-country operations that can only continue at the pleasure of the national governments in question. Overtly naming and shaming many national governments might well get Oxfam kicked out of the country, jeopardizing the security of its missions (and its staff in the country). This is a serious concern for organizations which have historically viewed hunger as a development problem and are attempting to refocus to rights frameworks while maintaining active development or humanitarian operations on the ground. Shaming national governments is a dangerous business, and it is one that may not be well suited to organizations which retain in-country missions and programming. In the case of civil and political human rights campaigns, groups like Amnesty International do not have to worry about jeopardizing in-country development programs, as they do not run any. In the case of activists around economic and social rights (like food), the safety and security of in-country missions is a very real concern. Refocusing blame toward corporations is one way to retain a naming and shaming mobilization strategy without running the risk of getting staff members' visas denied or in-country programing put in jeopardy.

---

59. Interview, Oxfam America 1, May 2013.

At the same time, there is a compulsion within these organizations, in using this rights rhetoric, to implicate the government in some way. But putting some degree of "discomfort" on national governments is a very different strategy than the overt naming and shaming we have come to expect from human rights organizations which engage in civil and political rights campaigns. This tension came up when this senior Oxfam America official and I discussed the "facilitating" versus "pressuring" roles that Oxfam has when working with governments and I asked what percentage of its engagement with governments fell on the "pressure" end of the spectrum:

> OXFAM AMERICA SENIOR OFFICIAL: Pressure versus facilitate? Um, honestly, honestly . . .
>
> MICHELLE JURKOVICH: Are we talking five percent? Are we talking less?
>
> OXFAM AMERICA SENIOR OFFICIAL: No, no. God, no. On pressure?
>
> JURKOVICH: On pressure of the nonfacilitating type.
>
> OXFAM AMERICA SENIOR OFFICIAL: Yes! Oh, well, hold on. I think you still mean marching down the streets.
>
> JURKOVICH: I kind of do. I mean . . . because I'm juxtaposing . . . to put it on a spectrum is what I'm trying to do. If one end is "Bad, bad Pinochet, stop forcibly disappearing your people. We're going to hold protests in the street." And the other end is we turn the other way . . .
>
> OXFAM AMERICA SENIOR OFFICIAL: I think, if you're asking me for extreme . . . I'd say zero . . . I'm saying what Human Rights [Watch] and Amnesty [International] do. There is none that fall in the top ten percent. None in the top ten percent.[60]

There is considerable path dependence at work inside these hybrid INGOs.[61] They maintain active in-country missions and often very traditional development programs while at the same time engaging in advocacy work under a "rights framework." These development legacies matter a great deal in shaping the nature of advocacy inside this new generation of INGOs, however. They use the language of human rights and adopt, to some extent, the hallmark mobilization strategy of rights organizations (naming and shaming), but need to protect their in-country programming, which means aggressive shaming of national governments is often too risky.

ActionAid is another advocacy INGO which has made the transition from what they called a "charity" focused on development work to one adopting a human rights–based approach (HRBA) to programming.[62] In an organizational handbook

60. Interview, Oxfam America 1, May 2013.

61. On the concept of path dependence, see Hall and Taylor 1996; and Pierson 2000.

62. Hargreaves et al. 2010, 9.

Needs based (with welfare features) approach to development

FIGURE 4.1. ActionAid as Charity Organization. Source: Hargreaves et al. 2010, 11. Illustration by Alastair Findlay.

to staff, this hybrid INGO portrays its evolution from a "charity" organization to one with an HRBA, as shown in figures 4.1, 4.2, and 4.3.

In the 1990s ActionAid understood itself primarily as an actor who would provide goods and services to meet the direct needs of specific communities. The national government, as can be seen figure 4.1, was not a part of its work: "Instead," the organization notes, "we *substituted* for government by providing the services for which government was ultimately responsible" (Hargreaves et al. 2010, 11, emphasis added).

This approach had changed by 2005, as illustrated in figure 4.2. Using another example of an education campaign, ActionAid notes that by 2005, their philosophy had changed to incorporate greater partnerships with local communities and a greater level of engagement with governments. In its own words, "We worked to empower (build capacity and knowledge of) communities to fulfill governments' responsibilities locally by providing public services, or by supporting state-community-ActionAid partnerships through which services were delivered and maintained. In addition to working on the feeder schools, we worked in partnership with government to improve infrastructure—classrooms and desks—in government schools. ActionAid

Empowerment approach to development

FIGURE 4.2. The ActionAid Empowerment Approach. Source: Hargreaves et al. 2010, 14. Illustration by Alastair Findlay.

topped up the money provided by government to upgrade schools" (Hargreaves et al. 2010, 13).

Finally, ActionAid illustrates its human rights approach as shown in figure 4.3. Under this philosophy, ActionAid states that its understanding of the role of government has changed significantly:

> Government is not neutral, but is instead strongly influenced by those who have power. Because of this we need to be strategic in how we work with the different arms of the government. At times we helped build the capacity of government structures such as school management and school governing bodies. At other times we needed to push government to change its policies and we needed to hold government accountable— so we entered into a campaign with others to influence a change in policy on user fees to hold government accountable to its commitments regarding the right to education.

Through our HRBA we build a wide movement for change

FIGURE 4.3.   The ActionAid Human Rights Approach. Source: Hargreaves et al. 2010, 17. Illustration by Alastair Findlay.

> When government introduced free primary education, the challenge shifted to ensuring quality education and retention of learners. The network focused on working closely with social audit groups to ensure government transparency and accountability in the use of education resources. (Hargreaves et al., 2010, 17)

While the empirical example given in the staff handbook was education campaigns (and feeding programs associated within broader educational objectives), it illustrates nicely how the organization perceived its own transformation from charity to HRBA programming over the past couple decades. At the same time, however, the manual highlights some of the murkiness over who constitutes "duty bearers" for the economic and social rights around which ActionAid campaigns. Under its current paradigm, it encourages employees to "think and act globally and locally; constraints to social change lie beyond the local in a complex and interconnected global system" (Hargreaves et al. 2010, 19). Campaigns are not always targeting national level officials, but look to broader global injustices.

Moreover, ActionAid highlights that under its current HRBA, there are multiple "duty bearers" to the given human right the organization is campaigning to realize. While the national government is "often the primary, or ultimate, duty bearer," in cases where the government is weak (or failed), the international community (namely, the UN or NGOs) become duty bearers. ActionAid also perceives a secondary level of duty bearers to rights, noting, "Secondary duty bearers are non-state actors who also have power and duties in relation to rights—for example, traditional and religious authorities, corporations and employers, and even individuals" (Hargreaves et al. 2010, 36).

When considering the hunger issue area in particular, one senior ActionAid USA official noted that blame is shared among five different actors, in the following order: national governments, outside governments (such as the governments of developed states), transnational corporations, a lack of capacity for national governments, and price speculators.[63] The understanding of blame in the hunger issue area within ActionAid (and economic and social rights more broadly) is more complicated than the neat diagrams in the manual suggest. Here, as was the case at Oxfam, there is a noticeable tension within the organization between the desire to use rights rhetoric and shaming strategies and the need to protect local programming.

At ActionAid, as at Oxfam, no national-level shaming campaign can be approved without the consent of the local ActionAid office. If the local office perceives the risk and threat to be too high in blaming governments (or other actors) in a given country, it has the power to veto such an action. This was the case, for instance, in Tanzania, when ActionAid wanted to launch a campaign against a U.S. company that was engaging in land grabbing. According to one senior ActionAid USA official,

> If we wanted to work on any campaign that said anything about somebody else's government, we'd have to ask them first. . . . We actually had a case in Tanzania where we were about to launch this huge report we had written on a U.S. company that was grabbing land in Tanzania and basically the, like, moments before we, you know, we hit Send, ActionAid Tanzania said you can't send it, the Tanzanian government is going to retaliate. And . . . we've gotten almost kicked out of a number of, I mean, ActionAid Uganda staff face violence from the Ugandan government for what they're doing. So it's really a pretty sensitive safety issue . . . local offices can say, "No, absolutely not. It's too politically sensitive."[64]

---

63. Survey results, senior staff member of ActionAid USA, June 2013.
64. Interview, ActionAid USA 1, June 2013.

In these hybrid INGOs, overt naming and shaming is still a risky enterprise, and the need to protect local offices and programs means that the nature of advocacy will necessarily be guided by different calculations than by organizations who do not have such operations to protect.[65] And these organizations will often target the Global North in their anti-hunger campaigns. For instance, ActionAid supported a "caravan of women" who walked from West Africa to South Africa to bring attention to the serious impact of climate change. The objective of this campaign was not to target national governments in Africa but to cause "global north governments to take action on climate change."[66] Similarly, the organization has engaged in the Tax Justice campaign, where ActionAid argues that financial firms such as Barclays deprive African countries of necessary tax revenue by facilitating the use of tax havens. ActionAid supported a march in Zambia "to stop corporations like Barclays from depriving people living in poverty in Zambia of basic social services."[67] Here, again, a corporation is to blame for the lack of social services in Zambia.

Even when ActionAid does feel it is safe to target a specific national government for high hunger rates, it often does so in ways that reflect its legacy as a development organization. For example, ActionAid has trained citizens—particularly women—in developing countries in Africa on how to read national budgets and hold governments accountable to spending the 10 percent on agricultural development that they promised to do in 2003 with the Maputo Declaration on Agriculture and Food Security. ActionAid has worked on public financing for agriculture campaigns in partnership with the Bill & Melinda Gates Foundation, as it sees agricultural development (and state funding for agricultural development) as central to hunger relief. When I asked one senior ActionAid USA official why ActionAid prioritized spending in agricultural development as the solution to hunger as opposed to pressuring governments for social safety nets, the following exchange took place:

> ACTIONAID USA SENIOR OFFICIAL: I just don't think it's as big of need in many of these, to me it's not the number one need in many of these communities, social safety nets.
>
> MICHELLE JURKOVICH: So the bigger need, you were saying, is gender equality and dealing with small scale ag production.

---

65. This does not mean that ActionAid never targets national governments. As one senior ActionAid USA official noted, their strategy is context specific. ActionAid India, for instance, does participate in rallies with advocacy targeting national governments (Interview, ActionAidUSA 1, June 2013).

66. Interview, ActionAid USA 1, June 2013. See also ActionAid International, n.d.

67. ActionAid USA 2013. For information on ActionAid UK's position on how Barclay's facilitates the use of tax havens to divert financial resources from African countries, see: ActionAid UK 2013.

ACTIONAID USA SENIOR OFFICIAL: Yeah, yeah.

JURKOVICH: And do you mean it, is it ag development because the assumption is people can—whatever they generate on this plot of land—they can sell and make a better livelihood for their family? Or is the assumption they're not, these are subsistence farmers so, it's that that they can better feed themselves? We're more interested in them growing a nutritionally balanced diet on their own land, right, than growing coffee and then selling it?

ACTIONAID USA SENIOR OFFICIAL: Yeah, we are more interested in that . . . we take a food sovereignty approach . . . people growing their own food on their own land.[68]

Agricultural development is a way for local communities to feed themselves and not need to rely on the government to provide assistance. It is, moreover, consistent with earlier development approaches to hunger where NGOs invested in irrigation training, seeds, and the like to help local communities improve agricultural industries. ActionAid, for instance, continues to help local communities create seed banks.[69] That the right to food is accomplished through pressuring governments to provide resources to agricultural development (as opposed to providing job training that is not tied to needing to work in agriculture, or social safety nets more generally) is consistent with previous development approaches to hunger. In the case of hybrid INGOs in the hunger issue area, such as Action-Aid and Oxfam, development legacies shape the nature and structure of advocacy within the organizations in the present day.

For issue areas like hunger, which can be (and are) conceptualized as both development and human rights problems, advocacy work will be shared across different types of organizations with inherent differences in the way they have historically mobilized and campaigned around the problem area. Understandings of who is to blame for the problem will vary, and even as organizations shift from development to human rights frameworks the legacy of prior development work will continue to affect the nature of their advocacy. Civil and political rights issue areas do not cross the (at times competing) frameworks of rights and development. Many economic and social rights live at the intersection of these two frameworks.

The lack of a norm around hunger makes it difficult (and unlikely) that campaigns will centralize around a single target, and the existence of multiple

68. Interview, ActionAid USA1, June 2013.
69. Interview, ActionAid USA1, June 2013.

conceptual frameworks around the issue area perpetuates this lack of a norm. Put differently, when issue areas can be conceptualized as, at the same time, development and human rights problems, these frameworks will enable complex and varied understandings of blame, responsibility, cause, and solutions in an issue area. Development frameworks on the one hand and human rights frameworks on the other both seek a solution to hunger, but answer the question of *who* should do *what* in different ways. The existence of multiple analytical frameworks around a problem area (i.e., "Of what is this problem an instance?") makes it challenging for a single norm to emerge around which activists can rally.

There remains, however, the puzzle of why existing international law does not serve to generate a norm in this issue area. Development legacies and competing analytic frameworks may explain why constructing a norm has been challenged, but in theory international law has resolved this dispute by attributing responsibility to national governments for the provision of food to their people. And yet, despite the existence of international law around the right to food, international anti-hunger organizations rarely leverage the law and it has failed to generate a corresponding norm that could focus advocacy efforts squarely on the state. Why is this the case? Chapter 5 turns to the puzzling role of international human rights law in attributing blame and responsibility for chronic hunger.

5

THE LIMITS OF LAW

The right to food has been codified in international law in several legally binding covenants and conventions, beginning with the International Covenant on Economic, Social and Cultural Rights (ICESCR), which was adopted in 1966 and entered into force in 1976, though the right to food was included earlier in the legally nonbinding Universal Declaration of Human Rights (1948). It has since been recognized in numerous other international conventions and agreements, such as the Convention on the Elimination of All Forms of Discrimination against Women (CEDAW) and the Convention on the Rights of the Child (CRC), as well as in 2004 with the nonbinding Voluntary Guidelines to Support the Progressive Realization of the Right to Adequate Food in the Context of National Food Security.[1]

In international law, primary obligation rests with national governments for ensuring the right to food. And yet, as discussed in chapters 2–4, despite the existence of international law, this issue area lacks a norm (i.e., a shared social expectation of appropriate behavior by a specific actor) among top international anti-hunger organizations. There is no consensus among activists on a unitary actor to blame for the persistence of the hunger problem, despite law providing a clear target, and advocacy campaigns reflect this lack of a consensus, targeting such diverse actors as transnational corporations, outside states, and international

---

1. While CEDAW and the CRC do not explicitly state a right to food for all, they recognize state obligation to ensuring adequate food and nutrition to specific populations (in CEDAW, pregnant and lactating women; in the CRC, children).

financial institutions, among others. The distinction between human rights law and norms is particularly glaring in this case, and yet scholarly conversations in the field of international relations (IR) frequently conflate codified law with norms around human rights, as though one necessarily presupposes (or automatically leads to) the other. The hunger case clarifies the important conceptual differences between law and norms around human rights and challenges the assumption that law and norms walk hand in hand, or that generating a law necessarily leads to the creation of a corresponding norm. Put differently, the hunger case reminds us that *not all human rights codified in law have corresponding norms* and that the existence of one does not presuppose the existence of the other.

The lack of a norm around hunger despite the prevalence of existing international law surrounding the human right to food presents scholars with two puzzles. First, what is the conceptual relationship between formal law and norms, particularly around questions of human rights? And second, why is existing international law unable to focus activist pressure on national governments for the violation of the right to food when their obligation in this issue area is already established in law? Despite the existence of international law ascribing responsibility to national governments for ensuring the right to food, such law is rarely referenced by international anti-hunger organizations. While scholars generally expect law to be used by activists to compel states to comply with their legal commitments, at least through the use of shaming or social sanctions, this is not the case here. Examining the disconnect between law and norms around hunger matters for more than abstract theorizing about the conceptual distinction between the two, though this is certainly important. This disconnect forces new thinking on the limits of law for human rights advocacy and the power of law to compel states to ensure that human rights are fulfilled.

This chapter begins with a conceptual discussion of the distinction between formal law and norms, underscoring the importance of not conflating the two concepts. The discussion then turns to the specific legal frameworks available in the case of the human right to food and examines why law has not generated a norm in this issue area. I argue that (1) in contrast to more oft-studied human rights campaigns focusing mostly on civil and political rights, many international anti-hunger organizations still do not conceptualize food as a human right, making international human rights law less relevant; (2) when activists do conceptualize food as a human right, they often root their understanding of this right in moral, not legal, terms; and (3) activists face the very practical concerns of continued debates (particularly when dealing with Canada and the United States) regarding the justiciability of the right to food and continued debates over the precise definition of the right itself, which makes leveraging law challenging. Underlying each of these three explanations, however, is the glaring disconnect between the attribution of a responsibility in international law and the generation of any norm. In other words, the hunger case suggests there is nothing automatic about *law* generating *norms* among activists or society at large. And, moreover, in the hunger case, international law cannot substitute for a lack of a norm in focusing advocacy pressure on a common target.

Conflating Formal Law and Norms

What is the conceptual relationship between formal law (rules codified in law) and norms? In the human rights literature, the two concepts are often conflated, with the terms *human rights law* and *human rights norms* used interchangeably.[2] As I will argue here, this is problematic, as it implies (incorrectly) that all human rights, once codified in law, have corresponding norms. As the hunger case has shown, not all human rights codified in law have norms, with important implications for human rights advocacy.

IR scholars have long been interested in conceptualizing law and legalization of rules,[3] though less attention has been paid to parsing the difference between norms and formal law. Max Weber (1978, 33–35) grapples with this distinction as he argues with legal philosopher Rudolf Stammler (1896) over where to set the conceptual boundary between orders understood as "convention" verses "law." Weber's "convention" matches what constructivists refer to as "norms," noting, "An order will be called . . . *convention* so far as its validity is externally guaranteed by the probability that deviation from it within a given social group will result in a relatively general and practically significant reaction of disapproval" (34, emphasis in the original). Stammler, according to Weber, posits that the distinction between convention and law is found in whether or not an individual followed the relevant rule voluntarily, or did so because their obedience was compelled through some enforcement mechanism (as would be the case in law, he argues, but not convention). Taking issue with this distinction, Weber notes that obedience is just as coerced in social conventions as it is in law. The distinction

---

2. The phrase "human rights norms" has become ubiquitous in the human rights literature, but it is generally left undefined, making it difficult to determine precisely what is meant by its usage (e.g., the phrase is used without definition in Fariss [2014], Greenhill [2010], and Lupu [2015], though in the case of Risse and Sikkink [1999, 1] and Keck and Sikkink [1998, 80], "human rights norms" seems to refer to rights codified in human rights law or included in the Universal Declaration of Human Rights. When "human rights norms" is used by Moravcsik [2000, 228, 238] it appears to reference human rights included in the European Convention for the Protection of Human Rights and Fundamental Freedoms [ECHR]). The use of the blanket phrase "human rights norms" is problematic as it suggests all human rights have norms and obscures the uneven progress of norm construction across human rights, especially in the case of economic and social rights.

3. Abbott et al. 2000; Finnemore and Toope 2001.

between law and convention, to Weber, is whether or not one is compelled to obedience by a "staff of people" employed specifically for the purpose of monitoring compliance—a rather technical and bureaucratic distinction (34).

Indeed, there is often an assumption in IR scholarship that a given law should be preceded by a norm if the law is to be effective.[4] But whether law is preceded by norms, or serves to generate those norms after laws are codified, scholars agree that laws and norms have a close conceptual relationship.[5] Perhaps because of the assumption that laws and norms must walk hand in hand, scholars have begun to use these terms interchangeably.

And yet, laws and norms are not the same thing, and the existence of one does not provide evidence of the existence of the other. In the case of some human rights, especially economic and social rights, international (and at times, even domestic) law obliges governments to ensure a right without any norm existing alongside this legal obligation within a relevant domestic population, or even among the society of states that ratified the law. This is certainly the case with the right to food, though the distinction likely also holds in many countries for other economic and social rights like housing, clothing, and health care.

One important dimension on which the concepts of law and norms differ is the need for a given belief in the appropriateness of specific behavior by a specific actor to be *socially shared* (referred to by constructivist scholars as intersubjectivity). While laws can be imposed on a society without that given society internalizing a belief that a specific behavior by a specific actor is appropriate or right, norms by definition must be intersubjectively held. Legal scholar H. L. A. Hart grapples with how to define and conceptualize law, noting that law has the important characteristic of existing even when society may neither know about the law's existence nor independently believe that a particular behavior ought to be expected of a particular actor. As Hart notes, "It may indeed be desirable that laws should as soon as may be after they are made, be brought to the attention of those to whom they apply. The legislator's purpose in making laws would be defeated unless this were generally done, and legal systems often provide, by special rules concerning promulgation, that this shall be done. But laws may be complete as laws before this is done, and even if it is not done at all" (2012, 22).

Norms are *socially shared* expectations of particular behavior by particular actors. They exist only when they are shared widely among members of a given society. It would be impossible, in other words, to have a norm that was only known by one individual, as this would be an individual belief, but not a norm.

---

4. Brunnée and Toope 2010, 55–87.
5. For a helpful review article on the recursivity of law, see Halliday 2009. See also Biersteker et al. 2007; and Reus-Smit 2004.

The Hart quote above is not meant to rehash debates about "secret laws" but rather to highlight the important insight that law by definition requires no shared social consensus.[6] Laws can exist without people knowing about them *or internalizing any belief that a particular expected behavior is morally right or good*. In this way, while law may articulate an actor, action, and sense of oughtness, it does not need to meet the necessary condition of being a socially shared belief (as was discussed in chapter 3), which is a requirement of norms. Conceptually, this is an important distinction between laws and norms.

Ratifying law at the level of the state, then, does not necessarily reflect any norm among a given society. Consider, for example, laws governing media piracy. There are formal laws prohibiting individuals from illegally downloading movies on the internet in the United States, and these laws are likely widely known among Americans. The existence of these laws, however, does not guarantee that a norm automatically exists in American society that downloading movies without paying for them is morally bad, such that if an individual did download a movie they would be socially shamed for their behavior. As was very apparent in my own college dormitory, downloading media without paying for it did not violate a social norm (as the behavior generated no social shaming for deviance), even though it violated a law. Laws and norms may exist side by side, but they also may not.

Returning to the topic of human rights, consider the distinction between laws and norms regarding the use of torture. The United States has ratified the United Nations (UN) Convention against Torture, which prohibits states from engaging in torture. Scholars remain divided, however, on whether there is any norm among the American public that torture ought to be prohibited by the state.[7] Public opinion data on the appropriateness of the state engaging in torture remains mixed, but encourages caution in assuming there is an anti-torture norm among the American public, despite the existence of law. According to a 2016 Reuters poll, for example, 63 percent of American respondents stated torture was either "often" or "sometimes" justified, with only 15 percent stating it should never be undertaken.[8]

Some might argue that while the existence of international law may not reflect a norm at the level of a given domestic society, it *would* reflect a norm among the states that ratified the law. For this reason it would be seen as appropriate to

---

6. Though legal scholars would note that if there is no social buy-in, we should expect law not to function well in societies. But the efficacy of law is a separate question from whether by definition laws must reflect shared social beliefs. Legal philosophers such as L. L. Fuller (1969) would remind us that law is inherently a moral enterprise (with morality being inseparable from law). While there may be some sense of morality in the concept of a rule of law, this is not the same thing as law always serving to reflect socially shared beliefs about appropriate behavior by specific actors.

7. Gronke et al. 2010; Mayer and Armor 2012; Wallace 2013.

8. Kahn 2016.

use the concepts of laws and norms interchangeably, as evidence of one could be seen as evidence of the other, even if only at the level of the state. And yet, much scholarship has challenged the idea that states are always "sincere ratifiers" of international law, arguing instead that some states may ratify international covenants and treaties without ascribing to a normative belief that they are appropriate and without any intention to actually abide by them in the first place.[9] According to this logic, ratifying a human rights treaty should not be seen necessarily as evidence of a norm but rather as a calculated strategic choice by states.[10]

Even if a group of states has internalized a norm surrounding a human right also codified in law, should we assume that this normative commitment necessarily continues as long as the legal commitment does? Conceptually, if we are willing to use the two terms interchangeably, we must. Yet Rosemary Foot skillfully challenges such an assumption in the case of torture, asking: "Why, then, given the rhetorical, moral and legal status of this prohibition, is torture being debated, contemplated and even resurrected as an unsavoury and allegedly necessary course of action in this counter-terrorist era?" (2006, 131). Formal law surrounding a prohibition against torture still exists but, Foot notes, the anti-torture *norm* may be eroding.

Whether a norm exists around a human right already codified in law should be an empirical question, not an assumed given. Laws and norms are not only conceptually distinct, but one does not presuppose the other. And when scholars write in terms of norms surrounding legal commitments, they should be clear *among whom* they expect this norm to exist. Is the norm expected to exist among states, activists, domestic publics, or some other community? Highlighting the distinction between laws and norms matters for more reasons than conceptual integrity or abstract theorizing. Understanding that laws and norms are not the same thing and do not necessarily walk hand in hand improves our ability to understand the limits of legal frameworks for human rights which lack norms and enables us to question the value of law in improving human rights if no corresponding norm is present. I will continue this discussion at the end of this chapter.

The Right to Food in International Law

Let us return briefly to existing state obligations in international law around the right to food. Previous chapters discussed the historical process of including the right to food in the Universal Declaration of Human Rights and the ICESCR

---

9. Simmons 2009.
10. Hathaway 2007.

TABLE 5.1 International Human Rights Instruments that Recognize a Right to Food

ABBREVIATION	FULL NAME	YEAR ADOPTED	YEAR ENTERED INTO FORCE	NUMBER OF STATES THAT HAVE RATIFIED AS OF JANUARY 2017	LEGALLY BINDING?
UDHR	Universal Declaration of Human Rights	1948 (UN General Assembly)	N/A	N/A	No
ICESCR	International Covenant on Economic, Social and Cultural Rights	1966 (UN General Assembly)	1976	165	Yes
CEDAW	Convention on the Elimination of all Forms of Discrimination against Women	1979 (UN General Assembly)	1981	189	Yes
CRC	Convention on the Rights of the Child	1989 (UN General Assembly)	1990	196	Yes
—	Voluntary Guidelines to Support the Progressive Realization of the Right to Adequate Food in the Context of National Food Security	2004 (FAO)	N/A	N/A	No

Source: This table is modified from the helpful chart in Eide and Kracht 2007, xxxix.

Note: While CEDAW and the CRC do not explicitly state a right to food for all, they recognize state obligation to ensuring adequate food and nutrition to target populations (in CEDAW, pregnant and lactating women; in the CRC, children).

(chapter 1) and the creation of the Voluntary Guidelines to Support the Progressive Realization of the Right to Adequate Food in the Context of National Food Security (chapter 2). For ease of reference, I have reproduced here the table that is provided in chapter 1, documenting the varied covenants and agreements recognizing the right to food (see table 5.1).

The precise language of what the right to food constitutes varies by covenant and convention but in all of them states are the actors who adopted and ratified the law and states, with a primary focus on the national government, are the actors obliged to ensure adequate food for their people. Readers looking for a detailed discussion of all references to the right to food in international law need look no further than Wenche Barth Eide and Uwe Kracht's seminal two-volume collection on the subject, *Food and Human Rights in Development*.[11] For

---

11. See Eide and Kracht 2005, 2007. For a detailed discussion of international legal frameworks around food security, and especially those related to trade, see Orford 2015.

our purposes here I highlight only a few important mentions of the right to food relevant to our discussion on state obligation and refer to their important text for a more sustained discussion of international law surrounding the right to food.

The International Covenant on Economic, Social, and Cultural Rights

Article 2 of the ICESCR lays out the general nature of the obligation of states to direct "the maximum of its available resources" toward "achieving progressively the full realization of the rights" listed in the covenant. Article 11 addresses the nature of the obligation surrounding the right to food specifically.

Article 2

1. Each State Party to the present Covenant undertakes to take steps, individually and through international assistance and co-operation, especially economic and technical, to the maximum of its available resources, with a view to achieving progressively the full realization of the rights recognized in the present Covenant by all appropriate means, including particularly the adoption of legislative measures.
2. The States Parties to the present Covenant undertake to guarantee that the rights enunciated in the present Covenant will be exercised without discrimination of any kind as to race, colour, sex, language, religion, political or other opinion, national or social origin, property, birth or other status.
3. Developing countries, with due regard to human rights and their national economy, may determine to what extent they would guarantee the economic rights recognized in the present Covenant to non-nationals.

Article 11

1. The States Parties to the present Covenant recognize the right of everyone to an adequate standard of living for himself and his family, including adequate food, clothing and housing, and to the continuous improvement of living conditions. The States Parties will take appropriate steps to ensure the realization of this right, recognizing to this effect the essential importance of international co-operation based on free consent.
2. The States Parties to the present Covenant, recognizing the fundamental right of everyone to be free from hunger, shall take, individ-

ually and through international co-operation, the measures, including specific programmes, which are needed:

(a) To improve methods of production, conservation and distribution of food by making full use of technical and scientific knowledge, by disseminating knowledge of the principles of nutrition and by developing or reforming agrarian systems in such a way as to achieve the most efficient development and utilization of natural resources;

(b) Taking into account the problems of both food-importing and food-exporting countries, to ensure an equitable distribution of world food supplies in relation to need.[12]

General Comment 12 of the ICESCR, though nonbinding because it is a recommendation adopted by the Committee on Economic, Social, and Cultural Rights (CESCR), more clearly articulates the state's obligations to respect, protect, and fulfill the right to food for its citizens:

> The right to adequate food, like any other human right, imposes three types or levels of obligations on States parties: the obligations to *respect*, to *protect* and to *fulfil*. In turn, the obligation to *fulfil* incorporates both an obligation to *facilitate* and an obligation to *provide*.* The obligation to *respect* existing access to adequate food requires States parties not to take any measures that result in preventing such access. The obligation to *protect* requires measures by the State to ensure that enterprises or individuals do not deprive individuals of their access to adequate food. The obligation to *fulfil* (*facilitate*) means the State must proactively engage in activities intended to strengthen people's access to and utilization of resources and means to ensure their livelihood, including food security. Finally, whenever an individual or group is unable, for reasons beyond their control, to enjoy the right to adequate food by the means at their disposal, States have the obligation to *fulfil* (*provide*) that right directly. This obligation also applies for persons who are victims of natural or other disasters.[13]

---

12. United Nations General Assembly 1966.

13. United Nations Committee on Economic, Social and Cultural Rights 1999, para. 15, emphasis in the original. The asterisk in the original leads to the following explanation for the inclusion of the "facilitation" addition:

> * Originally three levels of obligations were proposed: to respect, protect and assist/fulfil. (See *Right to adequate food as a human right*, Study Series No. 1, New York, 1989 [United Nations publication, Sales No. E.89.XIV.2]). The intermediate level of "to facilitate" has been proposed as a Committee category, but the Committee decided to maintain the three levels of obligation.

General Comment 12 continues to articulate what would constitute a *violation* of the ICESCR as it relates specifically to the right to food:

> Violations of the Covenant occur when a State fails to ensure the satisfaction of, at the very least, the minimum essential level required to be free from hunger. In determining which actions or omissions amount to a violation of the right to food, it is important to distinguish the inability from the unwillingness of a State party to comply. Should a State party argue that resource constraints make it impossible to provide access to food for those who are unable by themselves to secure such access, the State has to demonstrate that every effort has been made to use all the resources at its disposal in an effort to satisfy, as a matter of priority, those minimum obligations.[14]

References to human entitlement to food are also included, albeit with relatively brief mentions, in CEDAW and the CRC. Article 12.2 of CEDAW articulates the state's obligation to ensure "adequate nutrition during pregnancy and lactation."[15] The CRC begins by calling upon the Universal Declaration of Human Rights and recognizing the full score of human rights already articulated in the covenants, including the ICESCR. Article 24.2(c) of the CRC then highlights the state's obligation to "combat[ing] disease and malnutrition" through "the provision of adequate nutritious foods" to all children as essential to the right to health.[16]

Recognizing that existing international covenants and conventions did not go far enough in defining the parameters of the right to food, civil society groups working through the UN's Food and Agriculture Organization (FAO) brought states together to develop and agree to the Voluntary Guidelines to Support the Progressive Realization of the Right to Adequate Food in the Context of National Food Security, adopted in 2004,[17] which reiterate, "The progressive realization of the right to adequate food requires States to fulfill their relevant human rights obligations under international law." The Voluntary Guidelines comprise nineteen guidelines surrounding the right to food (in roughly ten thousand words), the purpose of which is to "aim to guarantee the availability of food in quantity and quality sufficient to satisfy the dietary needs of individuals; physical and economic accessibility for everyone, including vulnerable groups, to adequate food,

---

14. United Nations Committee on Economic, Social and Cultural Rights 1999, article 11, para. 17.
15. United Nations General Assembly 1979.
16. United Nations UN General Assembly 1989.
17. Additional discussion of the crafting of the Voluntary Guidelines is provided in chapter 2.

free from unsafe substances and acceptable within a given culture; or the means of its procurement."[18] The guidelines cover topics as diverse as social safety nets, food security during natural disasters, and food safety and consumer protection. They are legally nonbinding, but "represent the first attempt by governments to interpret an economic, social and cultural right and to recommend actions to be undertaken for its realization. The objective of the Voluntary Guidelines is to provide practical guidance *to States in their implementation of the progressive realization of the right to adequate food in the context of national food security.*"[19]

The vast majority of states have ratified at least one legally binding convention or covenant recognizing the responsibility of national governments for ensuring the right to food for their people. As of 2018, 169 countries had ratified the ICESCR. Every state, with the sole exception of the United States, has ratified the CRC, which recognizes state obligation to ensure adequate nutrition of children specifically. As of 2015 the right to food had also been included in thirty national constitutions, though as Courtney Jung, Ran Hirschl, and Evan Rosevear (2014) note, many national constitutions, even when they do include economic and social rights, do not identify them as domestically justiciable rights. Across the various legal instruments referencing a right to food, however, there are mentions of the need for some degree of international collaboration especially by other states in assisting with the realization of this right. And yet, according to the FAO, "The primary responsibility for ensuring the right to adequate food and the fundamental right to freedom from hunger rests with national governments."[20]

Despite international law surrounding the right to food ascribing responsibility to national governments for ensuring this right, there is no corresponding anti-hunger norm, at least among top international anti-hunger organizations, as was documented in chapters 3–4. This lack of a norm extends to the community of states who have ratified these laws, as evidenced by the lack of social sanctions or pressure among states when faced with violations of the law. Should a norm exist among states who have ratified international law ascribing responsibility to national governments for ensuring the right to food of their citizens, we would expect a social response to violation when states fail to fulfill their expected obligations. And yet there is no such social response. The United Kingdom is not shamed at UN meetings, for instance, for the persistent hunger of four million people within its population, despite having ratified the ICESCR.[21] In India, 38 percent of children under the age of five were stunted as of 2015, an indicator

18. Food and Agriculture Organization of the United Nations 2004, 6.
19. Food and Agriculture Organization of the United Nations 2004, foreword, emphasis added.
20. Food and Agriculture Organization of the United Nations, n.d.
21. McGuinness, Brown, and Ward 2016; the data on hunger in the United Kingdom is from 2012.

used by the UN Children's Fund (UNICEF) and the World Health Organization to estimate malnutrition rates.[22] And yet India is not shamed by other states who have similarly ratified law recognizing state obligation to ensuring the right to food.[23] The only exception to the nonexistence of state shaming for persistent hunger has been cases where there was clear evidence that governments had *intentionally* withheld food from their citizens (such as former president Robert Mugabe of Zimbabwe), but international law does not require such a high degree of barbarism to constitute a failure to ensure the right to food. For the vast majority of the world's hungry, hunger is not caused by active withholding of food but through poor and neglectful government policy. Nonetheless, there is rarely any social cost incurred for "violating" any claim that good governments ought to ensure that their people have enough food to eat. There is certainly formal law which articulates this obligation, but that does not mean this law has translated into a norm—*even among the society of states*—that, indeed, good governments ought to ensure that all their people have enough to eat to avoid the pangs of hunger.

Certainly one could claim international law around the human right to food is largely unenforced and comparatively weak, but international law around all human rights struggles with enforceability and yet the violation of some rights will still elicit shaming among the society of states (such as violations of free and fair elections and enforced disappearances) while others will not. My modest aim here is to call attention to the conceptual difference between codifying a human right in law and any norm existing around that right, even among the society of states who ratified that law. There may be a great many cases of overlap (human rights codified in international law that have been translated into norms as well), but there is not *always* an overlap such that we should interchange the concepts of laws and norms.

When Law Does Not Serve as an Enforcement "Whip"

In theory, one of the great benefits of international law, at least to activists, is its ability to ascribe responsibility to a specific actor for a specific action. In the case of international human rights law, scholars expect that once a state ratifies a spe-

---

22. United Nations Children's Fund, World Health Organization, and World Bank, 2015.

23. It is possible that there is a domestic norm in Indian society that the Indian government is obliged to ensure a right to food for its citizens. This would be an empirical question. Given the increase in domestic civil society groups in India advocating for a right to food and state responsibility in ensuring the right to food, the existence of a domestic norm is possible. On the international stage, however, among international nongovernmental organizations and the society of states who have ratified the ICESCR, there remains insufficient evidence that an anti-hunger norm exists.

cific convention or treaty activists will leverage this (very public) commitment to hold states accountable when they fail to live up to their commitments.[24]

In the case of many human rights we often see activists leverage the authority and legitimacy that comes with international law in order to hold states accountable for complying with its legal obligations. This has certainly been the case with campaigns against violations of the right to seek asylum, and the abuse of protestors, even when enforcement mechanisms (beyond shaming or reputational costs) surrounding these laws remain relatively weak.[25] In the case of international anti-hunger campaigns, however, international law has *not* served to focus international activism on a unitary target actor, despite the fact that the vast majority of states have ratified at least one legally binding international covenant or convention attributing responsibility to national governments for the right to food.

While scholars may disagree about the efficacy of shaming tactics in compelling behavioral change, there is an expectation in the literature that such tactics will be used by activists to hold states accountable for their commitments under international law.[26] Given the potential reputational if not material costs to non-compliance with international law, much of the human rights literature is interested in explaining why states would ratify human rights treaties in the first place.[27] Why limit state sovereignty and expose yourself to activist campaigns? Put more pithily by Nigel Rodley, former legal adviser and head of the Legal and Intergovernmental Organizations Office at Amnesty International, "Why do states give us these whips to flagellate themselves with?"[28] And yet, scholars rarely stop to examine cases where international law exists but human rights activists rarely use it to shame or attempt to "whip" states into compliance.

In the hunger case, law surrounding the right to food exists but is rarely referenced by international anti-hunger organizations, and this law has not translated into an anti-hunger norm among advocates, as documented in previous chapters. The remainder of this chapter examines why this is the case. I argue that (1) in contrast to more oft-studied human rights campaigns focusing mostly on civil and political rights, many international anti-hunger organizations still do

---

24. Brunnée and Toope 2010; Gurowitz 2004; Hafner-Burton 2008; Keck and Sikkink 1998; Simmons 2009.

25. For instance, Amnesty International has shamed the U.S. government for its child detention policies when families cross the southern border seeking asylum; see Amnesty International 2018. Human Rights Watch also released its *Punished for Protesting* report, shaming the Venezuelan government for "violations of the right to life; the prohibition on torture and cruel, inhuman and degrading treatment; the rights to bodily integrity, security and liberty; and due process rights"; see Human Rights Watch 2014, 1.

26. Brunnée and Toope 2010; Gurowitz 2004; Hafner-Burton 2008; Keck and Sikkink 1998; Simmons 2009.

27. See Goodliffe and Hawkins 2006; Moravcsik 2000; and Simmons 2009.

28. Nigel Rodley, quoted in Clark 2001, 4. At the time of the comment, Rodley was the UN special rapporteur on torture.

not conceptualize food as a human right, making international human rights law less relevant; (2) when activists do conceptualize food as a human right, they often root their understanding of this right in moral and not legal terms; and (3) activists face the very practical concerns of continued debates (particularly when dealing with Canada and the United States) regarding the justiciability of the right to food and continued debates over the precise definition of the right itself, which make leveraging this law challenging.

Framing Hunger without Rights

Despite the existence of international legal instruments articulating the human right to food, many international anti-hunger organizations do not use "rights rhetoric" in their advocacy. Hunger, like many economic and social rights, could be conceptualized in a variety of ways. As has been discussed in chapter 4, it can be understood primarily as a human rights violation or as a humanitarian or development problem independent of a rights issue. International human rights covenants open up the door for anti-hunger organizations to leverage right-to-food language (or frame hunger as the observable implication of a *violation* of this human right). But it is not essential that this language be used. International anti-hunger organizations can engage in advocacy in this issue area *without reference to any human right at all*. And they do.

In the case of many civil and political rights (such as enforced disappearances, suffrage, physical integrity), it is far less common to see international advocacy campaigns that do not reference the violation of a specific human right. In the hunger issue area, however, rights rhetoric is used more sparingly across the network of anti-hunger organizations. World Vision, for example, does not generally refer to hunger as a violation of a right to food. When a senior official at the Bill & Melinda Gates Foundation was asked if the foundation used right-to-food language, she responded, "No . . . it's just not the lens that we approach this work with."[29] Moreover, staff within the same international anti-hunger organization may also hold varied views on whether or not hunger is an example of a violation of a human right and what that means. In the case of some international anti-hunger organizations, right-to-food rhetoric may be leveraged in some advocacy efforts but not others. While Bread for the World has at times used right-to-food language in its advocacy,[30] one senior employee noted that she did not think it

---

29. Interview, Bill & Melinda Gates Foundation 2, May 2013.
30. See Simon (2009, 79) for a discussion by Art Simon, founder of Bread for the World, on the organization's first advocacy campaign in 1974 aimed at encouraging the U.S. Congress to pass a "Right to Food" resolution.

did so when focused on hunger internationally. When I asked why that was the case, she responded: "Why is that? I don't . . . do you think that it's important that we use it internationally—'right to food'? Well, we don't see that, there's not . . . there's not, it's not a food availability, it's a food access issue. Right? And so I don't know if there is a rights issue there. I think those translate to gender issues, sociological issues."[31] Another official at Bread for the World stated right-to-food language "just doesn't resonate."[32] The reasons for why international anti-hunger organizations may not use rights rhetoric or conceptualize hunger as a human rights issue are varied. Some organizations view rights language as too politically sensitive. Others simply do not see hunger as a human rights issue. The right to food is codified in international law, but this does not automatically translate into an understanding among all international anti-hunger organizations that food *is* (really) a human right. And if an organization does not view hunger as a human rights issue, it should not be surprising that international law regarding the right to food is not used to center advocacy on a single actor as responsible or to blame for violations of this right.

When "Rights" Have Little to Do with Law

While some international anti-hunger organizations do not use rights rhetoric, others, like Oxfam, will champion the right to food and understand themselves as doing "rights-based" work but not focus on international human rights law. According to Raymond Offenheiser (then president of Oxfam America) and Susan Holcombe, "Part of the *problem* is that our understanding of human rights has been filtered by legal discourse during the past half-century" (Offenheiser and Holcombe 2003, 296, emphasis added).[33] Rather, a preferred "broader view of human rights look[s] beyond state responsibilities and a legalistic approach and grounds itself in the concept of human dignity" (286). This was especially apparent in discussions with one Oxfam America senior official, as she spoke of the then relatively recent turn toward a rights framework within Oxfam and the little faith she put in international human rights law:

> OXFAM AMERICA SENIOR OFFICIAL: If you go from an organization which in the 1990s—which is a relatively short period of time—didn't know rights from their elbow . . .

31. Interview, Bread for the World 2, February 2013.
32. Interview, Bread for the World 1, February 2013.
33. Offenheiser and Holcombe also reference the work of Steiner and Alston (2000) on this point.

MICHELLE JURKOVICH [*laughing*]: Though food has been a right since 1948. And Oxfam has been around since . . .

OXFAM AMERICA SENIOR OFFICIAL: Food has been a right since, I'm sorry, since . . .

JURKOVICH: Well, legally, since 1948, in the UN Declaration.

OXFAM AMERICA SENIOR OFFICIAL: We're not that legal. I mean, the reason—honestly—the reason we do rights-based work is, I walk into every room . . . I go in to any place anywhere and just say, "Listen. I'm not going to tell you anything about the law. Who in here has the right to enough basic food to eat everyday so that they can live with dignity?" Everybody. "What convention is it in?" "I haven't a clue, but I have the right!" That's what you need to know, okay? I don't care if you know the name of the convention, I need you to know that the people we serve have that right and *somebody is responsible.* Sorry, I only have so much time . . . I only have so much time, because, partly I don't have that much faith in the international legal enforcement of human rights.[34]

Oxfam's turn to a rights approach is relatively new and, as is the case with many international anti-hunger organizations, Oxfam's history is rooted in viewing hunger outside of a rights framework. When the organization did turn toward such a rights approach (as discussed in chapter 4), it did not choose to root its understanding of the right to food in human rights law but rather on moral grounds. And these moral grounds do not single out national governments as solely responsible or to blame for hunger. Rather, as this senior official noted, "*somebody is responsible.*"

As was discussed in depth in chapter 4, Oxfam has focused much effort into its Behind the Brands campaign, where it targets transnational corporations. And blaming a corporation, according to Oxfam, is seen as entirely consistent with a rights approach. When I asked the same Oxfam America senior official what a right to food meant, she explained:

OXFAM AMERICA SENIOR OFFICIAL: It means that you are capable of identifying who is responsible, talking about the nature of their responsibilities, and doing something about it.

MICHELLE JURKOVICH: So, who is responsible?

OXFAM AMERICA SENIOR OFFICIAL: I've just told you.

JURKOVICH: Lots of people, then?

---

34. Interview, Oxfam America 1, May 2013, emphasis added.

OXFAM AMERICA SENIOR OFFICIAL: Yeah, and you hold them all responsible. . . . You launch Behind the Brands to hold corporations accountable. You launch national campaigns to hold governments
accountable. You call out foundations like the Gates Foundation even
though they give you money. . . . If you can't blame anyone, you're not
rights-based.[35]

In our human rights literature, we often understand human rights as legitimated through international law. For this reason, we would assume activists would
ascribe responsibility to whomever that law ascribes it for ensuring a given human
right is fulfilled.[36] Here, however, we have a senior official within Oxfam America, who does not attribute the right to food to a human rights legal framework,
and a corresponding campaign throughout the Oxfam confederation (Behind the
Brands) which targets corporations for contributing to hunger.

This is not to say that international human rights law is never referenced in
any anti-hunger campaigns. FIAN International, as discussed in chapter 4, will
regularly cite international human rights law to legitimate campaigns targeting
national governments. According to one senior official at FIAN, the primary solution to chronic hunger is indeed found in "the primacy of human rights law."[37]
And yet, FIAN will also target transnational corporations or outside states that
fund, to reference the example given in chapter 4, tree plantations in Mozambique
that displace peasant farmers as to blame for hunger.[38] Similarly, Amnesty International certainly cites international human rights law in its economic and social rights campaigns. But it goes above and beyond the attribution of responsibility
to national governments in these covenants to claim responsibility of other actors as well. As discussed in chapter 3, in their 2005 *Human Rights for Human
Dignity: A Primer on Economic, Social, and Cultural Rights*, Amnesty International
notes that "responsibility for denial of economic, social, and cultural rights frequently lies not only with governments but also with individuals, groups, and
enterprises."[39] International human rights law, in other words, provides *one perspective* on who is to blame for hunger, but it is not the sole authoritative voice
on the subject to international anti-hunger organizations. Interestingly, even the
former UN high commissioner for human rights, Mary Robinson claims, "Human
rights will not provide all of the answers, however. Some of the dilemmas we face
today present *moral* and *ethical* questions which human rights standards help to
identify but not always resolve. Consider, for example, the role of the food and

---

35. Interview, Oxfam America 1, May 2013.
36. See Goodliffe and Hawkins 2006; Moravcsik 2000; and Simmons 2009.
37. Interview, FIAN International 1, July 2013.
38. See FIAN Netherlands 2012.
39. Amnesty International 2005, 43.

agricultural industry. The actors involved in addressing hunger and access to food are not only states but also multinational corporations" (2005a, xx, emphasis added).

Despite the existence of international legal frameworks which attribute responsibility to national governments for right-to-food violations, responsibility and blame for hunger continues to be shared across many actors, even among rights-based international anti-hunger organizations.[40]

Why might groups claim to have a "rights" focus and yet not necessarily legitimate their campaigns in international human rights law? Why would they not restrict their campaigns to targeting actors to which binding international law ascribes responsibility? The Oxfam America senior official made passing reference to a lack of faith in any enforcement of international human rights law, and this certainly is a concern. And yet, enforcement is relatively weak for all human rights treaties and conventions, including those codified in the International Covenant on Civil and Political Rights.

At a more foundational level, however, the relative lack of use of international human rights law in international anti-hunger advocacy reflects again the discussion in chapter 3 of the lack of an anti-hunger norm. There is no consensus on a single actor as responsible for this problem. And law, moreover, has not provided an authoritative answer to the question of responsibility. Human rights law, in other words, does not necessarily create new norms, or codify existing norms; nor can it substitute for a lack of a norm in centering advocacy on a single target. Activists continue to construct campaigns, blaming a diverse array of actors, as there is no common consensus—despite the attribution of responsibility to national governments in human rights law—regarding a single *appropriate* target for international anti-hunger campaigns.[41]

Robinson's quote above highlights one reason for this: there are simply more actors that may be, to use her words, "involved in addressing hunger and access to food" than national governments. If international law does not implicate all actors that activists (or societies) believe may be involved in both *causing* and *solv-*

---

40. Interestingly, however, it is not that international law per se is seen as useless in combating hunger. Indeed, many nongovernmental organizations were actively involved in the construction and promotion of the Norms on the Responsibilities of Transnational Corporations and Other Business Enterprises with Regard to Human Rights, as discussed in chapter 3, though the Norms failed to gain the support of the Commission on Human Rights. Moreover, FIAN invested significantly in the construction of the Voluntary Guidelines to Support the Progressive Realization of the Right to Adequate Food in the Context of National Food Security. On the Norms initiative, see Ruggie 2013, xvii.

41. Though, as noted earlier, while national governments carry the primary obligation to ensure the right to food, there is recognition in international law that some degree of international collaboration will be required by outside states, particularly when dealing with hunger inside less developed countries.

ing a particular rights violation, then it will not be the sole authoritative voice in legitimizing campaign targets.

Moreover, as was discussed in previous chapters, campaigns against hunger continue to confront questions of *capabilities*. If activists do not believe a national government is *capable* of bettering the food situation in their country, they may be less likely to target them, even though they are responsible under international law. Former secretary general of FIAN International, Michael Windfuhr, notes the difficulty "of how to adequately measure the effective use of resources by a government" (2007, 346). For this reason, in FIAN, "there is a slight over-representation of victim groups that suffer from violations of *respect-* and *protect-bound* obligations" but not necessarily the final state obligation (under General Comment 12) to *fulfill* (340–41, emphasis original). According to Windfuhr, "The proof of a violation of fulfillment-bound obligations is therefore more difficult, as it involves potentially complicated resource-and policy discussions, including, for example, the burden of proof that the *government could in fact spend more resources for these groups than it actually does*" (341, emphasis added). In the case of economic and social rights like food, activists find themselves making the (somewhat subjective) determination regarding state capability to ensure this right.[42]

International human rights law does not lead international anti-hunger organizations to centralize pressure on a single actor in part because some organizations still do not see hunger as a human rights issue and in part because those that do conceptualize hunger as a rights violation root their understanding of these rights outside of a strict legal interpretation in international law, as other actors, notably corporations, are understood to be meaningful targets as well. Additionally, activist groups may find the burden of proof too steep to prove governments have failed to meet their fulfillment obligation under law.

Practical Concerns with Definitions and Justiciability

Activists also face very practical concerns when considering the usefulness (or not) of international human rights law around food. What, *precisely*, does the right to food constitute? Since the right is to be "progressively realized," according to international law, how much "progress" is sufficient to show that governments are

---

42. While states certainly require resources to ensure civil and political rights within their borders, in the case of economic and social rights, international law was written to permit the "progressive realization" of these rights—noting, however, that states should use the "maximum of available resources" to do so. As Windfuhr notes, however, this clause (from article 2 of the ICESCR) "makes it even more complex to assess if a government has fulfilled its obligation or not" (2007, 346n27).

not in violation of respecting, protecting, and fulfilling this right? Is the right to food judiciable? Should it be?[43]

Debates surrounding these questions were perhaps nowhere more apparent than in the attempts at crafting the Voluntary Guidelines to Support the Progressive Realization of the Right to Adequate Food in the Context of National Food Security. In an effort to further operationalize the right to food and provide greater clarity to this right, the FAO, with the support of civil society partners (including FIAN International) and states (notably, Germany, Norway, and Switzerland, with the active support of the G77),[44] facilitated a series of workshops from 2002 to 2004 to finalize wording on the Voluntary Guidelines.

On the one hand, a gesture such as this signals at least some desire of participants to utilize a human rights approach to food, or else there would be no interest in hashing out specific guidelines on the subject. On the other hand, however, the two years of deliberations over these guidelines made apparent the very real disagreement among states about what the right to food constitutes, how it should be ensured, and by whom.

In terms of definition, the United States made clear in the lead-up to the negotiations of the Voluntary Guidelines that they took a rather narrow interpretation of what the right to food constituted:

> The United States believes that the issue of adequate food can only be viewed in the context of the right to a standard of living adequate for health and well-being, as set forth in the Universal Declaration of Human Rights, which includes the opportunity to secure food, clothing, housing, medical care and necessary social services. Further, the United States believes that the attainment of the right to an adequate standard of living is a goal or aspiration to be realized progressively that does not give rise to any international obligation or any domestic legal entitlement, and does not diminish the responsibilities of national governments towards their citizens. Additionally, the United States understands the right of access to food to mean the opportunity to secure food, and not guaranteed entitlement.[45]

That the United States wanted to ensure that the right to food was neither justiciable nor seen as an individual entitlement is not especially surprising. After all, the United States has yet to ratify the ICESCR, rejects any legal standing to General Comment 12, and continues to stress the voluntary nature of the Volun-

---

43. For an excellent collection of essays on legal and political issues surrounding the right to food, see Eide and Kracht 2005, 2007. See also Dowell-Jones 2004.

44. See Oshaug 2005, especially 267.

45. Food and Agriculture Organization of the United Nations 2002.

tary Guidelines themselves. What is more intriguing is that a state such as Canada, which has ratified the ICESCR, also opposed reference to language used in General Comment 12 and rejected the justiciability of the right to food.[46]

There is, moreover, the very practical challenge of enforcement. At the most basic level, it is still extremely challenging for anyone to claim their right to food through any international body, as economic and social rights lacked an individual complaint procedure in the CESCR until May 2013, when the Optional Protocol went into force. In other words, individuals who were unable to feed themselves and their families had no legal grounds to submit *any formal complaints* to the CESCR to review state behavior or policies. Even now the complaint procedure is limited in its usefulness, as only individuals in states that have signed on to the Optional Protocol to the ICESCR can submit a complaint, and only for violations that occurred after May 2013, and where the CESCR finds the given state in question has exhausted all domestic legal processes.[47] It is similarly difficult to enforce the right to food in most domestic court systems. One notable exception is in India, where in 2001 its Supreme Court accepted public interest litigation submitted by the People's Union for Civil Liberties on the violation of the right to food leading to starvation deaths in the state of Rajasthan. While the Supreme Court issued a number of rulings, including orders to distribute stored grains through public assistance schemes, the case was ultimately dismissed in 2017.[48]

There are very real practical challenges, therefore, to leveraging international law in the case of the right to food. There remains uncertainty regarding the scope of the right itself (particularly in Canada, the European Union, and the United States), countries like Canada and the United States remain opposed to the right to food being justiciable, and international mechanisms for expressing individual grievances are limited.

The hunger case highlights the disconnect between laws and norms and the inability of law to substitute for a norm in focusing advocacy on a common target actor. International law attributes responsibility to national governments for the

---

46. Oshaug 2005, 268–69 and 268n17. Justiciability surrounding any right to food in domestic constitutions varies considerably. For variation in "aspirational" and justiciable rights in domestic constitutions, as well as a helpful discussion of how much variation exists across economic and social rights in terms of justiciability in domestic law, see Jung, Hirschl, and Rosevear 2014.

47. For an excellent essay on the need for the Optional Protocol see Alston 1991.

48. For more on the People's Union for Civil Liberties (PUCL) v. the Government of India and Others, Writ Petition (Civil) No. 196 of 2001, Supreme Court of India, see Birchfield and Corsi 2010; and Hertel 2015. The Court cited the passage of India's National Food Security Act of 2013 as the reason for the dismissal of the case.

human right to food. While there is debate over what the right precisely means, it is clear, at least in international human rights law, that the national government is ultimately responsible for hunger within its borders. Despite this attribution of responsibility, we see active efforts by international anti-hunger organizations to construct campaigns against a diverse array of actors (corporations, outside states, etc.). As chapter 3 discussed, there is no anti-hunger norm among top international anti-hunger organizations which serves to center responsibility on a single actor, and international law in this issue area has neither generated one nor can it substitute for the lack of one.

We spend a considerable amount of time in the human rights literature focusing on the importance of law and courts for addressing human rights abuses. The case of the right to food encourages us to reconsider the primacy of law for improving all types of human rights abuses. Law does not automatically generate norms. Activists can, and do, understand the meaning of "rights" outside of any legal framework and find legitimacy in nonlegal forms for these rights, focusing for instance on a moral legitimacy and not a legal one. Economic and social rights may share many common attributes with the right to food: they are rights which activists can choose to frame in nonrights ways (e.g., as development problems), making human rights law less salient; international legal covenants surrounding economic and social rights place a higher burden of proof on activists to document cases of violation (i.e., documenting that states are using the "maximum available resources" to "progressively realize" the right in question, which requires judgment calls about state capacity); and debates surrounding the justiciability and definition of economic and social rights continues to be politically contentious.

POLICY IMPLICATIONS AND THE ROAD AHEAD

This book has examined international advocacy around hunger and the right to food, provided a new analytical model to describe and explain this area and explored how it is possible that international anti-hunger advocacy would behave differently from human rights advocacy already documented in the literature. International anti-hunger activists are working in an environment without a norm around hunger. This lack of a norm is not only constitutive of the diffusion of blame around chronic hunger but also makes less possible certain campaign behavior (namely, the centralized pressure on one target actor we have come to expect in the transnational advocacy literature). Hunger's placement between two different analytic frameworks (development and rights) makes the construction of such a norm difficult, and for international anti-hunger organizations with in-country operations there are strong incentives not to blame national governments for fear of jeopardizing the safety and security of staff and active programs.

Moreover, international human rights law has not generated a corresponding norm to this right. While civil and political rights activists often call upon international law in legitimizing one central actor on which to target advocacy campaigns, advocates reference law far more sparingly in their work to reduce hunger. Chapter 5 provided three reasons why, in the case of international anti-hunger advocacy, international human rights law functions differently than it does for civil and political rights campaigns: (1) regardless of the existence of a right to food in international law, some activists still do not perceive hunger as a human rights violation; (2) when activists do conceptualize food as a human right, they often consider this right in moral but not legal terms; and (3) ongoing disputes between states over the definition of the right to food and its justiciability make leveraging international human rights law challenging for international anti-hunger activists.

Theoretical Implications

This study of international anti-hunger advocacy has important theoretical implications for how we understand such core concepts as norms, human rights, and law, as well as the impact of norms and law on the logic and shape of advocacy work.

For constructivist scholars, this book has highlighted the importance of norms in advocacy campaigns but argued that the absence of norms and its effect is poorly theorized. The human rights literature often discusses "human rights norms" as though there either was a norm that surrounded all human rights collectively or each human right individually, but the hunger case begs caution on this point. Not all human rights have norms. Chapter 3 deconstructed the key component parts of norms, arguing that their power is not in a vague sense of appropriateness but instead in ascribing a specific appropriate action to a specific actor. In the constructivist literature, this important function of norms is often overlooked, as norms are at times conflated with moral principles (which lack an actor from whom a behavior is expected).

Aside from the risk of stretching the concept of the norm so far as to render it analytically meaningless, the conflation of norms with moral principles makes it possible to ignore the very difficult task of linking socially expected appropriate behavior to a specific actor. In the case of the right to food, and likely other economic and social rights, constructing norms is extremely challenging. Doing so would require constructing both responsibility for the right by a particular actor as well as a concrete appropriate behavior the responsible actor would be expected to perform. When responsibility for a given right could be conceptualized as falling on the shoulders of several actors (spanning both the public and private sectors) or no actor at all, and the possible solutions or appropriate responses to the problem are understood as vast and varied, norm development will be especially challenging. If we believe that norms can be powerful in enabling and constraining action, as constructivist scholars certainly do, then understanding the challenges to norm construction, especially in articulating an actor-action link around many human rights, is important to those seeking to understand advocacy.

As the constructivist literature continues to probe questions like why some norms affect policy change while others do not, it is worth asking if we are really comparing like cases. In the United States, for example, most people may believe that everyone *ought* to have housing, for instance, but are unclear about *who* should do *what* about it. That same society may believe that universal primary education is morally good and believe that good governments ought to provide free primary education to all of its citizens. Moral principles are at play in both issue areas, but they do not both have norms. If we conflate moral principles with norms we fail to understand why, in the case of primary education, activists may have an easier time isolating and shaming a norm violator (the national government) than they would in shaming the same government for failing to provide, for instance, adequate low-income housing.

Moving beyond the distinction between moral principles and norms, this book brings philosophical insights on the concept of the supererogatory to bear on political science thinking about appropriate behavior. Supererogatory behavior, or behavior by specific actors that a social group deems morally praiseworthy but nonobligatory, complicates the social environment around some human rights, such as the right to food. This book challenges constructivist scholars in particular to carefully distinguish between socially shared standards of appropriate behavior of particular actors which are *obligatory* (norms) and those which are *optional* (supererogatory). Especially when considering activist strategies aimed at leveraging social pressure or shaming, understanding where norms are and are not present is essential.

While constructivist scholars often highlight the power of norms to enable and constrain action, they generally do not look at the impact of a lack of a norm on a given issue area. If norms make some behavior possible or even more likely, does a lack of a norm make other behavior less possible or less likely? As I argue in this book, the lack of an anti-hunger norm constitutes the environment in which international advocates are working, and this environment enables a particular pattern of advocacy behavior (as described in my "buckshot model") but not others (namely the "boomerang" and "spiral" models of advocacy). In the hunger case, the lack of a norm is perpetuated by competing analytic frameworks around the problem, strategic interests brought upon by the need to protect on the ground missions by international anti-hunger organizations, and the inability of international human rights law to generate such a norm.

These are characteristics that are more likely to be found in the case of economic and social rights, as these rights frequently cross development and human rights frameworks where organizations struggle to protect active on the ground missions. And yet, the human rights literature in international relations rarely examines economic and social rights or their advocacy trajectories, focusing instead almost exclusively on civil and political rights campaigns and using insights from this more narrow empirical domain to generate larger theories about how and why human rights advocacy functions the way it does. Comparing the hunger case to dominant human rights models in the literature suggests that there are significant theoretical and analytical payoffs to expanding the scope of our inquiry beyond the domain of civil and political rights. As we have seen in this book, international anti-hunger advocacy behaves differently from the expectations of our models, and these differences have allowed us to challenge key assumptions in our advocacy literatures, such as the assumptions that all human rights have norms and that advocacy around human rights necessarily focuses on one sole violator (generally the national government), as well as to problematize the belief that international law has translated into norms for all human rights.

To human rights and transnational advocacy scholars, this study highlights the need for additional research on economic and social rights and their advocacy campaigns. International anti-hunger campaigns do not fit the models expected in our literature, but does the alternative buckshot model apply to advocacy around other issue areas? Paul Nelson and Ellen Dorsey's study of international advocacy around HIV/AIDS and the right to water suggests it might. In their article, they find activists targeting diverse actors, including corporations, intergovernmental organizations, and states. In the case of these rights, advocacy efforts are "not constrained by the sole focus on the state as duty bearer and violator of human rights," with activists instead "targeting many institutions, including international financial institutions (IFI), transnational corporations, trade regimes, rich county governments, and poor country governments themselves" (Nelson and Dorsey 2007, 191). Recent advocacy around health care, especially in the United States, has also highlighted diffuse targets across the private and public sectors in addition to efforts by some activists to construct a norm that national governments ought to ensure their citizens have access to adequate health care.[1]

For scholars of advocacy, this study also raises new questions: Can advocacy transition from buckshot to boomerang or spiral patterns over time? If so, how? It may be the case that in the evolution of advocacy, issue areas buckshot (when there is no norm present) before they boomerang (when there is a norm around the right that activists can leverage). Instead of focusing synchronically on individual transnational advocacy campaigns, additional work on changing patterns of advocacy over time for the same issue area would be valuable. Building off insights from social movement theory, there remains much to be learned about how and why activists change directions in campaigns from targeting diverse private sector actors to focusing responsibility solely on the state, especially when dealing with economic and social rights.[2]

---

1. On competing issue frames of private property versus the right to life around HIV/AIDS medicines, see Sell and Prakash 2004.

2. McAdam et al. 1996; Minkoff 1999.

Finally, for legal scholars, this book has documented an important issue area for which international law is infrequently leveraged by international nongovernmental organizations (INGOs) to legitimate a specific campaign target. An important value of international human rights law is generally understood to be in providing a clear public commitment by national governments such that outside states, activists, and civil society groups can then use this commitment to shame these governments into compliance, or rally outside states to support sanctions in the event of noncompliance. On its own, international human rights law, whether for civil and political rights in the International Covenant on Civil and Political Rights (ICCPR) or economic, social, and cultural rights in the International Covenant on Economic, Social, and Cultural Rights (ICESCR) is relatively weak in terms of enforcement. In order for international human rights law to be effective, activist campaigns are essential. As scholars increasingly view international law not as an extraneous consideration in international affairs but rather as a core organizing principle,[3] it is especially important to understand these "deviant" cases where existing international law is shelved by activists. This book has discussed reasons why international law is largely ignored by international anti-hunger activists, many of whom opt instead to frame the right to food in moral instead of legal terms. Additional research is needed to explain variation in why international human rights law is used by activists of some human rights to legitimate particular approaches but frequently ignored or shelved by activists for other human rights.

Policy Implications

This study has important implications for activists and policy makers working on hunger and human rights. Below, I discuss concerns about the efficacy of shaming and blaming strategies in buckshot advocacy, the importance of questions of responsibility and blame in anti-hunger policy, and potential concerns with the turn toward ascribing responsibility for economic and social rights to corporations in international law.

In contrast to the boomerang and spiral models, blame is not centralized on a single actor in the buckshot model, as actors fan out blame among multiple campaign targets. The boomerang and spiral models are generally marketed as instances of *campaign success*. When campaigns fit these models, in other words, it is expected that the outcome of transnational advocacy is that the "violating" actor changes behavior (at least somewhat) and the human right is more fully

---

3. On the primacy of international law in international affairs, see Hurd 2017.

realized. Can shaming and blaming work effectively as an activist strategy if blame is diffuse? Kenneth Roth, executive director of Human Rights Watch, has expressed concern that it might not.

> Although there are various forms of public outrage, only certain types are sufficiently targeted to shame officials into action. That is, the public might be outraged about a state of affairs—for example, poverty in a region—but have no idea whom to blame. *Or it might feel that blame is dispersed among a wide variety of actors. In such cases of diffuse responsibility, the stigma attached to any person, government, or institution is lessened,* and with it the power of international human rights organizations to effect change. Similarly, stigma weakens even in the case of a single violator if the remedy to a violation—what the government should do to correct it—is unclear. (Roth 2004, 67, emphasis added)

Roth articulates well the challenges that activists face when there is no norm present. When it is unclear *who* ought to do *what*, it may be difficult for activists to effectively shame a target into compliance. Furthermore, in the absence of such a norm, the burden of proof to make a compelling case to their respective audiences is high, as activists cannot rely on what Roth calls the "stigma" already attached to a specific actor through the norm. We saw in chapter 5 the challenge FIAN International, in particular, has faced in providing enough evidence to sufficiently make the case that governments were failing to fulfill their right-to-food obligations. Our existing models assume centralized blame on a single target actor, but now that we know there are human rights for which this blame is diffuse it opens up avenues for new study into the effects of this diffusion on campaign success or failure. As Roth articulated from his experience as executive director of one of the most powerful human rights INGOs, there are good reasons to believe the diffusion of blame makes successful shaming more difficult and ultimately less effective.

Moreover, the lack of a norm, which enables the buckshotting of advocacy across multiple targets, may pose challenges for activist efforts at maintaining anti-hunger programs even once they have been successfully implemented. Brazil, for example, experienced an impressive reduction in malnutrition domestically after then president Luiz Inácio Lula da Silva launched his signature Bolsa Familia conditional cash transfer program and its related Fome Zero program.[4] Despite

---

4. Brazil met the UN's Millennial Development Goal 1C (to halve the number of hungry by 2015) several years ahead of schedule. Additionally, stunting rates among children under the age of five in Brazil dropped from 19.9 percent in 1989 to 6.8 percent in 2006; see Lutter, Chaparro, and Muñoz 2011, 23.

the success of these programs, however, public support in Brazil has shown evidence of decline. Among individuals who have received a postsecondary education support is particularly low—with less than 50 percent supporting the Bolsa Familia program in 2014.[5] In the aftermath of the 2018 presidential election of right-wing conservative Jair Bolsonaro, concerns remain about the future of funding for the Bolsa Familia program despite Bolsonaro's public statements of support. In the long run, if there is no norm in a society ascribing responsibility to national governments for the right to food, even effective social safety net programs may struggle to retain popular support. This may be problematic for activists down the line, as programs to combat hunger require substantial resources (and the approval of relevant domestic populations that these resources should be tasked to this purpose). Without a clear norm linking government responsibility to the amelioration of hunger, sustaining such initiatives may prove very difficult for activists.

In terms of anti-hunger policy, this book encourages policy makers, activists, and academics to reconsider the primary importance of constructing social understandings of responsibility for ensuring the right to food as a key part of any anti-hunger efforts. It is common to frame the hunger problem, especially among policy makers in the United States, as primarily a technical one. Framed in this way, the solutions to hunger arise from greater applications of agricultural technologies to reduce necessary inputs and increase agricultural outputs in shorter periods of time on smaller pieces of land. By this logic, hunger in developing countries could be solved if only farmers had access to better technology and markets, and thus our policies should be directed toward these ends. And yet, history reminds us that the market alone has never been able to solve the hunger problem and that hunger persists even in countries with extremely efficient agricultural industries and the very best technologies available for increasing agricultural output (such as in the United States). As the present study has suggested, an essential impediment to effective hunger reduction is the still unresolved question of who societies believe is ultimately responsible for ensuring everyone has access to adequate food, especially when they are unable to command that food through conventional means off the market. One cannot solve the hunger problem if it is unclear who is ultimately obliged to do so. U.S. policies abroad are hesitant to address questions of responsibility, obligation, and blame around the right to food, though the U.S. government is generally far less averse to commenting on state responsibilities, obligations, and blame around other human rights (especially civil and political rights). This is likely due to residual Cold War–era antagonisms between capitalist and communist approaches to governance. And yet, when the

---

United States joined with other United Nations (UN) Food and Agriculture Organization member states in support of the Voluntary Guidelines to Support the Progressive Realization of the Right to Adequate Food in the Context of National Food Security in 2004, it created an opening in which to reengage the question of state obligation for the right to food. The Voluntary Guidelines have been underutilized, and given the U.S. government's influence in international food assistance as the largest donor of food aid in the world, policy makers may find this particular framework especially fruitful in future efforts to develop more effective international anti-hunger policy.

Finally, there has been increasing interest among human rights lawyers and some activists in constructing international law ascribing responsibility to private corporations for human rights. Early efforts have included the construction of the Norms on the Responsibilities of Transnational Corporations and Other Business Enterprises with Regard to Human Rights as well as the Guiding Principles on Business and Human Rights, spearheaded by political scientist John Gerard Ruggie, discussed in chapter 3.[6] To date, no legally binding frameworks have been adopted, but this movement warrants additional thinking from within the legal community and human rights activists more broadly. What are the implications for economic and social rights if responsibility is bifurcated in international law between the public and private spheres? It is possible that even if such international law was codified it would be shelved by many anti-hunger and right-to-food activists, as existing covenants (most notably the ICESCR) frequently are. But if it were leveraged, how might the attribution of responsibility to the private sector for economic and social rights affect efforts to name and shame national governments? Does attributing responsibility to the private sector reduce government obligation to ensuring human rights? Might it provide governments with an actor on whom to credibly deflect such responsibility? Additional research on the implications of ascribing responsibility to the private sector for human rights protection and fulfillment is needed.

Brazilian archbishop and social justice advocate Dom Hélder Pessoa Câmara famously lamented, "When I give food to the poor, they call me a saint. When I ask why the poor have no food, they call me a communist." The hunger issue area resides in a complex social environment where there is a consensus on the moral principle that *nobody should go hungry* and that *it is good for everyone to have*

---

6. On the attribution of responsibility to corporations for human rights, see Mantilla 2009; and Ruggie 2013.

enough to eat but where there remains no consensus on who is obliged to ensure that hungry people are fed.

And yet, we do not live in a static world, and studies that focus on normative environments should be especially sensitive to the real possibility that social understandings of appropriate behavior may look very different even a few years from now than they do today.

The nature of this change, however, is always unknown, as normative landscapes do not necessarily evolve in ways that one might find inherently good or progressive. The present study has focused on the normative landscape surrounding international anti-hunger organizations and their advocacy up through 2014, but this landscape has and will continue to change over time. Today's challenges in declaring not only that all individuals are entitled to food but *from whom* individuals ought to be able to expect the fulfillment of this basic human right may find remedy in the coming years as societies increasingly grapple with the extent to which states are obliged to ensure the economic and social rights of their citizens. I hope so.

Appendix

NOTES ON RESEARCH METHODS

This project relies on the complementary work of three research methods: archival work, interviewing, and surveying. In order to understand how hunger as an issue area was placed on the international political agenda and how understandings of the problem have changed over time, I conducted archival research at the United Nations (UN) Food and Agriculture Organization archives in Rome, the UK National Archives, and the US National Archives. Utilizing different archives to study similar periods of time allows for a more nuanced understanding of different interests and perspectives on how hunger became a political issue. This archival research forms the basis of chapter 1.

It would have been impossible to conduct a study on international anti-hunger advocacy without the generosity, in particular, of contemporary anti-hunger advocates themselves, who sat for interviews, most averaging an hour to ninety minutes, and patiently answered my many questions about how they understood the problem of chronic hunger, its possible solutions, and who was to blame for the problem. In total, more than seventy staff members of top international anti-hunger organizations were interviewed for this project, most of whom were based at the following organizations: Action against Hunger; ActionAid; Amnesty International; the Bill & Melinda Gates Foundation; Bread for the World; CARE; the Food and Agriculture Organization (FAO) of the United Nations (UN); FIAN International; Médecins sans Frontières / Doctors without Borders (MSF); Oxfam; the

Rockefeller Foundation; Save the Children; the UN's World Food Programme; and World Vision.[1]

A smaller subset of interviewees, twenty-one individuals holding the most elite (senior and executive) positions were also surveyed on their beliefs about blame and solutions to chronic hunger. Surveys were all conducted one-on-one, between myself and the senior/executive staff member. Surveys were conducted between February and November of 2013, and most interviews took place between 2012 and 2015. The results of these surveys, as well as additional information on their methodology, can be found in chapter 3. Individuals were selected to participate in the surveys if they held elite positions in the organizations in question and were influential for the issue area at hand. (Some large organizations may have multiple elite staff, but some of those staff may have no overlap with the anti-hunger work of the organization). Interviewees, including those not surveyed, were selected as individuals within the organizations that I had identified through the organization's reports or websites as relevant to the anti-hunger work of the organization or who were referred to me by others in the organization as relevant to this work.[2]

Interview Method

> The most fundamental privilege that all researchers enjoy is gaining entrée into people's worlds. Choosing what to do with that privilege is an issue no researcher should take lightly.
>
> —Lee Ann Fujii, *Interviewing in Social Science Research: A Relational Approach (2017)*

The bulk of this project relies on the use of interviews, almost always with senior and executive staff of international anti-hunger organizations. It is indeed a privilege to spend so many hours in dialogue with international anti-hunger advocates. This privilege, as noted by Lee Ann Fujii (2017) comes with responsibilities, such as treating your research participants with dignity and respect, ensuring you have met ethical responsibilities that go above and beyond those required by your university's Institutional Review Board, carefully considering your own biases and questions of positionality in conducting your research, and considering how to

---

1. For a list of the country affiliate offices (where applicable) where I conducted interviews and surveys, see table 0.1 in the introductory chapter of the book.

2. Of course, I would not convey who referred me to an individual without the referrer's prior consent.

fulfill your own obligations regarding the population you have relied on for your research project.

My interview participants were, for the most part, senior officials at anti-hunger international nongovernmental organizations (INGOs) and intergovernmental organizations (IGOs). They held high ranking positions within the organizations, and many had been working in the field for many years. Some interviewees were either recently retired from the organization or about to retire, but most were current employees of the specific organization I was studying. This meant being aware of potential employment risks that a participant might face if they were to disclose information that other senior staff might view as sensitive. Mitigating these risks required extensive collaboration with my university's Institutional Review Board, where my project was approved through an expedited review. Interviewees were always given a choice to meet at a nearby coffee shop or the location of their choice if they did not want to talk within their organizational offices. When I met with multiple individuals in the same office, it was important to keep private the names of any other coworkers I may have met with, unless the individuals gave permission to use their name. As part of gaining informed consent, I agreed not to use names or specific position titles when attributing quotes or information but rather to use a more general attribution such as a "senior official from [organization name]." All pronouns were made feminine in this study when referring to an official who was directly quoted, as not doing so would have betrayed the identity of individuals in organizations where there is only one man or woman in a senior position.

At the beginning of each interview I asked participants if I could audio record our conversation to ensure I was capturing their responses accurately. In nearly all cases, participants agreed to audio recording. To facilitate record keeping, I used a Livescribe pen in much of my interviewing, which allowed me to synchronize my written notes with the audio recording simultaneously and upload digital images of my written notes to my computer along with the audio recording, all of which were kept password protected. This greatly assisted in record keeping and in allowing me to use the time when interviewing participants to pay attention to and make notes on body language, the setting of the room, pauses, and laugher in ways that would have been challenging if I was struggling to keep track verbatim of dialogue only by hand.[3]

My interviews always began with me asking the interviewees if they had any questions for me. While I had anticipated reluctance to speak to an outsider, in

---

3. As noted in Fujii 2010, 231, "metadata" such as silences can provide important information about interviewees' "thoughts or feelings," which are lost if interviewers pay attention only to what is verbally communicated.

nearly every case interviewees were surprisingly candid and enthusiastic to talk about the work of their organizations and their own perspectives on hunger and food security. Perhaps because I was an academic, interviews would often start with an interviewee looking to their bookcase, pulling out a couple of books or IO or nongovernmental organization (NGO) pamphlets they had read on hunger and asking if I had read them too. When I had already read the material, this allowed for finding some common ground in discussing the book or pamphlet at the beginning of our conversation. When I had not, it meant I learned about new materials that were important to my interviewees, and this highlighted how much I had to learn from the interviewees themselves.

My interviewees led very busy lives, and respecting their time was important. This often meant needing to reschedule our interviews at the last minute, as time-sensitive tasks would come up and interviewees would need to postpone our meetings. I estimate this happened about 50 percent of the time with my interviews, and it meant my schedule had to be flexible even at the last minute. Living in Washington, DC, the city where most interviews took place, allowed for this flexibility; when I traveled to London, New York, Oxford, or Rome for additional interviews it always meant adding in several days of buffer time during the travels for potentially rescheduled meetings.

When conducting the interviews and interpreting the interview data, I needed to consider questions of positionality as well as both my own potential biases and those of the interviewees. I was an outsider, a woman, a political scientist who had not previously worked as an IGO or INGO staff member, and I was an American. I was also young(ish) at the time. Being young and a woman did affect how I was perceived by some, with a few individuals assuming, perhaps because of my age or gender, that I knew very little about the topic area. On one occasion an interviewee invited a colleague to stand in the doorway of his office during our interview "to watch how he explained this problem to someone who does not know very much about it." To the contrary, I happened to know quite a lot about the topic at hand that day, but his assumption of my ignorance had the positive effect of him feeling very confident in talking to me and in explaining his positions in detail. Being American was challenging when interviewing at the FAO and WFP, in particular, when it was necessary to reiterate I had no government position whatsoever and was very open to disagreement with U.S. policies within the organization.[4] I worried that introducing myself as a *political* scientist would raise concerns over partisan angles to the project, but in part because the issue of

---

4. From 2017 to 2018, some years after the interviews for this book were conducted, I would find myself working at the U.S. Agency for International Development for a year on a fellowship with the American Association for the Advancement of Science, returning to the WFP for official business. At the time these interviews were conducted, however, I had no government affiliation.

hunger has avoided much of the political limelight, and in part because the scope of the project and my intent with it was explained thoroughly before beginning each interview, this rarely appeared to be an issue.

Scholars of violence and sensitive topics more generally have generated an important body of literature on how to consider the veracity of interviewee responses.[5] Interviewees may misremember historical events; their memories may be altered over the years by political, cultural, or social events; and they may have incentives to lie or misrepresent the past or present.[6] For the most part, my interviews covered contemporary anti-hunger advocacy work and campaigns that were often ongoing within the organizations when and where I interviewed staff. In this way I worried less about misremembering historical events, when the events at hand were often taking place in the present day or had taken place within the last few years. On a few occasions I did interview individuals who had spent decades within their organization, and on these occasions we did spend more time discussing the origins of policies that reached back thirty or more years. One individual had spent several decades working at the FAO and had kindly invited me to travel to her home to talk for a full day (nearly ten hours) to retell the history she remembered from the early years of her time at the FAO. As encouraged by Layna Mosley (2013b, 20–24), I considered interviews in light of each other and of historical documents I reviewed in the archives in order to compare responses and "triangulate" data.

When dealing with contemporary events or ongoing advocacy work, there was frequently an effort, especially in the beginning of our interviews, for interviewees to speak back information from an interviewee's organization's webpage or other public documentation, much of which painted the organization's work in very favorable light. Some interviewees took greater efforts than others to make their organizations look especially good, evidence-based, or effective. I planned to conduct interviews at an organization only after I had spent time researching the organization using other methods (secondary literature, the organization's own publications and reports, and discussions with other organizations about the work of the organization in question) and extensive prior knowledge of the organization's work and its history became a valuable tool in moving beyond the "public talking points" soon after the interview began. I would generally share a bit of information on what I had done so far in my research process at the beginning of our conversation and would mention, for instance, if I had already visited the organization's archives or read specific reports or spoken to other organizations (which should be done without giving the names of interviewees).

---

5. Cohen 2016; Fujii 2010; Wood 2003.
6. Fujii 2010; Loftus 1979; Mosley 2013a; Portelli 1991; Wood 2003.

Asking very specific and detailed questions which conveyed prior knowledge of the organization's work also helped in moving beyond superficial responses early on in the interviews and to engage more deeply in the interviewees' own experiences and understandings of the organizations.

When an interviewee's account did not comport with other information I had received (e.g., from secondary materials or other interviews), I would highlight points of disagreement and probe further. Contradictions often yielded much deeper insight into how an interviewee viewed a particular policy or position of her organization. As evident in the opening conversation in the introduction to this book, it was through pushing back on the comments of a senior staff member of Oxfam America and highlighting where I was perplexed by the response (and why) that allowed me greater understanding, in this particular case, of how the organization viewed the difference between a moral and legal right to food.

I was aware in interviewing and interpreting the interview data that it was impossible to be entirely objective. I was neither detached nor neutral about the subject matter of the study. Quite the opposite, I came to graduate school because I cared a great deal about understanding the persistence of hunger in a world with plenty of food. In order to ensure that I was interpreting what interviewees were saying appropriately, I would frequently repeat back to them in the interview what I heard them say to ensure it was a fair characterization. They would correct where necessary and push back on assumptions I had made if they felt they were inappropriate or inaccurate. This took additional time in the interview process, but I found it both useful to ensure that I was interpreting information in the way the interviewee intended, and it was a way of ensuring that I respected my interviewee as a partner in the research process. When I personally disagreed with an interviewee, after I ensured that I understood her position I would (if it was appropriate in the particular context) push back and ask why something should not be viewed another way. Had this approach ended up generating a hostile environment I would have stopped, but fortunately it did not. Interviews would often become vibrant debates by the end, and on several occasions interviewees would end our conversation saying, "That was fun!" I believed their remarks to be genuine. Given the right context and working relationship (this would not work in all contexts or with all interviewees), these debates served to be extremely valuable in allowing me to see the boundaries of how interviewees viewed, in particular, questions of blame and responsibility for hunger. For an example of this sort of exchange, see the remarks about why one might consider the rights of education, food, health care, and housing differently in my interview with an Oxfam America senior staff member in chapter 2.

References

Abbott, Kenneth, Robert Keohane, Andrew Moravcsik, Anne-Marie Slaughter, and Duncan Snidal. 2000. "The Concept of Legalization." *International Organization* 54, no. 3: 401–19.

Abbott, Kenneth, and Duncan Snidal, D. 1998. "Why States Act through Formal International Organizations." *Journal of Conflict Resolution* 42, no. 1: 3–32.

Action against Hunger USA. n.d. "Countries" (webpage). Retrieved January 17, 2020. https://www.actionagainsthunger.org/countries.

Action against Hunger USA. n.d. *2014 Annual Report and Financials.* New York: Action against Hunger USA. https://www.actionagainsthunger.org/2014-annual -report.

ActionAid International. n.d. "Caravan of Hope, Africa 2011" (webpage). Retrieved May 2014. http://www.actionaid.org.br/en/hungerfree-campaign/follow-caravan -hope-through-africa.

———. 2013. *#TaxPower—ActionAid's Campaign Explained.* Johannesburg: ActionAid International, July 12, 2013. https://actionaid.org/publications/2013/tax-power -actionaids-campaign-explained.

ActionAid UK. n.d. *Community Campaigning with ActionAid.* London: ActionAid UK. https://www.actionaid.org.uk/sites/default/files/publications/community _campaigner_network_a5_web_single_page.pdf.

———. 2013. "Time to Clean Up: How Barclays Promotes the Use of Tax Havens in Africa." November 2013 report. https://actionaid.org/sites/default/files/barclays_report _final_2.pdf.

———. 2019. "Become a Community Campaigner" (webpage), last updated August 12, 2019. https://www.actionaid.org.uk/campaign/become-a-campaigner.

ActionAid USA. 2013. "The People of Zambia Tell Barclays to Clean Up Their Act!," December 9, 2013. Accessed May 2014. http://www.actionaidusa.org/2013/12/people -zambia-tell-barclays-clean-their-act.

Adler, Emmanuel, and Vincent Pouliot. 2011. "International Practices." *International Theory* 3, no. 1: 1–36.

Albin-Lackey, Chris. 2013. "Without Rules: A Failed Approach to Corporate Accountability." Human Rights Watch. http://www.hrw.org/sites/default/files/related_material /business.pdf.

Alston, Philip. 1991. "No Right to Complain about Being Poor: The Need for an Optional Protocol to the Economic Rights Covenant." In *The Future of Human Rights Protection in a Changing World: Fifty Years since the Four Freedoms Address, Essays in Honour of Torkel Opsahl,* edited by Asbjørn Eide and Jan Hegesen, 79–100. Oslo: Norwegian University Press.

Alston, Philip, and Mary Robinson, eds. 2005. *Human Rights and Development: Towards Mutual Reinforcement.* Oxford: Oxford University Press.

Amnesty International. 2011. "Bringing George W. Bush to Justice: International Obligations of States to which Former US President George W. Bush May Travel." https:// www.amnesty.org/download/Documents/28000/amr510972011en.pdf.

Amnesty International. n.d. "Torture" (webpage). http://www.amnestyusa.org/our-work
/issues/torture.

———. 2005. *Human Rights for Human Dignity: A Primer on Economic, Social, and Cultural Rights.* Oxford: Alden.

———. 2014. *Human Rights for Human Dignity: A Primer on Economic, Social, and Cultural Rights: Second Edition.* Amnesty International Publications. https://www.amnesty
.org/download/Documents/8000/pol340012014en.pdf.

———. 2018. "Take Action for Human Rights: Free #theBerksKids" (web petition). https://
act.amnestyusa.org/page/13951/action/1.

Arsenault, Chris. 2015. "Climate Change, Food Shortages, and Conflict in Mali." *Aljazeera*, April 27, 2015. http://www.aljazeera.com/indepth/features/2015/04/climate-change
-food-shortages-conflict-mali-150426105617725.html.

———. 2016. "Fears for Poor as Brazil Cuts 'Minha Casa, Minha Vida' Housing Plan." Reuters, June 24, 2016. http://www.reuters.com/article/us-brazil-politics-landrights
-idUSKCN0ZA03C.

Associated Press. 1943. "Roosevelt Letter on Food." *New York Times*, May 19, 1943.

Ausderan, Jacob. 2014. "How Naming and Shaming Affects Human Rights Perceptions in the Shamed Country." *Journal of Peace Research* 51, no. 1: 81–95.

Bailey, Robert. 2011. *Growing a Better Future: Food Justice in a Resource-Constrained World.* Nairobi: Oxfam International, June 2011.

Baldos, Uris Lantz C., and Thomas W. Hertel. 2014. "Global Food Security in 2050: The Role of Agricultural Productivity and Climate Change." *Australian Journal of Agricultural and Resource Economics* 58, no. 4: 554–70.

Barrett, Christopher. 2001. "Does Food Aid Stabilize Food Availability?" *Economic Development and Cultural Change* 49, no. 2: 335–49.

Barrett, Christopher, and Dan Maxwell. 2005. *Food Aid After Fifty Years: Recasting Its Role.* New York: Routledge.

Barry, Colin M., K. Chad Clay, and Michael E. Flynn. 2013. "Avoiding the Spotlight: Human Rights Shaming and Foreign Direct Investment." *International Studies Quarterly* 57, no. 3: 532–44.

Beetham, David. 1995. "What Future for Economic and Social Rights?" *Political Studies* 43, no. 1: 41–60.

Benford, Robert D., and David A. Snow. "Framing processes and social movements: An overview and assessment." *Annual Review of Sociology* 26, no. 1 (2000): 611–639.

Biersteker, Thomas J., Peter J. Spiro, Chandra Lekha Sriram, and Veronica I. Raffo, eds. 2006. *International Law and International Relations: Bridging Theory and Practice.* Abingdon, UK: Routledge.

Birchfield, Lauren, and Jessica Corsi. 2010. "Between Starvation and Globalization: Realizing the Right to Food in India." *Michigan Journal of International Law* 31: 691–764.

Black, David. 1999. "The Long and Winding Road: International Norms and Domestic Political Change in South Africa." In *The Power of Human Rights: International Norms and Domestic Change*, edited by Thomas Risse, Stephen C. Ropp, and Kathryn Sikkink, 78–108. Cambridge, UK: Cambridge University Press.

Black, Robert E., Cesar G. Victora, Susan P. Walker, Zulfiqar A. Bhutta, Parul Christian, Mercedes De Onis, Majid Ezzati et al. 2013. "Maternal and child undernutrition and overweight in low-income and middle-income countries." *The Lancet* 382, no. 9890: 427–451.

Blyth, Mark. 2003. "Structures Do Not Come with an Instruction Sheet: Interests, Ideas, and Progress in Political Science." *Perspectives on Politics* 1, no. 4: 695–706.

Boadle, Anthony. 2014. "Brazil Leader's Popularity Slips, Still Favored to Win 2nd Term." Reuters, June 19, 2014. http://uk.reuters.com/article/2014/06/19/uk-brazil-election -idUKKBN0EU1S620140619.

Bob, Clifford, ed. 2010. *The International Struggle for New Human Rights.* Philadelphia: University of Pennsylvania Press.

Bommarco, Riccardo, David Kleijn, and Simon G. Potts. 2013. "Ecological Intensification: Harnessing Ecosystem Services for Food Security." *Trends in Ecology and Evolution* 28, no. 4: 230–38.

Brauer, Markus, and Nadine Chaurand. 2010. "Descriptive Norms, Prescriptive Norms, and Social Control: An Intercultural Comparison of People's Reactions to Uncivil Behaviors." *European Journal of Social Psychology* 40, no. 3: 490–99.

Brunnée, Jutta, and Stephen J. Toope. 2010. *Legitimacy and Legality in International Law: An Interactional Account.* Cambridge, UK: Cambridge University Press.

Buchanan, Ronald. 2009. "Guatemala Declares 'State of Calamity.'" *Financial Times*, September 11, 2009. https://www.ft.com/content/8571db1a-9d7c-11de-9f4a-00144 feabdc0.

Bunch, Matthew J. 2007. "All Roads Lead to Rome: Canada, the Freedom from Hunger Campaign, and the Rise of NGOs, 1960–1980." PhD diss., University of Waterloo.

Burke, Marshall, and David B. Lobell. 2017. "Satellite- Based Assessment of Yield Variation and Its Determinants in Smallholder African Systems." *Proceedings of the National Academy of Sciences* 114, no. 9: 2189–94.

CARE India. n.d. *A Million Faces of Hope: Annual Report 2014.* Noida, India: CARE India. https://www.careindia.org/wp-content/uploads/2017/05/CARE-India-Annual -Report-2014.pdf.

CARE International. n.d. "Where We Work" (webpage). http://www.care.org/work/where -we-work.

——. 2012. "Japan: One Year After Tsunami from Relief to Recovery." Press release, March 9, 2012. https://www.care-international.org/news/press-releases/japan-one -year-after-the-tsunami-from-relief-to-recovery.

——. 2014. *Fighting Poverty by Empowering Women and Girls in the Poorest Communities around the World: CARE International Annual Report.* Geneva: CARE International. https://www.care-international.org/files/files/publications/CARE-International -Annual-Report-2014.pdf.

Carnemark, Curt. 2012. "Four Steps to Feeding the World in 2050." World Bank, October 16, 2012. http://www.worldbank.org/en/news/feature/2012/10/16/four-steps -feed-world-2050.

Carpenter, Charli. 2014. *"Lost" Causes: Agenda Vetting in Global Issue Networks and the Shaping of Human Security.* Ithaca, NY: Cornell University Press.

Carpenter, R. Charli. 2011. "Vetting the Advocacy Agenda: Network Centrality and the Paradox of Weapons Norms." *International Organization* 65, no. 1: 69–102.

Chappell, M. Jahi. 2018. *Beginning to End Hunger: Food and the Environment in Belo Horizonte, Brazil, and Beyond.* Berkeley, CA: University of California Press.

Checkel, Jeffrey T. 1997. "International Norms and Domestic Politics: Bridging the Rationalist-Constructivist Divide." *European Journal of International Relations* 3, no. 4: 473–95.

Claeys, Priscilla. 2015. *Human Rights and Food Sovereignty Movement: Reclaiming Control.* New York: Routledge.

Clapp, Jennifer. 2012. *Hunger in the Balance: The New Politics of International Food Aid.* Ithaca, NY: Cornell University Press.

Clapp, Jennifer, and Marc J. Cohen, eds. 2009. *The Global Food Crisis: Governance Challenges and Opportunities.* Waterloo, ON: Wilfrid Laurier University Press.

Clark, Ann Marie. 2001. *Diplomacy of Conscience: Amnesty International and Changing Human Rights Norms*. Princeton, NJ: Princeton University Press.

Cohen, Dara Kay. 2016. *Rape during Civil War*. Ithaca, NY: Cornell University Press.

Cullather, Nick. 2010. *The Hungry World*. Cambridge, MA: Harvard University Press.

De Haen, Hartwig. 2005. "Foreword." In *Food and Human Rights in Development*, vol. 1, *Legal and Institutional Dimensions and Selected Topics*, edited by Wenche Barth Eide and Uwe Kracht, xxiii–xxiv. Oxford: Intersentia.

De Waal, Alex. 2004. *Famine That Kills: Darfur, Sudan*. New York: Oxford University Press.

Donnelly, Jack. 2007. *International Human Rights*. 3rd ed. Boulder, CO: Westview.

Dowell-Jones, Mary. 2004. *Contextualizing the International Covenant on Economic, Social and Cultural Rights: Assessing the Economic Deficit*. Leiden: Nijhoff.

Drèze, Jean, Amartya Sen, and Athar Hussain. 1995. *The Political Economy of Hunger: Selected Essays*. Oxford: Oxford University Press.

Drèze, Jean, and Amartya Sen. 1989. *Hunger and Public Action*. Clarendon Paperbacks. Oxford: Oxford University Press.

Dworkin, Ronald. 1978. *Taking Rights Seriously*. Cambridge, MA: Harvard University Press.

Eide, Asbjørn. 2007. "State Obligations Revisited." In *Food and Human Rights in Development*, vol. 2, *Evolving Issues and Emerging Applications*, edited by Wenche Barth Eide and Uwe Kracht, 137–58. Oxford: Intersentia.

Eide, Wenche Barth, and Uwe Kracht, eds. 2005. *Food and Human Rights in Development*. Vol. 1, *Legal and Institutional Dimensions and Selected Topics*. Oxford: Intersentia.

——, eds. 2007. *Food and Human Rights in Development*. Vol. 2, *Evolving Issues and Emerging Applications*. Oxford: Intersentia.

Elster, Jon. 1989. "Social Norms and Economic Theory." *Journal of Economic Perspectives* 3, no. 4: 99–117.

——. 2011. "Reciprocity and Norms." In *Social Ethics and Normative Economics*, edited by M. Fleurbaey and J. Weymark, 327–37. Berlin: Springer.

Epstein, Jessica. 2014. "Scientizing Food Safety: Resistance, Acquiescence, and Localization in India." *Law and Society Review* 48, no. 4: 893–920.

ETO Consortium. 2013. *Maastricht Principles on Extraterritorial Obligations of States in the Area of Economic, Social, and Cultural Rights*. Heidelberg: FIAN International. https://www.etoconsortium.org/nc/en/main-navigation/library/maastricht-principles/?tx_drblob_pi1%5BdownloadUid%5D=23.

Fariss, Christopher. 2014. "Respect for Human Rights Has Improved over Time: Modeling the Changing Standard of Accountability." *American Political Science Review* 108, no. 2: 297–318.

Ferguson, Kevin. 2013. "Lessons Learned: Growing Rice in Haiti and Vietnam." Oxfam America, December 30, 2013. http://www.oxfamamerica.org/explore/stories/lessons-learned-growing-rice-in-haiti-and-vietnam/.

FIAN International. 2014. "Philippines: Right to food of 6,212 farmers threatened despite the issuance of land titles" (webpage). Accessed April 2014 from: http://www.fian.org/get-involved/take-action/urgent-actions/urgent-action-philippines-hacienda-luisita/#c1585.

FIAN Netherlands. 2012. "Urgent Action—Mozambique: Swedish Development Cooperation Violates the Rights of Peasants in Niassa Province" (webpage), October 16, 2012. https://fian.nl/mozambique-swedish-development-cooperation-violates-rights-of-peasants-in-niassa-province/.

Finnemore, Martha. 2003. *The Purpose of Intervention: Changing Beliefs about the Use of Force*. Ithaca, NY: Cornell University Press.

Finnemore, Martha, and Kathryn Sikkink. 1998. "International Norm Dynamics and Political Change." *International Organization* 52, no. 4: 887–917.

Finnemore, Martha, and Stephen J. Toope. 2001. "Alternatives to "Legalization": Richer Views of Law and Politics." *International Organization* 55, no. 3: 743–58.

Fisher, William F. 1997. "Doing Good? The Politics and Antipolitics of NGO Practices." *Annual Review of Anthropology* 26, no. 1: 439–64.

Florini, Ann. 1996. "The Evolution of International Norms." *International Studies Quarterly* 40, no. 3: 363–89.

Foley, Jonathan. 2014. "A Five-Step Plan to Feed the World." *National Geographic,* May 2014. http://www.nationalgeographic.com/foodfeatures/feeding-9-billion/.

Food and Agriculture Organization of the United Nations. n.d. "Making Rights a Reality" (webpage). http://www.fao.org/FOCUS/E/rightfood/right2.htm.

———. 2002. *Annex II: United States of America, Reservation.* Rome: Food and Agriculture Organization of the United Nations. http://www.fao.org/docrep/MEETING/005/Y7106e/y7106e03.htm.

———. 2004. *Voluntary Guidelines to Support the Progressive Realization of the Right to Adequate Food in the Context of National Food Security.* Rome: Food and Agriculture Organization of the United Nations. http://www.fao.org/3/y7937e/y7937e00.htm.

———. 2009. "How to Feed the World in 2050: High-Level Expert Forum" (webpage). http://www.fao.org/wsfs/forum2050/wsfs-forum/en/.

———. 2010. "FAO Launches Anti-Hunger Petition." Press release, May 11, 2010. http://www.fao.org/news/story/en/item/42158/icode/.

———. July-September 2010. "FAO Uganda Information Bulletin," volume 3, issue 6. Retrieved from: http://www.fao.org/fileadmin/user_upload/emergencies/docs/FAO_Uganda_Information_Bulletin_october_2010_For_mail.pdf.

———. October 15, 2010. "FAO Director-General's Address at the World Food Day Ceremony," retrieved from: http://www.fao.org/fileadmin/user_upload/newsroom/docs/dgenglish.pdf.

Food and Agriculture Organization of the United Nations, International Fund for Agricultural Development, and World Food Programme. 2013. *The State of Food Insecurity in the World 2013: The Multiple Dimensions of Food Security.* Rome: Food and Agriculture Organization of the United Nations.

———. 2015. *The State of Food Insecurity in the World 2015: Meeting the 2015 International Hunger Targets: Taking Stock of Uneven Progress.* Rome: Food and Agriculture Organization of the United Nations.

Food and Agriculture Organization of the United Nations, International Fund for Agricultural Development, United Nations Children's Fund, World Food Programme, and World Health Organization. 2018. *The State of Food Security and Nutrition in the World 2018: Building Climate Resilience for Food Security and Nutrition.* Rome: Food and Agriculture Organization of the United Nations.

Foot, Rosemary. 2006. "Torture: The Struggle over a Preemptory Norm in a Counter-Terrorist Era." *International Relations* 20, no. 2: 131–51.

Fujii, Lee Ann. 2010. "Shades of Truth and Lies: Interpreting Testimonies of War and Violence." *Journal of Peace Research* 47, no. 2: 231–41.

———. 2017. *Interviewing in Social Science Research: A Relational Approach.* New York: Routledge.

Fuller, Lon L. 1969. *The Morality of Law.* Rev. ed. New Haven, CT: Yale University Press.

Gallas, Daniel. 2016. "If Rousseff Goes Will 47 Million Brazilians Lose Their Benefits?" BBC News, May 11, 2016. http://www.bbc.com/news/business-36216987.

Gauri, Varun, and Siri Gloppen. 2012. "Human Rights-Based Approaches to Development: Concepts, Evidence, and Policy." *Polity* 44, no. 4: 485–503.

Geneva Declaration Secretariat. 2011. *Global Burden of Armed Violence 2011: Lethal Encounters: Executive Summary.* Geneva: Geneva Declaration Secretariat. http://www

.genevadeclaration.org/fileadmin/docs/GBAV2/GBAV2011-Ex-summary-ENG
.pdf.

Gibbs, Jack P. 1965. "Norms: The Problem of Definition and Classification." *American Journal of Sociology* 70, no. 5: 586–94.

"The Global Political Economy of Food." 1978. Special issue. *International Organization* 32, no. 3. With contributions by Raymond F Hopkins, Donald J. Puchala, I. M. Destler, Robert L. Paalberg, Norman K. Nicholson and John D. Esseks, Gary L. Seevers, Cheryl Christensen, Henry R. Nau, James E. Austin, and D. Gale Johnson.

Godfray, H. Charles J., John R. Beddington, Ian R. Crute, Lawrence Haddad, David Lawrence, James F. Muir, Jules N. Pretty, Sherman Robinson, Sandy M. Thomas, and Camilla Toulmin. 2010. "Food Security: The Challenge of Feeding 9 Billion People." *Science* 327, no. 5967: 812–18.

Goertz, Gary, and Paul F. Diehl. 1992. "Toward a Theory of International Norms: Some Conceptual and Measurement Issues." *Journal of Conflict Resolution* 36, no. 4: 634–64.

Goffman, Erving. 1974. *Frame Analysis: An Essay on the Organization of Experience.* Cambridge, MA: Harvard University Press.

Goodliffe, Jay, and Darren G. Hawkins. 2006. "Explaining Commitment: States and the Convention against Torture." *Journal of Politics* 68, no. 2: 358–71.

Gränzer, Sieglinde. 1999. "Changing Discourse: Transnational Advocacy Networks in Tunisia and Morocco." In *The Power of Human Rights: International Norms and Domestic Change,* edited by Thomas Risse, Stephen C. Ropp, and Kathryn Sikkink, 109–133. Cambridge, UK: Cambridge University Press.

Greenhill, Brian 2010. "The Company You Keep: International Socialization and the Diffusion of Human Rights Norms." *International Studies Quarterly* 54, no. 1: 127–45.

Gronke, Paul, Darius Rejali, Dustin Drenguis, James Hicks, Peter Miller, and Bryan Nakayama. 2010. "US Public Opinion on Torture, 2001–2009." *PS: Political Science and Politics* 43, no. 3: 437–44.

Gurowitz, Amy. 2004. "International Law, Politics, and Migrant Rights." In *The Politics of International Law,* edited by Christian Reus-Smit, 131–50. Cambridge, UK: Cambridge University Press.

Haas, Peter M. 1992. "Introduction: Epistemic Communities and International Policy Coordination." *International Organization* 46, no. 1: 1–35.

Hafner-Burton, Emilie M. 2008. "Sticks and Stones: Naming and Shaming the Human Rights Enforcement Problem." *International Organization* 62, no. 4: 689–716.

Hafner-Burton, Emilie M., and Kiyoteru Tsutsui. 2007. "Justice Lost! The Failure of International Human Rights Law to Matter Where Needed Most." *Journal of Peace Research* 44, no. 4: 407–25.

Hall, Peter A., and Rosemary CR Taylor. 1996. "Political Science and the Three New Institutionalisms." *Political Studies* 44, no. 5: 936–57.

Halliday, Terence C. 2009. "Recursivity of Global Normmaking: A Sociolegal Agenda." *Annual Review of Law and Social Science* 5: 263–89.

Hambridge, Gove. 1955. *The Story of FAO.* New York: D. Van Nostrand.

Hargreaves, Samantha, KumKum Kumar, Shamim Meer, Laurie Adams, Adriano Campolina, Ramesh Singh, Sandeep Chachra, Anil Pant, Ennie Chipembere, and Carrie Pratt. 2010. *Action on Rights: Human Rights Based Approach Resource Book.* Johannesburg: ActionAid International. https://actionaid.org/sites/default/files/hrba _resourcebook_11nov2010.pdf.

Hart, H. L. A. 2012. *The Concept of Law.* 3rd ed. Oxford: Oxford University Press.

Hathaway, Oona A. 2007. "Why Do Countries Commit to Human Rights Treaties?" *Journal of Conflict Resolution* 51, no. 4: 588–621.

Hawkins, Darren. 2004. "Explaining Costly International Institutions: Persuasion and Enforceable Human Rights Norms." *International Studies Quarterly* 48, no. 4: 779–804.

Hendrix, Cullen, and Henk-Jan Brinkman. 2013. "Food Insecurity and Conflict Dynamics: Causal Linkages and Complex Feedbacks." *Stability: International Journal of Security and Development* 2, no. 2: 1–18.

Hertel, Shareen. 2006. *Unexpected Power: Conflict and Change among Transnational Activists.* Ithaca, NY: Cornell University Press.

——. 2015. "Hungry for Justice: Social Mobilization on the Right to Food in India." *Development and Change* 46, no 1: 72–94.

Heywood, Mark. 2009. "South Africa's Treatment Action Campaign: Combining Law and Social Mobilization to Realize the Right to Health." *Journal of Human Rights Practice* 1, no. 1: 14–36.

Hickey, Sam, and Diana Mitlin, eds. 2009. *Rights-Based Approaches to Development: Exploring the Potential and Pitfalls.* Sterling, VA: Kumarian.

Hoffman, Beth. 2013. *Behind the Brands: Food Justice and the "Big 10" Food and Beverage Companies.* Oxfam Briefing Paper 166. Oxfam International, February 26, 2013. https://policy-practice.oxfam.org.uk/publications/behind-the-brands-food-justice-and-the-big-10-food-and-beverage-companies-270393.

Holmes, John. 2008. "Losing 25,000 to Hunger Every Day." *UN Chronicle* 45, nos. 2–3. http://unchronicle.un.org/article/losing-25000-hunger-every-day/.

Hopf, Ted. 2010. "The Logic of Habit in International Relations." *European Journal of International Relations* 16, no. 4: 539–61.

Human Rights Watch. 2014. *Punished for Protesting: Rights Violations in Venezuela's Streets, Detention Centers and Justice System.* New York: Human Rights Watch. http://www.hrw.org/sites/default/files/reports/venezuela0514_reportcover_web.pdf.

Hurd, Ian. 2017. *How to Do Things with International Law.* Princeton, NJ: Princeton University Press.

Hyde, Susan. 2011. *The Pseudo-Democrat's Dilemma: Why Election Monitoring Became an International Norm.* Ithaca, NY: Cornell University Press.

International Food Policy Research Institute. 2010. "Policy Seminar: Food Security, Farming, and Climate Change to 2050" (webpage). http://www.ifpri.org/event/food-security-farming-and-climate-change-2050.

Jepperson, Ronald L., Alexander Wendt, and Peter J. Katzenstein. 1996. "Norms, Identity, and Culture in National Security." In *The Culture of National Security: Norms and Identity in World Politics,* edited by Peter J. Katzenstein. New York: Columbia University Press.

Jerven, Morten. 2013. *Poor Numbers: How We Are Misled by African Development Statistics and What to Do about It.* Ithaca, NY: Cornell University Press.

Jetschke, Anja. 1999. "Linking the Unlinkable? International Norms and Nationalism in Indonesia and the Philippines." In *The Power of Human Rights: International Norms and Domestic Change,* edited by Thomas Risse, Stephen C. Ropp, and Kathryn Sikkink, 134–171. Cambridge, UK: Cambridge University Press.

Juma, Calestous. 2015. *The New Harvest: Agricultural Innovation in Africa.* New York: Oxford University Press.

Jung, Courtney, Ran Hirschl, and Evan Rosevear. 2014. "Economic and Social Rights In National Constitutions." *American Journal of Comparative Law* 62, no. 4: 1043–94.

Jurkovich, Michelle. 2016. "Venezuela Has Solved Its Hunger Problem? Don't Believe the U.N.'s Statistics." *Washington Post,* September 21, 2016. https://www.washingtonpost

.com/news/monkey-cage/wp/2016/09/21/venezuela-has-solved-its-hunger
-problem-dont-believe-the-u-n-s-numbers/.

Jurkovich, Michelle. 2019. "What Isn't a Norm? Redefining the Conceptual Boundaries of 'Norms' in the Human Rights Literature." *International Studies Review*.

Kahn, Chris. 2016. "Exclusive: Most Americans Support Torture against Terror Suspects." Reuters, March 30, 2016. http://www.reuters.com/article/us-usa-election-torture -exclusive-idUSKCN0WW0Y3.

Katzenstein, Peter. 1996. *The Cultural of National Security: Norms and Identity in World Politics*. New York: Columbia University Press.

Keck, Margaret, and Kathryn Sikkink. 1998. *Activists beyond Borders: Advocacy Networks in International Politics*. Ithaca, NY: Cornell University Press.

Kelley, Judith. 2008. "Assessing the Complex Evolution of Norms: The Rise of International Election Monitoring." *International Organization* 62, no. 2: 221–55.

Kennedy, John F. 1963. "Remarks to World Food Congress Delegates, 4 June 1963." John F. Kennedy Presidential Library and Museum. https://www.jfklibrary.org/asset-viewer /archives/JFKPOF/044/JFKPOF-044-034.

Klotz, Audie. 1995. "Norms Reconstituting Interests: Global Racial Equality and US Sanctions against South Africa." *International Organization* 49, no. 3: 451–78.

———. 1999. *Norms in International Relations: The Struggle against Apartheid*. Ithaca, NY: Cornell University Press.

Kratochwil, Friedrich. 1989. *Rules, Norms, and Decisions: On the Conditions of Practical and Legal Reasoning in International Relations and Domestic Affairs*. Cambridge, UK: Cambridge University Press.

Lang, John. 2016. *What's So Controversial about Genetically Modified Food?* London: Reaktion Books.

Lappé, Frances Moore, Jennifer Clapp, Molly Anderson, Robin Broad, Ellen Messer, Thomas Pogge, and Timothy Wise. 2013. "How We Count Hunger Matters." *Ethics and International Affairs* 27, no. 3: 251–59.

Lazarev, Egor, and Kunaal Sharma. 2017. "Brother or Burden: An Experiment on Reducing Prejudice Toward Syrian Refugees in Turkey." *Political Science Research and Methods* 5, no. 2: 201–19.

Lebovic, James H., and Erik Voeten. 2006. "The Politics of Shame: The Condemnation of Country Human Rights Practices in the UNCHR." *International Studies Quarterly* 50, no. 4: 861–88.

Lipper, Leslie, Philip Thornton, Bruce M. Campbell, Tobias Baedeker, Ademola Braimoh, Martin Bwalya, Patrick Caron, Andrea Cattaneo, Dennis Garrity, Kevin Henry, Ryan Hottle, Louise Jackson, Andrew Jarvis, Fred Kossam, Wendy Mann, Nancy McCarthy, Alexandre Meybeck, Henry Neufeldt, Tom Remington, Pham Thi Sen, Reuben Sessa, Reynolds Shula, Austin Tibu, and Emmanuel F. Torquebiau. 2014. "Climate-Smart Agriculture for Food Security." *Nature Climate Change* 4, no. 12: 1068–72.

Loftus, Elizabeth F. 1979. "The Malleability of Human Memory: Information Introduced after We View an Incident Can Transform Memory." *American Scientist* 67, no. 3: 312–20.

Lopez, Virginia. 2013. "Venezuela Food Shortages: 'No One Can Explain Why a Rich Country Has No Food.'" *Guardian*, September 26, 2013. https://www.theguardian.com /global-development/poverty-matters/2013/sep/26/venezuela-food-shortages-rich -country-cia.

Lupu, Yon. 2015. "Legislative Veto Players and the Effects of International Human Rights Agreements." *American Journal of Political Science* 59, no. 3, 578–94.

Lutter, Chessa K., Camila M. Chaparro, and Sergio Muñoz. 2011. "Progress towards Millennium Development Goal 1 in Latin America and the Caribbean: The Importance of the Choice of Indicator for Undernutrition." *Bulletin of the World Health Organization* 89, no. 1: 22–30.

Lutz, Ellen, and Kathryn Sikkink. 2000. "International Human Rights Law and Practice in Latin America." *International Organization* 54, no. 3: 633–59.

Malthus, Thomas. 1798. *An Essay on the Principle of Population.*

Mantilla, Giovanni. 2009. "Emerging International Human Rights Norms for Transnational Corporations." *Global Governance: A Review of Multilateralism and International Organizations* 15, no. 2: 279–98.

March, James G., and Johan P. Olsen. 1998. "The Institutional Dynamics of International Political Orders." *International Organization* 52, no. 4: 943–69.

Margulis, Matias E. 2013. "The Regime Complex for Food Security: Implications for the Global Hunger Challenge." *Global Governance: A Review of Multilateralism and International Organizations* 19, no. 1: 53–67.

Marsh, David, and Gerry Stoker, eds. 2010. 3rd ed. *Theory and Methods in Political Science.* Basingstoke, UK: Palgrave Macmillan.

Mayer, Jeremy D., and David J. Armor. 2012. "Support for Torture over Time: Interrogating the American Public about Coercive Tactics." *Social Science Journal* 49, no. 4: 439–46.

McAdam, Doug, J. McCarthy, and Mayer N. Zald, eds. 1996. *Comparative Perspectives on Social Movements: Political Opportunities, Mobilizing Structures, and Cultural Framings.* Cambridge, UK: Cambridge University Press.

McCourt, David M. 2016. "Practice Theory and Relationalism as the New Constructivism." *International Studies Quarterly* 60, no. 3: 475–85.

McGuinness, Feargall, Jennifer Brown, and Matthew Ward. 2016. *Household Food Insecurity Measurement in the UK.* House of Commons Debate Pack CDP 2016-0238. London: House of Commons Library, December 2, 2016.

McKeon, Nora. 2009. *The United Nations and Civil Society: Legitimating Global Governance—Whose Voice?* London: Zed Books.

Messer, Ellen, and Marc J. Cohen. 2007. "Conflict, Food Insecurity and Globalization." *Food, Culture and Society: An International Journal of Multidisciplinary Research* 10, no. 2: 297–315.

Minkoff, Debra. 1999. "Bending with the Wind: Strategic Change and Adaptation by Women's and Racial Minority Organizations." *American Journal of Sociology* 104, no. 6: 1666–703.

Mitlin, Diana, and Sam Hickey. 2009. "Introduction." In *Rights-Based Approaches to Development: Exploring the Potential and Pitfalls,* edited by S. Hickey and D. Mitlin, 3–19. Sterling, VA: Kumarian.

Moloney, Anastasia. 2019. "Central America's 'Poorest of the Poor' Hit Hard by U.S. Aid Cuts: Charities." *Reuters,* October 3, 2019. https://www.reuters.com/article/us-central-america-aid-cuts-analysis/central-americas-poorest-of-the-poor-hit-hard-by-us-aid-cuts-charities-idUSKBN1WI2HA.

Moravcsik, Andrew. 2000. "The Origins of Human Rights Regimes: Democratic Delegation in Postwar Europe." *International Organization* 54, no. 2: 217–52.

Morrow, James 2007. "When Do States Follow the Laws of War?" *American Political Science Review* 101, no. 3: 559–72.

Morsink, Johannes. 1999. *The Universal Declaration of Human Rights: Origins, Drafting, and Intent.* Philadelphia: University of Pennsylvania Press.

Mosley, Layna, ed. 2013a. *Interview Research in Political Science.* Ithaca, NY: Cornell University Press.

——. 2013b. "Introduction: 'Just Talk to People'? Interviews in Contemporary Political Science." In *Interview Research in Political Science,* edited by Layna Mosley, 1–28. Ithaca, NY: Cornell University Press.

Mundy, Karen. 2010. "'Education for All' and the Global Governors." In *Who Governs the Globe?*, edited by Deborah Avant, Martha Finnemore, and Susan Sell, 333–55. Cambridge: Cambridge University Press.

Munro, Lauchlan T. 2009. "The 'Human Rights-Based Approach to Programming': A Contradiction in Terms?" In *Rights-Based Approaches to Development: Exploring the Potential and Pitfalls*, edited by S. Hickey and D. Mitlin, 187–206. Sterling, VA: Kumarian.

Murdie, Amanda. 2014a. *Help or Harm: The Human Security Effects of International NGOs.* Stanford, CA: Stanford University Press.

——. 2014b. "The Ties That Bind: A Network Analysis of Human Rights International Nongovernmental Organizations." *British Journal of Political Science* 44, no. 1: 1–27.

Murdie, Amanda and David David. 2012. "Shaming and Blaming: Using events Data to Assess the Impact of Human Rights INGOs." *International Studies Quarterly* 56, no. 1: 1–16.

Nelson, Paul, and Dorsey, Ellen. 2007. "New Rights Advocacy in a Global Public Domain." *European Journal of International Relations* 13, no. 2: 187–216.

New York Times. 1943a. "Average Relief Check to Rise 40% When Food Stamps End March 1." February 23, 1943.

——. 1943b. "43 Nations Accept Bid to Food Parley; Representatives to Take Part in Hot Springs Session Tuesday." May 12, 1943.

Offenheiser, Raymond C., and Susan H. Holcombe. 2003. "Challenges and Opportunities in Implementing a Rights-Based Approach to Development: An Oxfam America Perspective." *Nonprofit and Voluntary Sector Quarterly* 32, no. 2: 268–301.

Office of the United Nations High Commissioner for Human Rights. n.d. "Human Rights and the Post-2015 Development Agenda" (webpage). Accessed April 2014. http://www.ohchr.org/EN/Issues/MDG/Pages/MDGPost2015Agenda.aspx.

——. 1948. *Universal Declaration of Human Rights.* http://www.ohchr.org/EN/UDHR/Documents/UDHR_Translations/eng.pdf.

——. 2008. *Frequently Asked Questions on Economic, Social and Cultural Rights.* Fact Sheet No. 33. Geneva: United Nations, December 2008.

——. 2004. "Responsibilities of Transnational Corporations and Related Business Enterprises with Regard to Human Rights." Memorandum 2004/116. April 2004. http://ap.ohchr.org/documents/E/CHR/decisions/E-CN_4-DEC-2004-116.doc.

Orford, Anne. 2015. "Food Security, Free Trade, and the Battle for the State." *Journal of International Law and International Relations* 11, no. 2: 1–67.

Oshaug, Arne. 2005. "Developing Voluntary Guidelines for Implementing the Right to Adequate Food: Anatomy of an Intergovernmental Process." In *Food and Human Rights in Development*, vol. 1, *Legal and Institutional Dimensions and Selected Topics*, edited by Wenche Barth Eide and Uwe Kracht, 259–80. Oxford: Intersentia.

Oxfam International. n.d. "Behind the Brands: About" (webpage). https://www.behindthebrands.org/about/.

——. n.d. *Oxfam International Annual Report, 2012–2013.* Nairobi: Oxfam International. https://www-cdn.oxfam.org/s3fs-public/file_attachments/story/oxfam-annual-report-2012-2013.pdf.

——. 2014. "The Behind the Brands Scorecard Methodology," August 2014. https://oi-files-d8-prod.s3.eu-west-2.amazonaws.com/s3fs-public/file_attachments/btb_methodology_document_final_sept_2014.pdf.

Oxfam Great Britain. 2013. "Introducing . . . Enough Food for Everyone IF." Oxfam UK blog, January 23, 2013. https://oxfamapps.org/blog/2013-01-introducing-enough-food-for-everyone-if/.

Paarlberg, Robert. 2009. *Starved for Science: How Biotechnology Is Being Kept Out of Africa.* Cambridge, MA: Harvard University Press.

Parsons, Talcott. 1937. *The Structure of Social Action.* New York: McGraw-Hill.

Payne, Rodger. 2001. "Persuasion, Frames and Norm Construction." *European Journal of International Relations* 7, no. 1: 37–61.

Percy, Sarah. 2014. "The Unimplemented Norm: Anti-mercenary Law and the Problems of Institutionalization." In *Implementation and World Politics: How International Norms Change Practice,* edited by Alexander Betts and Phil Orchard, 68–84. Oxford: Oxford University Press.

Pew Research Center. 2014. *Brazilian Discontent Ahead of World Cup: President Rousseff Gets Poor Marks on Key Issues.* Washington, DC: Pew Research Center, June 3, 2014. https://www.pewresearch.org/global/2014/06/03/brazilian-discontent-ahead-of-world-cup/.

Phillips, Ralph W. 1981. *FAO: Its Origins, Formation and Evolution 1945-1981.* Food and Agriculture Organization of the United Nations.

Pierson, Paul. 2000. "Increasing Returns, Path Dependence, and the Study of Politics." *American Political Science Review* 94, no. 2: 251–67.

Pingali, Prabhu. 2016. "The Hunger Metrics Mirage: There's Been Less Progress on Hunger Reduction Than It Appears." *PNAS* 113, no. 18: 4880–83.

Pinstrup-Anderson, Per. 1987. "Macroeconomic Adjustment Policies and Human Nutrition: Available Evidence and Research Needs." *Food and Nutrition Bulletin* 9, no. 1.

——. 1988. *Food Subsidies in Developing Countries: Costs, Benefits, and Policy Options.* Baltimore: Johns Hopkins University Press.

——, ed. 2010. *The African Food System and Its Interaction with Human Health and Nutrition.* Ithaca, NY: Cornell University Press.

Popp, József, Károly Pető, and János Nagy. 2013. "Pesticide Productivity and Food Security: A Review." *Agronomy for Sustainable Development* 33, no. 1: 243–55.

Portelli, Alessandro. 1991. *The Death of Luigi Trastulli and Other Stories.* Albany: State University of New York Press.

Pottier, Johan. 1999. *Anthropology of Food: The Social Dynamics of Food Security.* Cambridge: Polity.

Price, Richard. 1997. *The Chemical Weapons Taboo.* Ithaca, NY: Cornell University Press.

——. 1998. "Reversing the Gun Sights: Transnational Civil Society Targets Land Mines." *International Organization* 52, no. 3: 613–44.

Rawls, John. 1971. *A Theory of Justice.* Cambridge, MA: Harvard University Press.

Reus-Smit, Christian. 2001. "Human Rights and the Social Construction of Sovereignty." *Review of International Studies* 27, no. 4: 519–38.

——, ed. 2004. *The Politics of International Law.* Cambridge: Cambridge University Press.

Ripples Nigeria. 2016. "We Hear Your Cry of Hunger, but It's Not Our Fault, FG Tells Nigerians." August 10, 2016. https://www.ripplesnigeria.com/hear-cry-hunger-not-fault-fg-tells-nigerians/.

Risse, Thomas. 2000. "'Let's Argue!': Communicative Action in World Politics." *International Organization* 54, no. 1: 1–39.

Risse, Thomas, and Stephen C. Ropp. 2013. "Introduction and Overview." In *The Persistent Power of Human Rights: From Commitment to Compliance,* edited by Thomas Risse, Stephen C. Ropp, and Kathryn Sikkink, 3–25. Cambridge: Cambridge University Press.

Risse, Thomas, Stephen C. Ropp, and Kathryn Sikkink, eds. 1999. *The Power of Human Rights: International Norms and Domestic Change.* Cambridge: Cambridge University Press.

——, eds. 2013. *The Persistent Power of Human Rights: From Commitment to Compliance.* Cambridge: Cambridge University Press.

Risse, Thomas, and Kathryn Sikkink. 1999. "The Socialization of International Human Rights Norms into Domestic Practices: Introduction." In *The Power of Human Rights: International Norms and Domestic Change*, edited by Thomas Risse, Stephen C. Ropp, and Kathryn Sikkink, 1–38. Cambridge, UK: Cambridge University Press.

Robinson, Mary. 2004. "Advancing Economic, Social, and Cultural Rights: The Way Forward." *Human Rights Quarterly* 26, no. 4: 866–872.

——. 2005a. "Foreword." In *Food and Human Rights in Development*, vol. 1, *Legal and Institutional Dimensions and Selected Topics*, edited by Wenche Barth Eide and Uwe Kracht, xix–xxi. Oxford: Intersentia.

——. 2005b. "What Rights Can Add to Good Development Practice." In *Human Rights and Development: Towards Mutual Reinforcement*, edited by Philip Alston and Mary Robinson, 25–41. Oxford: Oxford University Press.

Rogers, Simon. 2011. "War in Iraq: The Cost in American Lives and Dollars." *Guardian*, December 15, 2011. http://www.theguardian.com/news/datablog/2011/dec/15/war -iraq-costs-us-lives.

Roth, Kenneth. 2004. "Defending Economic, Social and Cultural Rights: Practical Issues Faced by an International Human Rights Organization." *Human Rights Quarterly* 26, no. 1: 63–73.

Ruggie, John Gerard. 2013. *Just Business: Multinational Corporations and Human Rights.* New York: W. W. Norton.

Sandholtz, Wayne. 2007. *Prohibiting Plunder: How Norms Change.* New York: Oxford University Press.

——. 2008. "Dynamics of International Norm Change: Rules against Wartime Plunder." *European Journal of International Relations* 14, no. 1: 101–31.

Sartori, Giovanni. 1970. "Concept Misformation in Comparative Politics." *American Political Science Review* 64, no. 4: 1033–53.

Scanlan, Stephen. J. 2003. "Food Security and Comparative Sociology: Research, Theories, and Concepts." *International Journal of Sociology* 33, no. 3: 88–111.

——. 2009. "New Direction and Discovery on the Hunger Front: Toward a Sociology of Food Security/Insecurity." *Humanity and Society* 33, no. 4: 292–316.

Scheper-Hughes, Nancy. 1993. *Death without Weeping: The Violence of Everyday Life in Brazil.* Berkeley: University of California Press.

Schiff, Jennifer. 2016. "Masquerading as Compliance: Tracing Canada's Policy Implementation Of The Human Right to Water." *Journal of Human Rights Practice* 8, no. 2: 264–83.

Schmid, Evelyne. 2015. *Taking Economic, Social and Cultural Rights Seriously in International Criminal Law.* Cambridge, UK: Cambridge University Press.

Schmitz, Hans Peter. 1999. "Transnational activism and political change in Kenya and Uganda." In *The Power of Human Rights: International Norms and Domestic Change*, edited by Thomas Risse, Stephen C. Ropp, and Kathryn Sikkink, 39–77. Cambridge, UK: Cambridge University Press.

Schweller, Randall, and Xiayou Pu. 2011. "After Unipolarity: China's Visions of International Order in an Era of U.S. Decline." *International Security* 36, no. 1: 41–72.

Sell, Susan, and Aseem Prakash. 2004. "Using Ideas Strategically: The Contest between Business and NGO Networks in Intellectual Property Rights." *International Studies Quarterly* 48, no. 1: 143–75.

Sen, Amartya. 1981. *Poverty and Famines: An Essay on Entitlement and Deprivation.* Oxford: Oxford University Press.

Sen, Binay Ranjan. 1982. *Towards a Newer World.* Dublin: Tycooly International.

Shiffman, Jeremy, Kathryn Quissell, Hans Peter Schmitz, David L. Pelletier, Stephanie L. Smith, David Berlan, Uwe Gneiting, David Van Slyke, Ines Mergel, Mariela A. Rodriguez, and Gill Walt. 2016. "A Framework on the Emergence and Effectiveness of Global Health Networks." *Health Policy and Planning* 31, supp. 1: i3–i16.

Shue, Henry. 1980. *Basic Rights: Subsistence, Affluence, and U.S. Foreign Policy.* Princeton, NJ: Princeton University Press.

Sikkink, Kathryn. 2011. *The Justice Cascade: How Human Rights Prosecutions Are Changing World Politics.* New York: W. W. Norton.

Simmons, Beth A. 2009. *Mobilizing for Human Rights: International Law in Domestic Politics.* New York: Cambridge University Press.

Simon, Art. 2009. "Enlisting Citizens to End Hunger: Bread for the World at 35," *Health Progress*, 90: 79–81.

Snow, David, and Robert Benford. 1988. "Ideology, Frame Resonance, and Participant Mobilization." *International Social Movement Research* 1, no. 1: 197–217.

Stammler, Rudolf. 1896. *Wirtschaft und Recht nach der materialistischen Geschichtsauffassung: eine sozialphilosophische Untersuchung.* Leipzig: Veit.

Staples, Amy. 2006. *The Birth of Development: How the World Bank, Food and Agriculture Organization, and World Health Organization Changed the World, 1945–1965.* Kent, OH: Kent State University Press.

Steiner, Henry I., and Philip Alston. 2000. *International Human Rights in Context: Law, Politics and Morals.* Oxford: Oxford University Press.

Stone, Kelly. 2015. *Mandating Hunger: The Impacts of Global Biofuels Mandates and Targets.* Washington, DC: ActionAid USA. https://www.actionaidusa.org/wp-content/uploads/2015/03/Mandating-Hunger-The-Impacts-of-Global-Biofuels-Mandates-and-Targets.pdf.

Stronthenke, Wilma, and Abby Carrigan, eds. 2013. *FIAN International Annual Report: 2012.* Heidelberg: FIAN International. https://www.fian.org/files/fian-ar-2012-enpdf.pdf.

Svedberg, Peter. 1999. "841 Million Undernourished?" *World Development* 27, no. 12: 2081–98.

Tasioulas, John. 2017. "Minimum core obligations: Human rights in the here and now." *World Bank.* https://openknowledge.worldbank.org/handle/10986/29144.

Taussig, Michael 1978. "Nutrition, Development, and Foreign Aid: A Case Study of US-Directed Health Care in a Colombian Plantation Zone." *International Journal of Health Services* 8, no. 1: 101–21.

Thomas, Daniel. 1999. "The Helsinki Accords and Political Change in Eastern Europe." In *The Power of Human Rights: International Norms and Domestic Change*, edited by Thomas Risse, Stephen C. Ropp, and Kathryn Sikkink, 205–233. Cambridge, UK: Cambridge University Press.

Tomasevski, Katarina. 1993. *Development Aid and Human Rights Revisited.* London: Pinter.

United Nations. 1986. *Declaration on the Right to Development.* UN Document A/RES/41/128. New York: United Nations, December 4, 1986.

———. 2003. *Commentary on the Norms on the Responsibilities of Transnational Corporations and Other Business Enterprises with Regard to Human Rights.* UN Document E/CN.4/Sub.2/2003/38/Rev.2. New York: United Nations. http://www1.umn.edu/humanrts/links/commentary-Aug2003.html.

———. 2013. "Food Security and Nutrition Should Top Development Agenda after 2015—UN officials." February 13, 2013. http://www.un.org/apps/news/story.asp?NewsID=44133#.UyTBTCgtBRc.

United Nations Children's Fund. 2013. *The State of the World's Children: Children with Disabilities.* https://www.unicef.org/publications/files/SWCR2013_ENG_Lo_res_24 _Apr_2013.pdf.

United Nations Children's Fund. n.d. "India: Nutrition" (webpage). http://www.unicef.org /india/nutrition.html.

United Nations Children's Fund, World Health Organization, and World Bank. 2015. "Joint Child Malnutrition Estimates (JME). Prevalence of Stunting, Height for Age (Percentage of Children under Five)." https://data.worldbank.org/indicator/SH.STA .STNT.ZS.

United Nations Committee on Economic, Social and Cultural Rights. 1999. *The Right to Adequate Food.* E/C.12/1999/5. Geneva: United Nations Committee on Economic, Social and Cultural Rights, May 12, 1999. https://www.refworld.org/pdfid/45388 38c11.pdf.

United Nations Conference on Food and Agriculture Hot Springs. 1943. *United Nations Conference on Food and Agriculture: Hot Springs, Virginia, May 18–June 3, 1943: Final Act and Section Reports.* Washington, DC: GPO.

United Nations Development Group. 2003. *The Human Rights Based Approach to Development Cooperation: Towards a Common Understanding Among UN Agencies.* New York: United Nations Development Group. https://unsdg.un.org/sites/default/files /6959-The_Human_Rights_Based_Approach_to_Development_Cooperation _Towards_a_Common_Understanding_among_UN.pdf.

United Nations Economic and Social Council. December 16, 1947. Commission on Human Rights, Second Session: Summary Record of Fortieth Meeting (E/CN.4/SR/40).

United Nations Economic and Social Council. May 24, 1948. Commission on Human rights, Third Session: India and the United Kingdom: Proposed Amendments to the Draft Declaration on Human Rights (E/CN.4/99).

United Nations Economic and Social Council June 28, 1948. Commission on Human Rights, Third Session: Summary Record of the Seventy-First Meeting (E/CN.4/SR.71).

United Nations General Assembly. 1966. *International Covenant on Economic, Social and Cultural Rights.* New York: United Nations. http://www.ohchr.org/EN /ProfessionalInterest/Pages/CESCR.aspx.

——. 1979. *Convention on the Elimination of All Forms of Discrimination against Women.* New York: United Nations. https://www.ohchr.org/documents/professionalinterest /cedaw.pdf.

——. 1989. *Convention on the Rights of the Child.* New York: United Nations. http://www .ohchr.org/EN/ProfessionalInterest/Pages/CRC.aspx.

——. 1997. *Renewing the United Nations: A Programme for Reform.* A/51/950. New York: United Nations, July 14, 1997. https://www.unicef.org/about/execboard/files/A-51 -950_Renewing_the_UN-ODS-English.pdf.

——. 2000. *UN Millennium Declaration A/RES/55/2.* September 18, 2000. https://www.un .org/en/development/desa/population/migration/generalassembly/docs /globalcompact/A_RES_55_2.pdf.

——. 2005. *Resolution Adopted by the General Assembly on 16 September 2005: 60/1, 2005 World Summit Outcome.* New York: United Nations. https://www.un.org/en /development/desa/population/migration/generalassembly/docs/globalcompact /A_RES_60_1.pdf.

United Nations General Assembly, Department of Public Information. 2011. "General Assembly Suspends Libya from Human Rights Council." Press release, March 1, 2011. http://www.un.org/News/Press/docs/2011/ga11050.doc.htm.

United Nations Office for the Coordination of Humanitarian Affairs. 2017. "Syria: Forty-One Donors Pledge a Combined US$6 Billion for 2017 in Immediate and Longer-

Term Support." Press release, April 5, 2017. United Nations Office for the Coordination of Humanitarian Affairs. https://www.unocha.org/story/syria-forty -one-donors-pledge-combined-us6-billion-2017-immediate-and-longer-term -support.

United Nations Sub-Commission on the Promotion and Protection of Human Rights. 2003. *Norms on the Responsibilities of Transnational Corporations and Related Business Enterprises with Regard to Human Rights.* E/CN.4/Sub.2/2003/12/Rev.2. Geneva: United Nations Sub-Commission on the Promotion and Protection of Human Rights, August 26, 2003. https://digitallibrary.un.org/record/501576/files/E_CN.4 _Sub.2_2003_12_Rev.2-EN.pdf.

Urmson, J. O. 1958. "Saints and Heroes." In *Essays in Moral Philosophy*, edited by A. I. Melden, 198–216. Seattle: University of Washington Press.

U.S. Agency for International Development. 2020. "Food Assistance Fact Sheet— Guatemala" (webpage). April 7, 2020. https://www.usaid.gov/sites/default/files /documents/1866/FFP_Fact_Sheet_Guatemala.pdf.

U.S. Department of Agriculture, Economic Research Service. 2019. "Definitions of Food Security" (webpage), last updated September 4, 2019. https://www.ers.usda.gov /topics/food-nutrition-assistance/food-security-in-the-us/definitions-of-food -security/.

Uvin, Peter. 1992. "Regime, Surplus, and Self-Interest: The International Politics of Food Aid." *International Studies Quarterly* 36, no. 3: 293–312.

——. 1994. *The International Organization of Hunger.* London: Kegan Paul International.

——. 1998. *Aiding Violence: The Development Enterprise in Rwanda.* Bloomfield, CT: Kumarian.

——. 2004. *Human Rights and Development.* Bloomfield, CT: Kumarian.

Vernon, James. 2007. *Hunger: A Modern History.* Cambridge, MA: Harvard University Press.

Wallace, Geoffrey P.R. 2013. "International Law and Public Attitudes Toward Torture: An Experimental Study." *International Organization* 67, no. 1: 105–40.

Wallerstein, Mitchel B. 1980. *Food for War—Food for Peace: United States Food Aid in a Global Context.* Cambridge, MA: MIT Press.

Walt, Stephen. 2009. "Alliances in a Unipolar World." *World Politics* 61, no. 1: 86–120.

Watts, Jonathan. 2016. "Brazil's Interim Government Wastes No Time Erasing Workers' Party Influence." *Guardian*, May 20, 2016. https://www.theguardian.com/world /2016/may/20/brazil-rightwing-government-michel-temer.

Way, Sally-Anne. 2005. "The Role of the UN Human Rights Bodies in Promoting and Protecting the Right to Food." In *Food and Human Rights in Development*, vol. 1, *Legal and Institutional Dimensions and Selected Topics*, edited by Wenche Barth Eide and Uwe Kracht, 205–26. Oxford: Intersentia.

Way, Wendy. 2013. *A New Idea Each Morning: How Food and Agriculture Came Together in One International Organisation.* Canberra, Australia: ANU E Press.

Weber, Max. 1978. *Economy and Society.* Vol. 2. Edited by Guenther Roth and Claus Wittich. Berkeley: University of California Press.

Wendt, Alexander. 1994. "Collective Identity Formation and the International State." *American Political Science Review* 88, no. 2: 384–96.

——. 1998. "On Constitution and Causation in International Relations." *Review of International Studies* 24, no. 5: 101–18.

Winders, Bill. 2009. "The Vanishing Free Market: The Formation and Spread of the British and US Food Regimes." *Journal of Agrarian Change* 9, no. 3: 315–44.

Windfuhr, Michael. 2007. "Experiences from Case Related Right to Food Work: Lessons Learned for Implementation." In *Food and Human Rights in Development*, vol. 2,

Evolving Issues and Emerging Applications, edited by Wenche Barth Eide and Uwe Kracht, 331–57. Oxford: Intersentia.

Wolf, Susan. 1982. "Moral Saints." *Journal of Philosophy* 79, no. 80: 419–39.

Wolfensohn, James D. 2005. "Some Reflections on Human Rights and Development." In *Human Rights and Development: Towards Mutual Reinforcement*, edited by Philip Alston and Mary Robinson, 19–24. Oxford: Oxford University Press.

Wood, Elisabeth Jean. 2003. *Insurgent Collective Action and Civil War in El Salvador*. Cambridge: Cambridge University Press.

World Bank and the Organisation for Economic Co-operation and Development. 2013. *Integrating Human Rights into Development: Donor Approaches, Experiences, and Challenges*. 2nd ed. Washington DC: World Bank and the Organisation for Economic Co-operation and Development.

World Food Programme. 2019. "Guatemala" (webpage). https://www.wfp.org/countries /guatemala.

Wright, Wynne, and Gerad Middendorf. 2007. *The Fight over Food: Producers, Consumers, and Activists Challenge the Global Food System*. University Park: Penn State University Press.

Young, Katharine G. 2008. "The minimum core of economic and social rights: a concept in search of content." *Yale Journal of International Law* 33: 113–175.

Zerbe, Noah. 2004. "Feeding the Famine? American Food Aid and the GMO Debate in Southern Africa." *Food Policy* 29, no. 6: 593–608.

Index

Page references in *italics* indicate illustrative content, such as figures and tables. Page references followed by an "A" indicate material in the Appendix.

CPSIA information can be obtained
at www.ICGtesting.com
Printed in the USA
LVHW011938050122
707898LV00003B/376

9 781501 751783